The Corrupt Society

From Ancient Greece to Present-Day America

Robert Payne

PRAEGER PUBLISHERS
New York

Published in the United States of America in 1975
by Praeger Publishers, Inc.
111 Fourth Avenue, New York, N.Y. 10003

Library of Congress Cataloging in Publication Data
Payne, Pierre Stephen Robert, 1911–
  The corrupt society.
  Bibliography: p.
  Includes index.
  1. Political ethics. 2. Corruption (in politics).
3. Social ethics. 4. Good and evil. I. Title.
JA79.P36   172   73-11782
ISBN 0-275-51020-4

Printed in the United States of America

For

RICHARD M. NIXON

Contents

Introduction

In the following pages I have attempted to set forth what has been said about corruption in the past, to sketch out a general theory of corruption, and to determine whether there exist any medicines to cure the disease in societies and individuals. By corruption I mean the working of those moral and social forces that bring about the decay and ultimately the death of societies and those other forces that arise within individuals and work toward the same end.

The reader will find himself in the position of a doctor dissecting a plague-ridden corpse. He will discover that many different plagues are at work, and even when he succeeds in identifying and isolating the plague bacilli he may be in no better position to prevent further outbreaks. He will discover that the processes of corruption are sometimes irreversible, and he may find himself agreeing with the great Arab philosopher Ibn Khaldun, the first to enquire deeply into the phenomenon of corruption as we understand it today, who wrote in the fourteenth century:

They think that the decay is the result of the incapacity or negligence of their predecessors. They are wrong. These accidents are inherent in empires and cannot be cured.

Ibn Khaldun's sweeping conclusion is not entirely true, for there are exceptions to all rules. On rare occasions the process can be halted or even reversed, or a society may lie dormant for a long time only to revive again in full splendor. Sometimes a corrupt and dying society will recover its health spontaneously and mysteriously, as though by a divine visitation. Ibn Khaldun, a devout Muslim, believed that such visitations of divine energy occurred very rarely, perhaps once in a thousand years.

The processes of corruption are rarely studied because exact evidence is generally unavailable and societies are so various that it is not possible to make exact comparisons. Nevertheless, I believe that general laws can be discovered and that the processes themselves can be charted. In theory, this should be a work in ten volumes, tracing the concept of corruption through all known civilizations and mythologies, but there are some advantages in writing a shorter book. I have not examined the whole forest but have examined many of the dead and dying branches. I have learned that nothing in the forest is what it seems to be, that dragons and goblins abound, and real tigers stalk the shadowy places.

I have been interested in trying to discover the laws and methods by which corruption operates and the various stages the corrupt individual passes through before he reaches the vertiginous stage of absolute corruption. If such laws exist, do they apply to all societies or are there exceptions? And if there are exceptions, why? And what country or people has paid most attention to corruption and done most to prevent it? Corruption appears to be a universal phenomenon that lays its own imperious claims on the world, and therefore it is the duty of all nations to prepare themselves against its onslaught by taking proper precautions. In the prison camps of Nazi Germany and the Soviet Union I found absolute corruption and wondered why one was so short-lived while the other has been able to prolong itself for generations.

I have been puzzled, too, by the fact that in recent years very little has been written on corruption, although it exists all over the world and in the very air we breathe, in the seats of government, in big business, in industrial organizations, and reaches down into the fragmented lives of ordinary citizens. We all know it and we have all seen it. Perhaps we have written so little about it because it is so familiar.

I have dedicated this work to Richard Nixon, a former president of the United States, not because he was the worst of corrupters—though he was certainly among the most successful—but because it was through the study of his works, his recorded conversations, and his ghostly writings that I first became aware that corruption had settled deeply in America and that only by heroic measures could it be halted. He was in office during most of the time this book was being written, and his shadow falls heavily over these pages.

For the rest, this is a study of a strange and terrible disease, which obeys its own laws and is nearly always fatal. Societies afflicted with it sometimes yield to treatment, but the cure is almost as terrible as the disease, for the cure involves a radical reorientation of the society away from the sources of corruption and the damming up of those sources until they no longer present a threat to the very existence of these societies. Corruption is contagious; it breeds on itself; once established, it is inhumanly difficult to remove. But unless a nation collectively wants to die, it must, once corruption has settled in it, grapple with the problem or perish.

Every good tree bringeth forth good fruit; but a corrupt tree bringeth forth evil fruit.

A good tree cannot bring forth evil fruit, neither can a corrupt tree bring forth good fruit.

Every tree that bringeth not forth good fruit is hewn down, and cast into the fire.

Wherefore by their fruits ye shall know them.

Matthew 7:17–20

There are sins, sins against the commonwealth of mankind, against the phenomenon of life itself, the stigma of which would cling through death, and for which there was pardon only in annihilation.

WINSTON CHURCHILL, in *Savrola*

An individual cannot assist or save a time; he can only express that it is lost.

SØREN KIERKEGAARD

The Form and
Nature of Corruption

The Corruptions of the Physical Body

When a man dies, strange things happen to him. But they happen in an orderly fashion, logically, according to scientific laws. The processes leading to birth require only nine months, but the processes of corruption, the processes by which he is withdrawn from any semblance of life, cover a much longer span of time.

All living creatures must die, and the processes of corruption are very similar whether it is a man, an elephant, a tiger, a cat, or an insect. Death jolts the machine in a new and hitherto unsuspected direction, for which the body is ill prepared and incapable of any resistance. Where previously there existed an intricate mechanism to sustain life, to move, to see, to understand, to adapt itself to its environment, there now takes place an irreversible disintegration of the mechanism. The processes of corruption do not act evenly. Each part of the body has its own timetable, and some parts of the body function mechanically long after death has taken place.

The dead body remains active, but it is in a state of passive activity. Things are happening within it, but they are not things over which the body has any control. It suffers these things to happen to it; it has become finally a creature of necessity, at the mercy of forces incomparably stronger than itself.

Significantly, corruption sets in first at the top. The brain cells are alive for only four minutes after the heart has stopped beating. Even though the heartbeat may be revived, the infinitely complex machinery of the brain begins to be dismantled within four minutes, and there exists no medicine capable of reviving the dead brain. The heart is more enduring than the brain, for the auricles continue to contract even when the ventricles have already ceased beating. Thus, the right auricle is called *ultimum moriens,* the last to die.

In this way, according to varying timetables, the body gradually enters a state of corruption. While the brain dies almost immediately, the stomach continues to digest food for twenty-four hours after the heart has stopped beating. The digestion of food is completely purposeless; intended to sustain life, it becomes after death merely the continuation of an autonomous action never controlled by the brain. These independent organisms continue to flourish; the hair, fingernails, and toenails continue to grow. The blood, too, retains its life-sustaining properties and remains liquid in the veins for a considerable time. It is functionally alive for at least two or three hours after death. A leg or an arm severed or torn from the living body and therefore to all outward appearances dead can be joined to the body if the operation takes place within two hours. The dead limb is resurrected, feels pain, cold, heat, touch, glows with health. What is dead becomes alive because it can be knit into the living organism.

At death the arteries empty themselves into the veins and capillaries, and the blood settles in the lowest part of the body by force of gravity. The strange pallor of the upturned face of a corpse is in stark contrast to the blood-red appearance of the back of the corpse when it is suddenly turned over.

Between two and six hours after death *rigor mortis* sets in, beginning with the head. Complex chemical processes in the nerves and muscles bring about an increasing rigor, but two or three days later the same processes bring about a softening of the body. *Rigor mortis* is thus a very temporary phenomenon.

The first visible signs of decomposition occur twenty-four to forty-eight hours after death with the appearance of greenish-blue discolorations of the veins and a diffused greenish-blue discoloration of the abdomen. Thereafter the processes of corruption begin to move rapidly. The stomach finally stops digesting food, putrefies;

the gases swell and push up the flesh. About the same time the cornea becomes completely opaque. The semen dies. The temperature of the body is now the same as that of the surrounding air. In time the soft parts of the body will assume the texture of glutinous jelly, then powder. The essential framework, the skeleton, may survive for many thousands of years.

Left alone, left to rot, the physical body assumes savage colors, purple, red, and green, with strange yellows and liquescent blacks. The skin pulls back from the lips in the familiar sardonic grin of death. The bloated flesh erupts, while worms and maggots carve tunnels through it. The decomposing corpse is a spectacle of the purest horror, which seems to have been designed as an ultimate punishment, an act of accusation against the once living flesh. A month after a man has died he is scarcely recognizable; he has become a monster. All, or nearly all, that was human in him has been effaced. The brilliantly constructed machine, trained to respond to millions of subtle stimuli, now responds to nothing at all, spills out gases, changes color, and serves no purpose except to manure a field.

The poets have found little consolation in death except to record its strange quietness. But this quietness is an illusion; activity is taking place all the time, signals are being passed along the dead roads, and all this activity is working toward the breaking down of the flesh, the cells, the muscles, and the dismantling of the millions of communication centers in the brain. The wreckers are destroying the house from within.

Just as ugly, and ultimately just as incomprehensible, are the corruptions of the mind and the corruptions of society. Sometimes societies die and putrefy long before they are pronounced dead, and sometimes men die of corruption long before they have taken to their deathbeds. Like a decaying corpse, a corrupt society festers and poisons the atmosphere; the essential life-giving saps and oils are absent, and while it continues to live it is more than half dead. It will die eventually or may miraculously recover, but just as we can observe the changing characteristics of a corpse, the discolorations, the rictus smile, the stiffening of the limbs and the darkening of the eyes, so we can observe in a corrupt society the way in which it gradually decomposes, dying its many deaths.

In the corrupt individual we observe the same processes that affect corrupt societies and corrupt bodies. There are general laws that apply both to societies and to individuals, but what might be called the curves of decay of societies and individuals do not follow identical patterns, nor are the symptoms exactly the same; yet they have enough in common to throw light on one another. Not all the mysteries of corruption can be explored: at the heart of these mysteries there are unspeakable horrors.

Although mysteries abound, there are many things that can be discovered. The form and nature of corruption can be defined; the critical points can be examined; we can indicate where the responsibility lies and where the rot begins; and sometimes it is possible to chart the progress of corruption in minute and intricate detail. Corruption takes hidden forms and wears brilliant coverings; we can strip it naked and see the horror for what it is. We learn how societies sometimes become aware of the corruption inside them, struggle against it, and even conquer it, and we learn what disposes them to surrender meekly to a comforting euphoria and a lingering death. We study the corrupt individual by studying his acts, beliefs, and innate prejudices. We discover that societies all over the world tend to be corrupted in the same way, and that corrupt individuals nearly always act in the same way. We learn that corruption is a universal phenomenon, which has appeared in all ages and all countries. We discover that contempt for one's fellow men lies very close to the heart of the mystery, and that human courage and dignity are always the most potent weapons against corruption.

The news, therefore, is not all bad. There are good and helpful things to be found in the study of corruption. Among other things, we learn to recognize it for what it is and to destroy it before it has overtaken a whole society. There exist sovereign remedies against the corruption of societies, and they are very simple. "The power which causes several portions of a plant to help each other we call life," wrote John Ruskin in *Modern Painters*. "Intensity of life is also intensity of helpfulness. The ceasing of this help is what we call corruption." It is precisely when we help one another that we gain our victories over corruption, but the victory is assured only when we help one another with all our strength.

Nearly everywhere we find societies tainted with corruption. It is in all governments, in the air we breathe, in the polluted rivers and the spoiled seas. The corrupt have all the shining weapons and the gaudiest uniforms, the power and the glory. In its ultimate form, corruption is a black-uniformed general wearing the insignia of a silver skull and crossbones on his military cap as he strides through the prison camps, knowing that the prisoners are too weak and helpless to rise against him. It amuses him that people die, that he can inflict torture at will, that he has added grievously to the weight of suffering in the world. In the military dictator we see corruption in its most extreme form. But even in the prison camps there are men who preserve their human dignity and fight back with all their resources, helping one another, refusing to accept for a single moment the claims of the dictator to impose his will upon them. They are the heroes of our time.

In our age we have seen more corruption than in any previous age. Never before have our societies been so riddled with this pervasive plague, but never before have men been so aware of the dangers confronting them. In defiance lies freedom; in the raw will of man we find our salvation. On a stone floor in the Tower of Constance at Aigues Mortes, in France, an unknown Huguenot prisoner carved with a nail a single word, *RÉSISTEZ*. Against corruption there is only one battle cry: Resist—resist to the uttermost—as you would resist death itself.

The Corruptions
of Society

A culture is not only the language and the arts of a people. It is all their history, all their hopes for the future. It is ancestors and graves, the shapes of houses and cradles, the colors of innumerable skies, the patterns of accumulated thoughts. It is made out of things as weightless as sounds and as heavy as iron, the songs of girls in the fields, the shapes of mattocks and hoes. Above all, it is the way men hold their heads.

By the very nature of things, cultures are fragile. They can sometimes be destroyed very easily by an order issued from above. A blow delivered at exactly the right place can devastate a culture that has grown slowly over many hundreds of years, producing a settled way of life unique in its own time and place. Societies are mortal and go down to defeat; the gift of immortality is not granted to them. But though cultures are fragile, they show on occasion extraordinary powers of survival. They can be deformed and defaced by conquerors and tyrants and yet survive as long as there are a few people determined to make them survive. Just as an oak tree struck by lightning will continue to send out new shoots and new branches, so people living under tyranny and forbidden to speak their own language or read their own books or practice their traditional rituals will sometimes live deeply within themselves, quietly nourishing their culture against the time when it will emerge into the sunlight.

The strength of cultures, and their weakness, cannot be measured exactly by any known measuring rods. We simply do not know how much residual strength lies in a culture when it is confronted by a powerful enemy determined to destroy it. When Hitler prepared to invade England, he drew up plans to dismember the British Empire and destroy the British people. The intellectuals and the Jews would be killed outright, the males would be transported to the Baltic, and the females would become the wives and concubines of German soldiers. We do not know and can hardly guess what would have happened if the German expeditionary force had made a successful landing and begun to carry out this program, prepared with great care and foresight. From everything we know about the British, however, it seems unlikely that the Germans would have succeeded in this ultimate test of strength. A million Britons would have been killed, but the German expeditionary force would have been torn to pieces, Great Britain would have been saved by the raw courage of its people, and the German army would have withdrawn to the continent to pursue easier conquests.

We shall never know what would have happened if the Germans had landed on the English coast. But there are lessons to be learned from the study of that catastrophe which was once so close to fulfillment—the Germans with their clear-cut plans, their vastly superior armaments, and their disciplined juggernaut of an army, and the British home guards, who were training with broomsticks and whose inadequate defenses consisted of a few coils of barbed wire along the seacoast. Britain was virtually defenseless. To all appearances Britain was doomed, and it must have seemed to the Germans only a matter of weeks or months before the island was transformed into a German colony. But appearances were deceptive. Not a single German soldier landed on British soil, and the German Army of the West finally surrendered to a British general. What saved Britain was the courage of its people, their faith in their thousand-year-old culture, their knowledge of their own invincibility. Irrational forces came into play. For a whole year, fighting alone, the British had held off the immense power of the German military machine.

A culture is not a rational thing and does not obey rational laws. When it appears strongest, it may be weakest. When it appears to be dying, it may be at the summit of its strength. The elements of a culture are so various that we cannot with any certainty say that this or that culture is superior to another. All we can do is isolate some of the factors that make for endurance: courage, willpower, vigor, the sense of the common traditions that bind a people together, and their determination to preserve a way of life that satisfies and enriches them. If the arts are flourishing, if the people have a common purpose, if their natural spontaneity is encouraged, we can be sure that the essential core of a nation is healthy. If the arts are stagnant, if the people's natural spontaneity is destroyed, and if they are oppressed from above, then we can be sure that the essential core is unhealthy. The artists are usually the indicators of the strength of a culture.

"When I hear the word 'culture,' " wrote Hans Johst, the German playwright whose works were admired by Hitler, "I reach for my revolver." He was saying in effect what Hitler had said many times: the master race had no need for traditional German culture. What it needed above all was the force and the disciplined army to dominate all Germany's real and imagined enemies. All other considerations could be abandoned. But no one in the National Socialist Party paused long enough to examine the consequences of this theory of domination once it was put into practice. Was it to be expected that the conquered people would acquiesce in their own defeat? Hitler liked to use the phrase "once and for all," as though acts and their consequences were final. The most elementary reading of history shows that nothing happens "once and for all," and consequences are often unpredictable.

A visitor to Munich in 1938 could have seen two museums that demonstrated the National Socialist attitude toward art. One enormous museum, erected at great cost, showed the art officially encouraged by the government. There were portraits of Hitler in shining armor, larger-than-life-size portraits of Nazi leaders, paintings and sculptures of German youth, full-breasted peasant girls and heroic workmen advancing toward an uncertain destiny. Everything was static, frozen, hard-faced. An extraordinary number of battle scenes showed expressionless German soldiers hurling themselves against enemy trenches amid shell-fire and the explosions of hand grenades. The features of their hapless enemies were always indistinct, so that it was impossible to tell whether they were intended to represent Frenchmen, Britons, Russians, or Chinese. Here and there in the museum were marble statues of the ancient Teutonic gods.

Not far from this museum was another, dedicated to "corrupt" art. Huge banners invited the public to view the art officially condemned by the National Socialists. In five or six galleries there were assembled many superb masterpieces of modern art, including works by Kokoshka, Franz Marc, George Grosz, Klee, and many German expressionists. These works were being held up to public contempt. But the aims of the organizers of the exhibition miscarried. Too many people were looking at these masterpieces with joy and delighted surprise. The organizers therefore called in about twenty storm troopers to discourage any enjoyment of the paintings. Along the galleries the storm troopers marched in their heavy boots, armed with pistols, amusing themselves by glaring threateningly at anyone who showed admiration for the paintings. Sometimes a storm trooper stood in front of a painting that was being examined a little too enthusiastically. Arrests were made. Suddenly, in one of the galleries, three or four storm troopers could be seen running toward a painting where three or four people were grouped in admiration. At all costs such groups must be broken up. Official National Socialist art must be vindicated, and it was impermissible to enjoy "corrupt" art, even though it was being officially displayed.

In the museum of "corrupt" art there was life and spontaneity, a sense of the wholeness of art, and great beauty. In the official museum there was only deadness. A bureaucratic, propagandist art had emerged at the dictate of Hitler, and it precisely mirrored his own incomprehension of art and his own vacuity. Similarly in Soviet Russia under Stalin there emerged a propagandist art designed to celebrate Stalin and the Communist Party. Not surprisingly, the arts of the Soviet Union and of National Socialist Germany had much in common: the same heroic workers, the same full-breasted peasant girls, the same glorious soldiers in the midst of battle against ill-defined enemies. These arts were almost interchangeable. Living art vanished; only stereotypes remained.

Confucius said that if you want to know the spirit of the people, you have only to listen to their songs. A modern observer has only to study the arts of a country to know whether it is fundamentally healthy or corrupt. Paintings, literature, and music tell us more than presidential speeches. Indeed, presidential speeches usually tell us more than we need to know about the ill health of a country. A speech should flow; it should have life in it; it should not be a thing of bits and pieces glued together from the work of a half-dozen paid speech writers. Stalin wrote a history of the Communist Party in the Soviet Union that was patched together from the works of many other writers and reads as though it was composed by a computer.

Similarly, Richard Nixon wrote an autobiography with the assistance of a ghostwriter. Occasionally an authentic sentence by Nixon can be found embedded within it. Both Stalin and Nixon were corrupt, each in his way, and the mark of their corruption was the lack of recognizable life in their speeches and writings. What gives art and literature their dignity is the abundant sense of life flowing through them. We cannot expect to find even a trace of this living quality in corrupt men.

Absolute corruption appears in states ruled by absolute tyrants. In colonial Africa freedom from the tyranny of the rulers rarely lasted for more than a few weeks. The tyranny of the colonial powers was often replaced by the tyranny of a local soldier who looted his own country and reduced it to slavery. President Idi Amin of Uganda, a former heavyweight boxing champion, came to power in the traditional way: he had been a member of the palace guard. Thereafter he raped, murdered, and tortured people at his pleasure. He was poorly educated and derived special enjoyment from punishing people who were better educated. One day he ordered all the Asians in Uganda to be deported; this was done, and most of the country's trade came to a standstill. He carried on continual vendettas against his own people, invaded the countries on his borders, announced great victories when he was retreating from his enemies, and amused himself by dispatching a stream of telegrams to heads of state all over the world, telling them how they should conduct their affairs. Corrupt, ignorant, and paranoid, Idi Amin reduced the once proud people of Uganda to beggary and misery. Jean-Bédel Bokassa, self-appointed President for Life of the Central African Republic and former sergeant in the French army, was, if possible, even more murderous and even more corrupt. Once, when there was a rash of burglaries, he marched his guards to the central prison in Bangui. The guards were armed with clubs, and they proceeded to beat all the prisoners to bloody pulp, leaving them to roast for six hours under the tropical sun. The bodies were later publicly exhibited on a platform in the marketplace.

But it is not only the military dictators who drive a people to despair. In his book *The Mountain People,* the anthropologist Colin Turnbull has described the Ik, an African tribe forced out of its traditional hunting ground and the territory it had owned for generations. As a result they lost their religion, their social organism, their will to live. They became completely heartless and watched brothers and sisters die with complete indifference. Turnbull tells of an Ik family watching a baby crawling toward a fire and burning itself. No one made the least effort to rescue the baby. When it was burned, the observers burst out laughing. Such things provided the only entertainment remaining to them.

These small, dark people were concerned only with grubbing for food and finding shelter. They hated vigorously, but it was a mindless hatred, almost without emotion. They would gaze for long hours in a stupor at the lands that once belonged to them, where they were no longer permitted to hunt. They stole from one another. They lied. They quarreled viciously. When an old blind man tried to reach a dead hyena for a share of the meat, they trampled him underfoot, laughing. If someone asked for love and kindness, the request was rejected out of hand as a matter of principle. An Ik fights for himself, rides roughshod over others, and is perfectly content if he can steal a leopard bone from a dying man.

The saddest thing was not that there was so little affection among the Iks but that they had outlawed affection. They were fragmented and had no common purpose. They had constructed a corrupt society, but the conditions were not of their own making. There was no President Idi Amin destroying them from above. A law had been passed saying, "Your hunting grounds are to be yours no more." Their reasons for living had been taken away from them. Something very similar happened to many tribes of American Indians. Uprooted, alienated, without resources and without hope, they live in a state of social collapse and decay.

How does one recognize a corrupt society? What signs does it show? If we traveled through it, would we know it for what it is?

Just as no one has the slightest difficulty recognizing a putrefying corpse, so no one in his senses has the slightest difficulty recognizing a corrupt society, for the marks of corruption are as indelible and as evident as the *livor mortis,* the blue discolorations that appear on a corpse. Like the Iks, a corrupt society only goes through the motions of living. Reflex actions continue; some habits survive; and a society faced with ruin may surrender briefly to an overwhelming feeling of euphoria before it dies.

A corrupt society is one where the forces of death are stronger than the forces of life, where hope has vanished, where the essential structure is in a state of dissolution and no new structure has evolved. One can imagine a society in which no babies are born because the parents have no hope that their offspring will survive; and indeed the rise and fall of the birth rate is very often a measure of the health or lack of health in a society. Human hopes revolve around the family, and the disintegration of family life also provides a measure of the corruption of a society.

A textbook on pathology can inform us step by step how corruption occurs in a dead body, but there are no textbooks to help us understand the processes of corruption in a civilization. The processes are complex, variable, not always easily identifiable. What may contribute to corruption in one civilization may act as a positive and curative force in another; just as arsenic in small doses may be beneficial to a patient while a large dose will kill him, so we must be careful not to assume that something inherently dangerous to a civilization must always be evil. Even a very powerful shock can sometimes be beneficial, and sometimes a small shock applied at the right time and place may bring about the ruin of a civilization or a culture. There are no absolute standards by which we can measure the poisons that infect a nation, nor are there any absolute standards by which we can measure the amount of harm done. Any theory of corruption involves standards of measurement that remain to some extent subjective, and when we describe the processes of corruption we must recognize that these processes do not follow absolute laws but contain within themselves the principle of indeterminacy. As Ibn Khaldun observed, the patient on his deathbed sometimes recovers miraculously "because God has willed it."

But while there are complexities, there are also simplicities. It is not difficult to recognize the stench of corruption. If we enter a city and see bodies lying in the streets and the survivors peering helplessly from shattered windows or cowering in cellars, we know that the city has been mortally wounded. It may recover in time—the stench of the dead may be wafted away by a liberal use of quicklime and by digging mass graves—but the wounds are clearly visible. So, too, with a corrupt civilization. The wounds cry out. We do not have to search for them. If the government announces that there is equal justice for all and the people are being arrested arbitrarily and thrown into prison camps, tortured and forced into hard labor, then we learn soon enough that the proclamations of governments are meaningless and that something has gone hideously wrong. At the entrance to the extermination camp at Auschwitz there was inscribed in iron letters WORK MAKES MEN FREE. The reality was very different: the prisoners were herded into gas chambers or worked to death. The psychological factors that led the National Socialists to put up this pious inscription tell us a good deal about the nature of corruption. None are so pious as the corrupt; moral adages are always on their lips; they practice cold-blooded deceit all the more hopefully when they can invoke morality and they are well aware that they are committing a fraud. The corrupt know that they are corrupt and glory in it.

Healthy societies and corrupt societies move according to different principles, which are diametrically opposed to one another. It is possible to draw up a rough balance sheet with the characteristics of a healthy society on one side of the ledger and the characteristics of a corrupt society on the other.

HEALTHY SOCIETY	CORRUPT SOCIETY
Rule by the greatest number, respect for the law fairly administered.	Dictatorship, rule by a clique of lawless and ruthless men.
The individual follows his own will.	The individual is bent to the will of the dictator.
The best brains in government.	Mediocrities in government.
The individual is free to work and dwell where he pleases.	The individual works for the government and dwells where the government orders him to dwell.
The individual travels where he pleases.	The individual's travels are restricted by the government.
Tolerance, acceptance and enjoyment of foreign cultures.	Intolerance, contempt for foreign cultures.
In religion: a steady faith, a single God.	In religion: worship of the dictator, proliferation of new gods.
In the arts: monumentality, creation of new forms, the human image as touchstone. Untrammeled government aid to the arts.	In the arts: portraits of the dictator, imitative forms, the human image becomes "the worker," "the believer," the follower of the dictator. Government interference in the arts.
In morals: lusty, heterosexual sex, strong family ties, respect for the father figure in the family.	In morals: controlled sexuality, homosexuality, weak family ties, the dictator as father figure.
In social organism: fluid, upward mobility, all organisms open to the talented.	In social organism: fixed, restricted mobility, all organisms filled by a closed elite.

HEALTHY SOCIETY	CORRUPT SOCIETY
In language: free expression, the flowering of the language, no censorship, sobriety.	In language: restricted expression, debasement of the language, censorship, grandiloquence.
In economy: a deliberate aim toward an egalitarian society.	In economy: extremes of wealth and poverty, the amassing of wealth by the dictator's party.
A sense of community and coherence giving stability to the society. Respect for traditions.	Divisiveness, no common feeling, instability. Traditional forms are officially jettisoned. New traditions are invented to serve the dictator.
Respect for life.	Senseless killings.
A sense of shame when wrongs are committed.	Cynicism when wrongs are committed.
The aim is to increase the welfare of the entire community. An open society looking to the future.	The aim is to celebrate the dictator. A closed society looking to the present.
An infinite value attached to human life.	Life becomes valueless: a man = a pack of cigarettes.
The dignity of the individual is maintained.	The dictator is indifferent to everyone's dignity except his own.
Succor for children, the old, and the infirm. They know they will be well cared for.	The state gives only minimal assistance to the young, the old, and the infirm.
The cult of kindness. The life wish.	The cult of brutality. The death wish.
Indifference to titles and modes of address.	Proliferation of titles and modes of address.
The elected ruler is engaged in public affairs to the utmost of his ability and with total dedication, indifferent to wealth and honors.	The dictator engages in public affairs when it pleases him, acquires great wealth and titles, and uses his position to advance his own fame.

These categories are not intended to be exhaustive. They define the differences between a human, stable, decent, and tolerable society and one that is inhuman, unstable, obscene, and intolerable. Although no society has ever existed that possesses every one of the categories in the left-hand column, we recognize in many totalitarian tyrannies the categories in the right-hand column. Nor are the categories defining a healthy society in any way utopian. Healthy societies have existed for longer or shorter periods in many countries and in many ages, usually coinciding with an outpouring of the arts. Thus we find societies based on respect for the individual and the laws in Periclean Athens, the Roman Republic, the India of King Harsha, the Florence of Lorenzo de' Medici, Queen Elizabeth's England, and the early years of the United States. If they were exceptional, it is because abundant good health is rare among nations, and if they often produced great art, it is because great art flourishes during the periods when the individual is most free to express himself. Few of these periods lasted for more than fifty years and nearly all of them were followed by periods of decline. Thus Athens fell from glory with the death of Pericles, Florence lost its preeminence with the death of Lorenzo, and Gupta India perished after the murder of King Harsha. Nor can we imagine Elizabethan England without the saving grace of Elizabeth. The personalities of the rulers spurred the times; they were the energizers; but nothing would have been accomplished if the people had not been equal to their tasks.

On the other side of the balance sheet are the corrupt societies ruled by corrupt men by force and terror. Unhappily, it is possible to compile a much longer list of corrupt than of healthy societies. Every military dictatorship is an example of a corrupt society. In its extreme form a corrupt society takes the form of a vast prison camp where the guards are the ruling elite and the secret police, informers, and *agents provocateurs* are everywhere in evidence. It is the world of Yevgeny Zamyatin's *We* and of George Orwell's *1984*. Its contours are well known and well defined. In the prison camps of the Soviet Union and Nazi Germany millions upon millions of men lived out their lives amid the stench of corruption.

The corrupt society has its own language, a corrupted form of an otherwise healthy language, and its own laws, which are the natural laws turned upside down. The basic law is a single word: *Obey*. The basic aim is conformity. The basic texts are those announced by the ruler, however illogical or senseless. The basic weapons are the well-tried weapons of military force, threats of arrest, and deceit. No one should underestimate the power of deceit to keep a terrified people in subjection. A tyrannical and corrupt government announces: "You are not terrified. You are not subjected. You are perfectly happy." There is no choice: the long-suffering population replies in chorus, "We are perfectly happy." Hitler, in an early edition of *Mein Kampf,* wrote, "You cannot believe how much you have to deceive a nation in order to govern it." He was wrong: one can believe it very easily, for even the democratic governments are not above using deceit for their own purposes.

In *1984* George Orwell described an imaginary tyranny that had an uncomfortable resemblance to existing tyrannies. It had its own language, its own laws, its own slogans. The slogans were totally meaningless: "Who controls the past controls the future; who controls the present controls the past," or the words inscribed in an elegant script across a 1,000-foot-high pyramid:

WAR IS PEACE
FREEDOM IS SLAVERY
IGNORANCE IS STRENGTH

The huge pyramid was the headquarters of the Ministry of Truth, known as Minitrue. Here was developed the new language called Newspeak, with its three separate vocabularies—one for elemental human needs, another for technical matters, and the third for political slogans and commands.

Orwell realized that a corrupt government inevitably corrupts language. Words are not so much separated from the truth as placed in direct opposition to the truth, in direct confrontation with logic. Hence WAR IS PEACE and FREEDOM IS SLAVERY. As Orwell observed in his classic essay "Politics and the English Language," "If thought corrupts language, language can also corrupt thought." It is not a question of shades of meaning or of a reinterpretation of accepted terms. The government gives its own precise and authoritative definitions of things, and anyone who refuses to accept these definitions is severely punished. In the Soviet Union the dictator addresses everyone as *tovarisch,* comrade, thus implying that everyone is a fellow worker and that there are no differences of degree between them. It is a simple and convenient formula; unhappily, it is merely a formula. When Hitler attacked the Soviet Union in the summer of 1941, Stalin, then living in his summer palace on the Black Sea, was silent for several days. He drank himself into a stupor. When he awoke from the stupor, he found it necessary to address the Russian people and made a tape-recorded speech. He began with the words "brothers and sisters." The words seemed incomprehensible. He had never used them before. People gazed at one another in disbelief, wondering why he was addressing them in this way, for "brothers and sisters" had no place in Stalin's lexicon. It was something so new and startling that it seemed to be an aberration, and the people were relieved when in later speeches he addressed them as *tovarischi*.

Orwell was not exaggerating when he invented Newspeak. The language fascinated him. He observed that it was designed to diminish the range of thought. It was permissible to say "This dog is free of lice" or "This field is free of weeds," but it was not permissible to use phrases like "intellectually free" or "politically free." Similarly the words "politically equal" were discouraged, but it was permissible to use "equal" in mathematical equations.

Just as the words in Newspeak lost any identifiable meaning, so did the official songs. The theme song of Big Brother was:

> *Under the spreading chestnut tree*
> *I sold you and you sold me:*
> *There lie they and here lie we*
> *Under the spreading chestnut tree.*

The merit of the song lay in its perfect inanity and hint of treachery. Who "I," "we," "you," and "they" are is never explained; it was enough that the people should recite the mindless words mindlessly. Nor was Orwell exaggerating to any great extent when he permitted O'Brien, the Grand Inquisitor, to address Winston Smith, his prisoner, with a homily based on the historical mistakes of recent tyrannies. Speaking with a kind of exaltation, he said:

The first thing for you to understand is that in this place there are no martyrdoms. You have read of the religious persecutions of the past. In the Middle Ages there was the Inquisition. It was a failure. It set out to eradicate heresy, and ended by perpetuating it. For every heretic it burnt at the stake, thousands of others rose up. Why was that? Because the Inquisition killed its enemies in the open, and killed them while they were still unrepentant. Men were dying because they would not abandon their true beliefs. Naturally all the glory belonged to the victim and all the shame to the Inquisitor who burned him.

Later, in the twentieth century, there were the totalitarians, as they were called. There were the German Nazis and the Russian Communists. The Russians persecuted heresy more cruelly than the Inquisition had done. And they imagined that they had learned from the lessons of the past; they knew, at any rate, that one must not make

martyrs. Before they exposed their victims to public trial, they deliberately set themselves to destroy their dignity. They wore them down
by torture and solitude until they were despicable, cringing wretches,
confessing whatever was put into their mouths, covering themselves
with abuse, accusing and sheltering behind one another, whimpering
for mercy. And yet after only a few years the same thing had happened again. The dead men had become martyrs and their degradation was forgotten.

Once again, why was it? In the first place, because the confessions
they had made were obviously extorted and untrue. We do not make
mistakes of that kind. All the confessions that are uttered here are
true. We make them true. And, above all, we do not allow the dead
to rise up against us. You must stop imagining that posterity will
vindicate you, Winston. Posterity will never hear of you. You will be
lifted clean out from the stream of history. We shall turn you into gas
and pour you into the stratosphere. Nothing will remain of you: not a
name in a register, not a memory in a living brain. You will be annihilated in the past as well as in the future. You will never have existed.

This is, of course, not prophecy. Such things had happened in
Orwell's lifetime. The Jews at Auschwitz were scientifically transformed into gas. Ultimate power is the power to destroy a man not
simply by killing him but by ensuring that he has never had any
existence or by transforming him into an invisible gas.

In all corrupt societies man tends to become not zero but a minus
sign.

Healthy societies are always different; corrupt societies are all
alike. This should not surprise us, since healthy societies manifest
the infinite variety of life, while corrupt societies have the sameness
of death. What corrupt societies have in common is precisely their
corruption; they smell the same, and the same contagion flows from
them.

But just as men die in different ways, so societies become corrupt
in different ways. The tyrant who destroys the spontaneous life of a
nation brings about almost from the moment he takes power a kind
of death that can be immediately recognized. Life, as men ordinarily
conceive of life, stops. Fear, caution, a wooden obedience take the
place of spontaneity. Men are reduced to things, numbers, nothings;
they are permeated with the death that comes from the top. When
Constantine Caramanlis was offered a cabinet post by the Greek
dictator, General Ionnis Metaxas, in 1936, he telegraphed: "Mister
Premier, all dictatorships contain the sperm of death. They are
doomed from the beginning, as will be yours." Although no one has

ever isolated the sperm of death or seen it, men are very well aware of its existence, and Caramanlis was saying no more than the truth. A military dictatorship, with all its attendant curses of regimentation, thought control, torture chambers, and prison camps, brings into existence the absolutely corrupt state.

In dictatorship we see corruption in its most obvious form. A healthy, uncorrupted society must necessarily be everything that a dictatorship is not. Where dictatorship imposes an apparent order from above, a healthy society imposes a real order from below, following the expressed will of the people. Where dictatorship places power in the hands of a dictator who rules through a small, closely knit group of his henchmen, a healthy society spreads power among the largest possible number of people. Where dictatorship exalts the dictator, a healthy society exalts all the members of the society. Where dictatorship employs instruments of terror, a healthy society resolutely rejects these instruments. Where dictatorship debases the language and invents an entire vocabulary in order to mask its arbitrary laws and to impose a new form of society on the people, a healthy society encourages the natural flowering of the language at its own pace without orders from above.

The democracies can take very little comfort from the fact that totalitarian societies are absolutely corrupt. The relative corruption within a democracy can be almost as damaging. A nation where the government is relatively corrupt quickly learns that corruption breeds corruption; once a single member of the government has been corrupted, there is a tendency for all the other members to follow in the same path. When Vice-President Spiro Agnew was charged with receiving payoffs from building contractors, no one in or outside the United States felt that Agnew alone in the government was guilty of corruption. There was a presumption that others were equally guilty but had the luck not to be found out. *Agnew* became synonymous with corruption, as *Quisling* had become a synonym for traitor, but unlike Quisling, Agnew received only a minimal punishment. And the fact that he received so light a punishment and was not sent to prison only fed the suspicions of the public that the powerful were rarely punished for their crimes.

The government sets the tone for the bureaucracy: a firm, honest government produces a firm, honest bureaucracy. When the bureaucracy discovers that the members of the government are corrupt and go unpunished, or receive only the lightest of sentences when their crimes are discovered, then it begins to follow the example of the government. Bureaucrats learn to interpret the laws for their own advantage and pursue their own gains, secure in the knowledge that they will go unpunished. They have vast powers over the common people. They enjoy the power vested in them by the authority of the government. Within limits they can interpret the laws as they please, but there are limits beyond which it is dangerous to go. When they realize that the government and their immediate superiors are corrupt, they gradually find themselves extending the limits. They promise, for a fee, to cut through red tape. They will issue a license at once if you hand them $100 under the table but will delay issuing it for six months if you refuse. They demand small sums of money for performing commonplace acts that are among their essential duties. They are in a position to institutionalize corruption, and for this reason governments have wisely introduced an inspectorate to oversee every branch of the bureaucracy. Unhappily, the government cannot inspect all the acts of a corrupt bureaucracy, and the inspectorate itself may be corrupt. Even more unhappily, the people who suffer most under a corrupt bureaucracy are the poor, who have no court of appeal.

Let us imagine a corrupt post office clerk in an imaginary country. He enjoys watching people standing in line, for this gives him a feeling of power and authority. He can keep the line waiting as long as he pleases. He can leave his little office for ten minutes and watch imperturbably from his hiding place as the line grows longer and the people become increasingly impatient and angry. "They are like sheep," he tells himself, "and they must be treated like sheep." He returns triumphantly, smiling at his own success. "I was called away —official business," he murmurs, and the long-suffering people who have been waiting to buy stamps sigh sympathetically.

The post office clerk begins to pilfer the mail. It amazes him how easy it is to slip a few registered letters into his pocket. He feels very little guilt. Many others are pilfering mail. The chief postal officer in the district is a notorious pilferer, but no charges have ever been brought against him. A few complaints have reached the post office, but they have been handled circumspectly. The chief of all the postal services, a member of the government, has made it known that a certain amount of pilferage is inevitable. He is himself corrupt. He receives money under the table from the airlines he has specially favored for transporting the mail. This is known to many of his colleagues, who demand their cut. The harassed chief of the postal service finally agrees to give 50 per cent of his takings to his colleagues and is certain that they will soon demand 75 per cent.

Everyone in the postal service knows that the chief is corrupt and that pilfering is taking place on a massive scale. By tacit agreement the postal officers, from the most junior clerk upward, join in a conspiracy of silence. At any moment one of them can reveal the full extent of the conspiracy to the police or to a judge, but the pilferage is so rewarding that anyone who is in the least inclined to reveal what is happening hesitates before admitting the crime. One thinks twice before admitting a crime of such magnitude. Nor is it safe to make such an admission. Gradually the postal service has become a conspiratorial organization with its own hierarchy, its own enforcers, its own secret rules and regulations. Throughout the organization there are men watching closely for the first open sign of disaffection. The postal service comes to resemble a totalitarian society ruled by the secret police. A few postal clerks, thought to be about to go to the police, are found murdered. The pilfering continues, and the postal clerks live in fear for their lives.

In a democracy an aroused and angry public can demand a commission of enquiry. Witnesses can be subpoenaed and compelled to answer questions on oath; the conspiracy will eventually be uncovered and the conspirators sentenced to long terms of imprisonment. Unfortunately, these commissions are necessarily very slow in reaching their verdicts, and the more astute conspirators are rarely punished to the full extent of the law. More terrible than the pilfering of millions of dollars' worth of mail is the weakening of the moral fiber that occurs whenever a conspiratorial organization comes into existence.

By its very nature, every bureaucracy tends to become a conspiratorial organization. Every bureaucracy becomes a closed society demanding implicit loyalty from its members. Implanted in all members is the need to serve the bureaucracy first and the public second. The bureaucracy's mistakes must be covered up, its black sheep removed as silently as possible. At all costs it is necessary to maintain the fiction that the bureaucracy works only for the public interest and is not in the least concerned with the perpetuation and increase of its own powers.

The power wielded by a bureaucracy is so great that the temptations of corruption must always exist. Power generates corruption. Wherever men exercise power there is the presumption that some of them will be corrupted by it. In the police, in the internal revenue service, and in the regulatory agencies the temptations of corruption will always remain until someone devises a foolproof plan for policing them effectively. These are the officials who bear down most heavily on the public and are therefore in a position to do the most harm. That many bureaucracies remain honest is a testimony to the common humanity of the men who staff them.

When the Knapp Commission met to enquire into police corruption in New York, it learned that there were two types of corrupt policemen—the "meat-eaters" and the "grass-eaters." The "meat-eaters" were those who devoted their working lives to corruption, extracting huge payoffs and using all the weapons at their disposal for enforcing their demands, while the "grass-eaters" simply accepted the comparatively small payoffs that came to them whenever there was a sharing of the proceeds from gambling, drug traffic, and prostitution. In the five police districts they studied they learned that the monthly share per plainclothesman ranged from $300 or $400 in midtown Manhattan to $1,500 in Harlem. The pattern of corruption was strikingly standardized and institutionalized. Books were kept, and each plainclothesman signed a receipt for his "nut." Newly assigned plainclothesmen received nothing during their first two months of service while their reliability and trustworthiness were being investigated, and it was made clear to them that on no account must they reveal the existence of the "pad." Some of the "meat-eaters" became millionaires, but the Knapp Commission wisely pointed out that the "grass-eaters" were at the heart of the problem, because their great numbers tended to make corruption respectable.

An extraordinary situation had arisen: it had become virtually impossible for a policeman to be uncorrupted. "The rookie who comes into the department is faced with the situation where it is easier for him to become corrupt than to remain honest." Since it was easier to be corrupt, and since he was in no position to fight against the entire police force, the rookie did exactly what the others were doing: he accepted his small share of the "pad," kept his mouth shut, and joined the conspiratorial organization. Since New York is the city with the greatest murder rate in the world and there are about two million hand guns owned by its private citizens, this meant that the city was virtually defenseless against its enemies. Arrests continued to be made, criminals were placed on trial, judges sentenced them to varying terms of imprisonment, but the police were arresting only those criminals who were not contributing to the "pad." New York continued to exist by the force of its own momentum, but it was dangerously wounded.

The Knapp Commission was invited to make its recommendations, and did so. It asked for the appointment of a Special Deputy Attorney General with powers to maintain a permanent investigation of police and judicial corruption throughout the state and the establishment of an independent inspectorate of the police. Five further recommendations were made:

> First, corrupt activity must be curtailed by eliminating as many situations as possible which expose policemen to corruption, and by controlling exposure where corruption hazards are unavoidable.
> Second, temptations to engage in corrupt activity on the part of the police and the public must be reduced by subjecting both to significant risks of detection, apprehension, conviction, and penalties.
> Third, incentives for meritorious police performance must be increased.
> Fourth, police attitudes toward corruption must continue to change.
> Fifth, a climate of reform must be supported by the public.

These recommendations were useful but paid no attention to one fact of overriding importance. Conspiratorial organizations, like corruption, tend to perpetuate themselves, and they can be broken only by methods of extreme severity, by punishments so harsh that only the most foolhardy would take the risk.

Newspaper accounts made much of the vast sums of money siphoned off by the police and of the strange alliances formed between the police and the criminals. But although these were bad enough, the real harm lay elsewhere, in the helplessness of the public confronted by police they could no longer trust. If the police were criminals, who were the defenders of the law? And the public realized that there were no defenders, that they lived in a lawless city, where each man survived only by a series of miracles, and that the city would become more lawless every year.

The terrible thing is that corruption exists wherever there are men yearning for an unfair advantage over their fellow men. That unfair advantage, acquired by force or threats or trickery, is one of the many aspects of power. It appears to be human nature to accumulate advantages, to yearn for power, to seek prominence and wealth to the detriment of others. We dream of becoming famous and of being millionaires, forgetting that fame is always illusory and that there are few millionaires who have not acquired their wealth dishonestly. In a more egalitarian society wealth would have less meaning and fame would perhaps be reserved for great artists and inventors, the true benefactors of humanity. A policeman acquiring a fortune by corruption might regard himself as a man of some considerable importance. A high police official, a witness at the Knapp

Commission hearings, pointed out that in the egalitarian society of the prison "a corrupt cop ranks lower than a child molester."

So far I have discussed corruption as it appears in the public sector. In the private sector corruption also flourishes, but it lacks the force that comes from the misuse of governmental and bureaucratic power. Corruption in the private sector is relative. It kills and wounds, blasts hopes, poisons the minds of the young, but it cannot destroy on the same scale as a well-entrenched bureaucracy. Big businesses tend to become corrupt, and they become all the more corrupt the closer they are to governmental power. They are corrupt when they make fraudulent claims in their advertisements, and they are capable of terrifying acts of corruption in their competitive wars with one another. President Eisenhower in his farewell address to the nation issued a solemn warning against the corruptions of the military-industrial complex. Apparently no one listened, for the corruptions continued.

In the private sector corruption appears in the most unlikely quarters. Let us imagine a meeting of a philanthropic society dedicated to the furtherance of some excellent aims: the cure of a disease, or the encouragement of arts and letters, or the advancement of antiquarian research. Twenty or thirty people come together to support a broad program of philanthropy. They are full of enthusiasm, prepared to sacrifice their time and money for the common cause. They elect a chairman, an executive secretary, a treasurer, and someone who will record the minutes of the meetings. For a year everything runs smoothly, there is no bickering, all the members of the society carry the same weight, all are equals, and all are heard. They raise money eagerly for their philanthropy and rejoice in their good works. They form a family of friends with one desire: to promote their cause.

Then gradually and imperceptibly a shadow falls over their meetings. They become aware of a sense of strain, arguments flare up, the chairman occasionally pounds the table with his gavel. The chairman and the executive secretary are at odds with one another. Soon power groups are formed, voices are raised, angry charges fly across the table, the chairman pounds his gavel more frequently. Then one group demands the expulsion of another as a matter of principle, and they are all fighting. The original purpose of the philanthropic society is forgotten in the violent exchanges and recriminations. The society, torn by factions, is now in its weakest state, and it is at this point that one of the members exerts himself to assume the leadership of the society "in order to heal the wounds and to prevent any further quarreling."

There had never been any need for leadership in the philanthropic society. It worked best when the members simply sat round the table and discussed the various projects dear to them. Now with its new leader the society grows powerful and influential, but the original aims have been forgotten. Power for its own sake becomes the goal of the small, self-perpetuating group in office. New projects are rammed through the executive board, and if the board raises objections the executive committee, dominated by the chairman, sees to it that the projects are put into operation. The leader selects the members of the executive board, hires a new executive secretary, controls the finances, and so dominates the society that it becomes the instrument of his own advancement. The philanthropic society is no longer philanthropic.

The society has gone through four stages:

First, all move in the same direction with a common goal.

Second, power groups emerge. They may have arisen naturally or they may have been manipulated.

Third, one power group dominates the rest, and out of this there emerges a leader.

Fourth, the philanthropic society becomes the vehicle of the leader, whose aim is personal domination to his own advantage. The original aims of the society are abandoned.

Something very similar to this happened to the Social Democratic Party in Russia, which split into the Bolshevik and Menshevik parties. The Bolsheviks, meaning "the majority," were in fact in the minority. When they seized power, they annihilated the Mensheviks and all other parties. The Social Democratic Party, which had begun as a philanthropic party of idealists, ended by becoming an instrument of ruthless repression employing all available social, military, and police techniques to dominate the people.

Only those who have actually seen the process in operation can realize the stranglehold that a determined and ruthless chairman can have on an organization. Much sooner than anyone might expect, he exerts complete domination. The bemused members of the board are transformed into sheep, blindly following him, and after a while they become accustomed to being led and even to rejoice in his leadership, for they no longer bear the responsibility of making decisions. Finally there comes the day when the chairman announces that the board has been of wonderful assistance to him but has now outlived its usefulness. He thanks them for their services, presents each of them with a plaque, and dismisses them from his office.

The chairman has corrupted the philanthropic society by the simplest of means and transformed it into a conspiratorial organization with himself as chief conspirator. At all times he has acted within the law. At times he has stretched the society's bylaws a little; he has not always permitted the members to speak; he cannot be said to have had the best interests of the society at heart. He has acquired power in the way in which it is nearly always acquired—he has taken it from others and in the process destroyed or radically altered something that belonged to others.

The corruptions of a society nearly always come about through the usurpation of power. There are men who find the temptations of power irresistible; they pull the levers and give commands, and to their astonishment they find that people immediately obey them. Obedience becomes a reflex action, meaningless and automatic, and at this point power loses its validity because it has become divorced from human associations and is no longer being wielded for the benefit of humanity but for the private enjoyment of the man who wields power. Throughout history men have rightly regarded power as something fearful and dangerous, to be used only with the utmost sense of responsibility, for power is deadly and unless used responsibly it corrupts everything it touches.

The Five Faces
of Corruption

The processes of decay and degeneration are always terrible; and the decay of a nation is no less terrible than the corruption of the physical body. What is especially terrible is that the people within the society are not responsible except in rare cases for the harm inflicted on them. They have not asked that their society should die or that it should be reduced to a kind of ignominious death-in-life. They are not corrupt. Corruption has worked on them as a result of historical forces over which they have no control, or it has seeped down through the government, or it has been brought about by treachery and subversion from within, or it arises from unstable cultural elements within the society. Conquest, tyranny, treachery, and the clash of cultures bring about corrupt societies, and so does old age. Sometimes the five faces of corruption are visible at the same time.

Just as a man is an unwilling victim of the processes of decay within his own body before and after his death, so societies are nearly always the unwilling victims of their own decay. The people bear only a limited responsibility, and very often they bear no responsibility at all. They may be conquered by surprise. A tyranny may have been imposed on them. They may have been totally unaware of the traitors in their midst. There may have been no available means to prevent the clash of cultures from tearing them apart and reducing them to a state of permanent civil war. Nor are the children born into an old and dying society responsible for its coming death. It may be argued that a society should be made so strong that it cannot be conquered under any conditions, or that the tyrant who poisons the society should be killed, or that it is the duty of the people to see that there are no traitors in their midst, or that they should make reasonable compromises to avoid a clash of cultures; but these arguments beg the question. A country can be very strong and yet be defeated by a weaker country. A tyrant may prove to be so well entrenched in the seat of power that it is virtually impossible to remove him. A great and proud nation may be infested with traitors in high places without the people knowing about it. In the study of corruption the innocence of the great mass of the people is the saddest thing of all. They bear the brunt of the misery, but only in democracies, where they are able to elect the leaders of their choice, can they be said to bear any responsibility for it.

There are many weapons that can be used to prevent the corruption of societies. The most powerful of these weapons are vigilance and knowledge. Hence the importance of the press, radio, and television to break through all imposed restrictions to discover how the government works, how it arrives at its decisions, how it manages its defenses, how it deals with traitors, especially the traitors in its midst. The free flow of information is essential if the people are to have any responsibility in their affairs; and unless they bear this responsibility, they are no more than the slaves of an irresponsible tyranny. A judiciary that can act decisively and quickly when high crimes and misdemeanors are committed is more than ever necessary when a nation is threatened by subversion and treachery. In the words of Thomas Paine: "Those who expect to reap the blessings of freedom must, like men, undergo the fatigue of supporting it."

The least corrupt societies are those that are completely open, where the responsibility is shared among all the people, where there is no privileged class, and where there are no vast differences in wealth. Corruption enters as soon as the government is managed on behalf of special interests against the interests of the people. Once the government is corrupt, then it will become all the more incapable of dealing with the corruption brought about by traitors within and subversives and still less capable of dealing with its foreign enemies.

Old age, conquest, tyranny, treachery, and the clash of cultures are all complex phenomena involving factors difficult to assess. What the military authorities call treachery is not always treachery, as the Dreyfus case demonstrated. A tyranny can be absolute or relative, murderous or aseptic, but in either case it is intolerable. What calls itself a democracy may in fact be a disguised tyranny or a plutocracy. Old age, as applied to nations, is not a measurable quality. Just as the human body is corrupted in subtle and terrible ways, so societies are corrupted in subtle and terrible ways; and there is always the stench of corruption in our nostrils to remind us of its presence.

CORRUPTION BY OLD AGE

We recognize an old and dying society by its creaking muscles, its rheumy eyes, and a certain disjointedness in its approach to the problems of the present day. It lives on its past glories, celebrates its ancient arts, and haughtily observes younger societies that do not have its advantages of wisdom and experience. Sometimes it speaks out with a voice of authority, loud and clear, as though it had acquired new vigor, but in fact the words are familiar words spoken hundreds of years ago, and the clarity of the voice is only an indication of the familiarity of the pronouncements.

Such old and decaying civilizations existed in both China and Japan in the early years of the last century. In Japan the way of life had not changed notably for eight hundred years. In China, too, in spite of the appearance of the remarkably able emperors K'ang Hsi and Ch'ien Lung during the Manchu dynasty, the society had become strangely static, as though caught up in an interminable dialogue with itself concerning whether it wanted to go on living. The great emperors had the effect of making their successors look pathetically small. The British were attempting to invade the south, the Russians were pressing heavily on the north, and the Japanese were pressing even more heavily along the eastern coastline. China seemed about to be torn apart and colonized, like Africa.

When war with Japan was imminent and funds for building a naval fleet were voted by the Chinese government, the empress dowager Tz'u-hsi sequestered a large part of the funds and built herself a marble pleasure boat to decorate her summer palace. Intelligent, venomous, and murderous whenever her will was crossed, the empress dowager presided over a corrupt court given over to constant attendance on her whims. Like the Japanese shoguns until the arrival of Commodore Matthew Perry, the empress dowager detested and feared all foreigners and was herself largely responsible for the Boxer Uprising, dedicated to the indiscriminate slaughter of all foreigners found on Chinese soil. She was wholly corrupt and wholly irresponsible. In the tradition of empresses, she fought her way to the throne by poisoning anyone and everyone who threatened her tenuous right to it.

The Manchu dynasty, founded in 1644, had started well and ended ingloriously. History would have been kinder to it if it had ended in 1796 with the death of Ch'ien Lung. The empress dowager resembled a ghost from the ancient feudal past. The Chinese were wasting their energies in civil wars when they should have been expending their strength fighting off the colonial demands of Japan and the Western powers. China was dying at the roots just at the moment when it was most necessary to be vigorously alive.

Nations grow old and tired, the bureaucracy becomes unworkable, the laws proliferate, the people lose their spirits, and the life-giving forces are outweighed by the deathly forces of contentment and indifference. The Chinese wanted a new form of government, but throughout their history they had been ruled by emperors and scarcely knew where to turn when the empress dowager died in 1908. They wanted something new but could not define it. Revolution broke out in 1911 and was followed by a restoration. Yüan Shih-k'ai, a close adviser of the empress dowager, proclaimed himself president and then very briefly emperor. China split into its constituent parts, and soon each province was under the command of a local warlord. The remedy was worse than the disease, and the patient was dying.

Poor Yüan Shih-k'ai! He was almost a caricature of the corrupt man in the position of power: rich, fat, ungainly, he derived his power from the army and from his successful intrigues with the empress dowager. He was forceful, intelligent, treacherous, completely out of touch with the modern world. He believed passionately in emperor worship and regarded himself as an ideal emperor. Happily, he died, or was poisoned, in 1915, and for the following twelve years China, in the words of Dr. Sun Yat-sen, became "a dish of shifting sand." The warlords proliferated. Their troops were paid by confiscating the property of citizens and exacting taxes for ten years ahead. There was no stability, no central government, no sense of achievement. Rival governments appeared in Canton and Hankow, while the "legitimate" government pretended to rule from Peking; and all the time the Japanese were waiting for the opportunity to strike.

China, so old, so venerable, so riddled with the diseases of age, seemed to be on the verge of death when Chiang Kai-shek drove his army northward in 1927 and conquered one by one the warlords in his path. By the end of the year China was united under the Kuomintang regime, and Nanking was selected as the new capital. Four years later, in 1931, the Japanese attacked in Manchuria, giving the new government no time to consolidate its strength. The Kuomintang government was corrupt, with half the important ministers coming from Chiang Kai-shek's immediate family.

Chiang Kai-shek acted like a feudal prince; his word was law; he demanded instant obedience, permitted no discussion, and therefore knew very little about what was happening in the country or what people were thinking. When the Japanese attacked China, he governed from Hankow and then from Chungking in the heart of Szechuan province. He was still the feudal prince, ruling by decree, incapable of understanding the forces at work, a strict Confucian who understood the arts of war as it was practiced in the Han dynasty. When he was a young man, Chinese armies were still fighting the tribesmen on the borders of Annam with bows and arrows. The Pacific war came to an end with the dropping of nuclear explosives on Hiroshima and Nagasaki, and Chiang Kai-shek believed he had inherited a united China. Within four years he was a refugee from the mainland on the island of Formosa. The old feudal ways were discredited, and the Chinese Communists powerfully asserted their right to cut the country off from its ancient past. The new China was like a young shoot, glorying in its youth.

How wistfully, over the centuries, have men dreamed of escaping from the old and embracing the new, as though men could be born again, as though like serpents they could slough off their ancient skins. The old yearn for their lost freshness and innocence, for clear eyes and clear aims. So John Dryden wrote:

> *All, all, of a piece throughout;*
> *Thy Chase had a Beast in View;*
> *Thy Wars brought nothing about;*
> *Thy Lovers were all untrue.*
> *'Tis well an Old Age is out,*
> *And time to begin a New.*

The desire to begin anew is so strong that it has given us the names of countries, historical epochs, and political movements. The Renaissance, the Reformation, the Restoration, Risorgimento, New Deal, New Frontier, New Life Movement, New World—all these names were intended to suggest separation from a dead or decaying past. The Russian poet Alexander Blok welcomed the Bolshevik Revolution because it was a new birth. "To build everything new," he exclaimed, "so that our lying, dirty, boring, monstrous life becomes a just and clean, a joyous and beautiful life!" Under the revolution he would starve to death, and long before he died he would grow disenchanted with the revolution, but his fierce hope for a new life for Russia remained.

The consolations of a new life are chiefly to be found in the imagination. President Woodrow Wilson, in his famous first inaugural address, believed it was the duty of Americans to build a new world. "Our duty," he declared, "is to cleanse, to reconcile, to restore, to correct the evil without impairing the good, to purify and humanize every process of our common life." The words are heavy with the customary clichés beloved by politicians, but there is no doubt that he hoped to purify and humanize the processes of life.

In much the same way Lorenzo de' Medici proclaimed the coming of a new age with the cry "Le tems reviens," meaning that a new time would bring a wonderful freshness to Florentine life. But the new time obstinately refused to come, and life went on as before except for the rich and feverish glow of his own presence, his own delight in his Florentines. The new time, if it existed at all, was Lorenzo himself. Nor was the Renaissance a new birth, for it is impossible to give a precise date to the beginning of that extraordinary marriage of the arts and sciences that came into existence under the Medicis, when it seemed that Florence was destined to become the intellectual capital of Europe.

We regard the New with something of the joy of a grandfather doting on his most recent grandchild. The New means a sudden spurt of energy, boisterous lungs, an explosion of ideas. It announces that it has come to supplant the old, the decaying, the corrupt. It is so strident and demanding that many feel uncomfortable in its presence and find themselves preferring the old and the corrupt because they are familiar presences.

When the New enters a society, it generally takes the form of a charismatic ruler or prophet, who releases forces hitherto unsuspected, unknown, or barely recognizable amid a welter of traditional forces. Lorenzo was not an innovator. He built on the past and channeled the learning of his time and all the known arts in the direction he desired. Gandhi, Mao Tse-tung, and Napoleon galvanized their people into actions that would not have taken place without them. They were all deeply rooted in tradition. They were revolutionaries who wore the robes of legitimacy. Gandhi was a Hindu possessing an incandescent faith in Hinduism and in his own people. Mao Tse-tung followed a long tradition of peasant leaders who overthrew the existing government when it no longer possessed the Mandate of Heaven. Napoleon restored the ancient monarchy and gave it a new and urgent life. What they gave to their people was a new aim, a new purpose. Quite suddenly the windows seemed to be thrown wide open and the life of the people was worth living again.

But sometimes there are no charismatic leaders to revive the dying spirits of a country. The old traditions die hard; the old gods demand to be worshiped; the old ways of life are woven into the fabric of society; and the thought that all this traditional knowledge must be supplanted by new ideas with their explosive consequences stirs the powerful lords of the country to fury. Nevertheless, the new ideas are necessary to keep the country alive, like fresh blood pouring into aged veins. In old age the muscles lose their flexibility, the sight grows dim, the legs totter, the mechanism of the brain begins to fail, while memory of the ancient past grows keener. So it is with nations, which forget that the memory of past glories provides no nourishment for the soul and that the future has a greater claim on them than the past.

CORRUPTION BY CONQUEST

On February 20, 1707, toward evening, the emperor Aurungzeb died in the small town of Ahmadnagar, having ruled India for nearly fifty years. A stern and bigoted man, determined to impose the Muslim religion on his subjects and to make the lives of the Hindus intolerable, he spent the greater part of his reign making war. He had come to power by imprisoning his father, Shah Jahan, and killing his older brother, the talented Dara Shikoh, and thereafter he habitually killed everyone who appeared in the slightest degree to threaten his authority. His crimes were so numerous that on his deathbed he was forced by his conscience to confront them. "I am so evil," he said, "that I fear God will have no place for me. Therefore bury me bareheaded, for they say that all those who come bareheaded into God's presence will receive His mercy. But I do not believe He will dare to look at me!"

Aurungzeb's crimes derived from his coldness of temperament, his calculating spirit, which led him to consider all actions only in terms of his immediate profit. He had no foresight, no feeling for people, no understanding of popular movements. He liked to say that he was an ascetic who wanted to live in the utmost simplicity, but in fact he was attended by the most luxurious court that had existed up to his time. He permitted his Mughal courtiers the greatest license: they drank heavily, took drugs, practiced all kinds of sexual excess, bribed their way to high office, and stole unashamedly from the Hindus, taking their women and possessions whenever it pleased them. The emperor, a small, squat, ugly man with a parrot's beak of a nose, approved of their wildest crimes. By his intense bigotry and intolerance he alienated the Hindus and aroused the fierce animosity of the Rajputs. One day, when he was in his ninetieth year, he turned to one of his advisers and said: "Why are the Mahrattas always rising against us? What have we done to them?" He had forgotten that he had been murdering them for half a century.

But Aurungzeb's greatest crime was that he left India weak and divided against herself. Unlike his great-grandfather Akbar he was not in the least concerned to find a common meeting ground between Muslims and Hindus; instead he rejected all efforts to do so, exhausted himself in inventing new punishments for the Hindus, and encouraged the Muslims to regard the Hindus as their slaves. In 1757, fifty years after his death, a small and obscure battle in the village of Plassey in Bengal decided the fate of India for the next 190 years. Robert Clive, a countinghouse clerk of the East India Company, with a very modest experience of soldiering, won the battle that made Bengal a British possession. Thereafter, slice by slice, India became the property of the East India Company and was ruled from its offices in London until in due course it became the property of the British crown and was ruled by a viceroy.

The imposition of British customs and ways of thought on the Indians, Muslims and Hindus alike, had shattering consequences. They became a subject people, taught to regard every British soldier as a superior being. "We are treated like gods here," wrote Winston Churchill from Bangalore, where he was posted as a young subaltern. He had some reason for satisfaction. Although he was not wealthy, he possessed a string of polo ponies and an army of servants attended to his wants. He had a large house, very few duties, and spent a good deal of his time cultivating his roses with the help of his Hindu gardeners. The British in India lived like lords, and in time the Indians came to regard their presence as natural and inevitable, like the monsoons.

In the high schools lessons were taught in English, examinations were held in English, and proficiency in English was necessary for entry into the civil service or in the administration of the railroads. As a boy Gandhi found his English teacher almost incomprehensible and discovered later that the teacher had learned English by rote. What he had thought to be English was a strange barbaric language made up of verbs, adverbs, nouns, pronouns, adjectives, and prepositions put together by main force in what appeared to be an intelligible order. Later Gandhi became a master of the English language, but his proficiency was not due to anything he had learned in school.

The most corrupting influence was not English, which served as a link-language in a country where there were at least fifteen separate tongues. Corruption came with the implied superiority of the British conquerors, the habits of acquiescence, the sterile attempt by cultivated Indians to be more British than the British. A glance at the map in the schoolroom showed that Britain was a world power, possessor of all the areas painted red, and therefore invincible. The viceroy was surrounded by the panoply of a king. A very small British garrison force ensured the security of the Indian Empire. In all the princely states, which remained theoretically independent while professing loyalty to the crown, British "advisers" saw that the maharajahs were aware of their responsibilities toward the British raj. The maharajahs were allowed to retain their enormous wealth, but remained in office at the pleasure of the crown and could be removed by an Order in Council. The aristocracy consisted of the British governors and civil servants with the viceroy at the top, the maharajahs, and a few rich industrialists, mostly Parsees from the region of Bombay. Knighthoods were scattered like confetti among the maharajahs and Parsees.

British rule was on the whole silent and conspicuously inconspicuous. The villagers in the five hundred thousand villages of India were scarcely aware of its existence unless they lived near the cantonments where the British officers trained their Indian mercenaries, permitting few Indians to rise to officer rank. But the damage lay precisely in the fact that the rule was invisible, faceless, remote. There was the continual sapping of the sense of national unity, the knowledge that a whole people were powerless and would remain powerless for centuries to come, the certainty that the longer the

British stayed in India the longer they would want to stay. The Indians had been corrupted into believing they were the permanent servants of a master race. ''

The surprising thing is that they took so long to revolt. Not until 1905, following the Japanese victory over the Russians, did they begin to rebel in earnest, although on a pitiably small scale. British officers were assassinated in Bengal. For the first time the word *swaraj,* self-rule, began to be heard as though it were within men's reach. When Gandhi returned to India in the early days of 1915, bringing with him the weapon of *ahimsa,* nonviolent protest, the revolutionary movement swung into action, with Gandhi and the Congress Party as the focus of revolt. The conquered were turning on their conquerors, and the end was in sight.

A whole generation passed before power finally fell into the hands of the conquered people. In 1947 the Indian subcontinent was divided into two sovereign nations, Pakistan and India, where the great majority of Pakistanis were Muslims and the great majority of Indians were Hindus. Then at last the centuries of foreign rule brought about the inevitable explosion as the Hindus and Muslims took up arms and fought each other *in extremis,* each side expressing the pent-up rage and frustration that had gathered strength over so many years. In the bloodbath that saw the deaths of perhaps eight million people the new nations were born.

The emperor Aurungzeb, by deliberately setting the Muslims against the Hindus, was ultimately responsible for this bloodbath, which took place 240 years after his death; nor were the British blameless, for they took no precautions against it, although they must have known it was coming; nor were Jinnah and Gandhi, the Muslim and Hindu leaders, altogether blameless, for they also knew it was coming. What had been corrupt and hidden for centuries now came out into the open in a massacre of unparalleled agony as the physical body of India was torn apart. Gandhi in his heroic old age attempted to heal the wounds, but without success. What should have been the joyful days of independence were given over to interminable sorrow.

Conquest, wherever it occurs, breeds corruption, the degradation of man, the stifling of the life of a nation. The British were more fair-minded than most conquerors. They introduced their judicial system to India. They collected taxes fairly and punished their own people with severity when they committed crimes. They followed Hindu and Muslim law as far as possible and so long as it did not conflict with their own law. They rarely permitted themselves the luxury of massacre, for they were not bloodthirsty by nature; the one massacre, at Amritsar, was ordered by a British officer who had lost his nerve and was terrified out of his wits. If they had not been fair-minded, the struggle would'have been far more bitter. They left India more bravely than they conquered it.

The Spanish conquest of Mexico and Peru was far more harmful to the conquered natives, for Cortes and Pizarro did their utmost to destroy the religion and social organisms that alone gave meaning to the peoples' lives. In Tenochtitlán the images of the gods were destroyed by fire or hurled into the canals or shattered into a hundred pieces to form the rubble foundations of churches and palaces. Every Aztec temple was leveled to the ground and the earth was raked over; everything that could conceivably relate to the cult of the gods was destroyed, and thereupon a church was erected on the same spot. In Cuzco in Peru the Temple of the Sun was made of monolithic stones; the symbol of the sun was removed, and the crucifix was substituted. The Incas became slaves, their holy books were destroyed, their written language perished, their leaders were murdered. Like Hitler's Germans in the Ukraine, the Spaniards murdered and plundered at will. Massacre was developed into a fine art in the hope that the population would be reduced to just enough servants and slaves to permit the new masters to live in comparative luxury. Corruption was deliberate and applied with ferocious cruelty. This time there was no possibility of revolt. The spirit of the people was broken, like an old stick broken across the knee.

In Africa in the nineteenth century the colonial powers employed the same methods. Local kings and tribal chieftains lost their authority to white men who abrogated to themselves the supreme power, pronounced laws, ordered fines and executions, introduced forced labor, destroyed the tribal temples, and permitted missionaries to compel the Africans to conform to Christian standards of morality. Uprooted, the Africans lost their faith in themselves and found themselves imitating the customs of the invaders, as though by simply following their customs they could be like them, as powerful as they were. They learned French, English, and German, dressed in uncomfortable European clothes, and swore allegiance to kings who lived far away, whom they had never seen and were never likely to see. Young district officers, fresh from Europe, ruled over hundreds of square miles of territory with efficiency and sometimes with kindness. In German Southwest Africa, the German district commissioners acted with predictable brutality, and the Belgians in the Congo were scarcely less brutal. In South Africa the

Africans were herded into the gold and diamond mines, receiving wages that allowed them to live on a bare subsistence level. But these economic crimes were perhaps the least important of the crimes committed against them. The real crime was that they were treated like animals. They had only one purpose: to work productively for the white men and to serve their interests.

To corrupt is to dehumanize, and the processes of corruption were carried out in colonial Africa with an extraordinary ruthlessness. When the tide turned and the colonial countries became independent, the whites sometimes asked themselves what they had done wrong to be greeted with so much hatred by the people to whom they had granted freedom and independence. What they had done wrong was very simple: they had regarded the Africans as their servants.

A political structure can tolerate and absorb an almost limitless amount of petty corruption. It cannot tolerate and absorb the corruption of the spirit that comes about when the conquerors assume the role of masters and the conquered accept the role of servants. Where there is no faith and trust, communication becomes merely a ritual made up of orders and acquiescence, and both masters and servants are corrupted. Usually the masters are corrupted to a much greater degree than the servants, because they begin to believe in their own mastery. The servants have the advantage of knowing that if they can retain their sense of identity and their spiritual freedom, they may outlast their masters.

When the Germans conquered France in 1940 they were surprised to see the French women behaving as though they had never been conquered. They dressed more elegantly than usual, wore feathers in their hats, and flaunted their beauty. They pretended more or less successfully that the Germans were not present, or that if they were present, they were no more than a nauseating gas mysteriously percolating through the atmosphere. Despising their conquerors, they showed their independence by cultivating fashions that annoyed and fascinated the Germans. Thus almost instinctively they came into possession of a weapon that effectively made a mockery of conquest.

Conquest, wherever it occurs, breeds corruption in the conqueror. Too often a people who have been defeated in war and then enslaved lose their essential characteristics. Torn up by the roots, their customs changed, their traditions obliterated, the government composed of foreigners or self-serving traitors, the conquered people acquiesce in their enslavement.

But sometimes it happens that the conquered people succeed in throwing off all the corruptions of conquest. France, twice conquered by Germany, is not the less France. No one walking through the streets of Paris can imagine that it was once the headquarters of the German Army of the West, that the street signs were once written in German, or that German soldiers paraded up and down the Champs-Elysées. Except for the small blue enamel plaques in the walls announcing that here or near here a Frenchman was shot down by the Germans, all traces of the former German rule were effaced, and this became all the easier because the Germans never penetrated or influenced French culture. The conquest was a temporary phenomenon: the beast scratched with his poisoned claws but the poison was sucked out in time, the wound was cleansed, and there was no scar.

Nor would anyone visiting Peking today find any evidence that it was occupied by the Japanese for eight terrible years, with a Japanese military governor ruling from within the Forbidden City. Thousands of Japanese patrolled the streets, street signs were in Japanese, many palaces and private houses were converted into Japanese houses by the addition of tatamis and sliding screens. The robust Chinese outer structure remained, while a delicate, paper-thin inner structure was built inside it. When the Japanese finally surrendered, there were only these paper houses to remind the Chinese that their land had been occupied and their people slaughtered in the millions. It took only a few minutes to throw the paper houses into the flames.

China remained uncorrupted by the Japanese invasion chiefly because the Chinese were aware of the immense size of their country and the permanence of their traditions. It was inconceivable to them that China would become for any length of time a Japanese province. Their pride in their past was rooted in the knowledge that they had cultivated their soil for nearly four thousand years, and it puzzled them that the Japanese should believe themselves capable of ruling over so vast an empire. Can the spider eat an elephant? They learned in 1937 that the Japanese military-industrial complex was led by men who were totally corrupt and totally ruthless, capable of setting in motion mass extermination campaigns on a hitherto unprecedented scale. The terror of the Japanese advance along the Yangtse River was followed by the sack of Nanking, where 100,000 people were murdered in cold blood; the Chinese learned there was no treachery the Japanese were incapable of committing in order to smash Chinese resistance. Nothing like this had happened since the time of Tamerlane. The Western powers, preoccupied by the rise of

Hitler, turned a deaf ear to China's appeals for aid. It was happening far away, in a country few people knew, at the other side of the world.

Although the Japanese had hoped to destroy China and transform it into a colony, the chief effect of their extermination campaigns was exactly the reverse of what they had intended. The Chinese were hardened against them and determined to throw off the Japanese yoke. The war against China was still unfinished when the Japanese government gave orders for a general attack against American and British bases in the Far East. In this way they overreached themselves and brought about the destruction of their empire.

CORRUPTION BY TYRANNY

When a country has either surrendered to a tyrant or been tricked into granting him full powers, the processes of corruption are immediately brought into play. The tyrant, ruling by decree, sooner or later comes to realize that his decrees are based on the small amount of evidence available to him and are effective only insofar as they reflect a real knowledge of the situation. There are many problems for which he simply does not know the answers. He chooses his advisers from among men as ignorant and unprincipled as himself, and therefore finds himself ruling blindly. The tragedy of the tyrant is that he is at the mercy of all the misinformation that comes to him and that even if he wanted to do good it would be impossible for him to do so because he is cut off from the people by the mere fact that he is a tyrant.

He may call himself President for Life, Leader, Dictator, Generalissimo, or Chairman of the Revolutionary Committee. It makes little difference what title he affects. He is the man who pretends he knows what is best for the country, and very often he is the man who knows least what should be done. He makes wild guesses. When confronted by internal troubles, he inevitably embarks on foreign wars. His solutions are always simplistic. The infinite complexity of modern society puzzles him. He simplifies it. One political party, one church, one organization for the youth of the country, one trade union, one system of farm management, one system of food distribution. "We must streamline everything," he tells his advisers. "In this way we can really control everything." Finally he discovers that he controls only the army and the secret police.

The concentration of power in the hands of a single man chokes off the best energies of the nation; all must become subservient to him; his lonely eminence removes him farther and farther from reality; and the power he may have seized for the best of reasons inevitably is used for the worst of reasons—to maintain him in power.

At the heart of the mystery of corruption lies the desire of one man to impose his will on others to the largest possible extent. His need to dominate overrides the public welfare. Power becomes an end in itself, and the dictator scarcely cares what happens to the people so long as he can maintain his domination over them. And it is precisely here that the greatest injury is inflicted on the people. For domination has nothing whatsoever to do with good government, and power as an end in itself destroys good government.

Thus in every dictator we discern a nihilistic core, a compacted emptiness. Ultimately he believes in nothing, and least of all does he believe in the people he rules over. He despises them for having submitted to his domination. Since power as an end in itself becomes increasingly unreal and since he regards himself as the sole arbiter and instrument of power, he becomes unreal even to himself, and it is all one to him whether he embarks on wars to add luster to his fame or puts a bullet into his skull. Meanwhile the dictator, the most unstable of creatures, puts on a mask of rigid stability.

In March 1971 General Yahya Khan, the dictator of Pakistan, decided upon a general massacre of the inhabitants of East Pakistan, who strenuously objected to his dictatorship. It was a comparatively simple matter to decide upon priorities. The first to be massacred were the students, then the professors, then the police, then the poor. On a single night tanks and troops poured through Dacca, and the massacres were carried out according to plan. The student dormitories at the University of Dacca were attacked, and everyone in them was killed. Professors were dragged out of their living quarters and shot. The police barracks were destroyed. The huts of the poor along the river bank were put to the flames, and the people were shot down by machine-gun fire as they tried to escape. General Yahya Khan was simplifying the processes of government.

In 1974 the committee of colonels that had been ruling Greece despotically for seven and a half years fell from power after attempting to organize a military coup on the island of Cyprus. Cyprus was an independent state ruled by a Cypriot prime minister, with a large Turkish minority. The aim of the colonels was to unite Cyprus with Greece and rid the island of Turks. The military coup failed; a Turkish army sailed to northern Cyprus and mounted a full-scale invasion, taking advantage of a situation that would never have arisen if the colonels had not embarked on one of those dangerous foreign adventures that are among the greatest joys of dictatorship. Cyprus, which the colonels hoped to possess, was now irretrievably lost. When they saw that the gamble had failed, the colonels vanished into the obscurity from which they had arisen, and within a few days all the visible symbols of their authority vanished from Athens, while a civilian government under Constantine Caramanlis took office.

To the surprise of the Athenians the seven-and-a-half-year nightmare left few traces. The wounds of corruption were not deep and soon healed. The world learned that if a military despotism is brief and does not kill too many people or uproot too many institutions it may leave no more than a scar on a country's history. The Greek historians are not likely to devote much space to the dictatorship of the colonels, who proved to be incompetent rulers, hiding behind their uniforms, shadowy and impersonal. Their tasks were easy: they dominated by terror, arrested and tortured whenever they pleased, closed newspapers, and ruled by decree. This was not history; this was murder. The mafiosi had taken over the government.

When the colonels stepped down in total disgrace, the 3,000-year-old civilization moved forward again. Only the broken bodies of tortured men and the white crosses on the prisoners' graves on the remote islands of the Greek archipelago testified to the fact that a dictatorship had existed. The air was clean again, and freedom returned to the country where it was born.

The colonels were military men who exulted in their power to give orders, which were obeyed only because they were enforced by armed power. They were ridiculous and ugly, but it was necessary to take them seriously. There was no dialogue between the colonels and the people. On all important matters concerning the development of the nation they had nothing to say. They ruled ineffectively, inefficiently, disastrously, but if they had not overreached themselves in Cyprus they might have remained in power for many more years. Fortunately, it is in the nature of dictators to overreach themselves.

There are many kinds of tyranny, ranging from a military dictatorship to the benevolent despotism of the philosopher-king, and all are intolerable. Plutocracy, or rule by the rich, suffers from the same defects as every other tyranny, for it stifles the natural growth of the community, affronts human dignity, and directs the energies of the nation toward inhuman goals.

The United States is dangerously close to being a plutocracy. A third of the private wealth is owned by less than 5 percent of the population. The great majority of the indigent poor, amounting to a fifth of the population, are living on a subsistence level or below the starvation line. Except for the very rich, the entire population is so caught in inflation and recession that it must bend all its energies to making ends meet. The great majority of the senators and congressmen are rich men who consciously or unconsciously identify their interests with those of the rich. The senators and congressmen generally refuse to allow their full incomes to be made public, and there is therefore no way of knowing the source of their emoluments outside their official salaries. They announce, "Our private incomes are our private concerns," though it is obvious that their private incomes concern the public they have been elected to serve.

Corruption among senators and congressmen is not unknown; lobbyists are continually at work attempting to corrupt them. The vast sums of money spent by the lobbyists are put down by the giant corporations as legitimate expenses in their income-tax returns. In this way big business acquires the ear of the government, but there are no lobbyists for the poor, the sick, the old, the disheartened, the people who believe that plutocracy is not a worthy form of government. Nelson Rockefeller is said to have spent $27,000,000 of his own money to be elected governor of New York; it is clear that the money is not a gift to charity. Money is power—power to influence people, power to create more money, power to embark on profitable wars. The cost of being elected is such that only comparatively rich men can afford to be candidates, with the result that the voters are sometimes forced to choose between two rival millionaires and would prefer to vote for neither of them.

Just as it is intolerable that the rich should buy their way to power, so it is intolerable that the poor should be powerless. It is said that their remedy lies in the ballot box, that since they form so large a proportion of the population they can turn out the rich men who rule them and put in men who will truly represent them. But the system works against them. The plutocrats are in charge and will not willingly surrender their power except in the event of catastrophe.

In a plutocracy money becomes the sole criterion of value. Because it takes precedence over life, because it is assumed to possess an inherent existence of its own, and has all the advantages of being readily manipulated through accounting systems so that the addition or subtraction of a few zeros effectively changes a balance sheet, money becomes both an instrument for wielding power and the lifeblood of the nation. But all this is shadow play. Money is not life; it deadens life. It is without form, without substance, without color. It breeds corruption. It cannot produce a child or a tree or a work of art. The accumulation of vast amounts of money in the hands of a man cuts him off from the living forces of society.

Worst of all, a plutocracy deadens the healthy aspirations of the young, who are the real source of a nation's strength. If the only criterion of value is money, why work except for money? Why not accept the values of the plutocrats, since they have the whole country in their grip? Why think about anything except the accumulation of money? But since money reposes on fictions and a man cannot satisfactorily spend his life among fictions, there is always the feeling that something has gone profoundly wrong. Especially among the young there is a loss of confidence, a loss of faith, an omnipresent, haunting fear that the shadow play of money may dissolve into nothingness and that it is not a play worth attending, that life itself, the energy of the nation, is of infinitely greater significance and cannot be purchased.

Money corrupts; vast sums of money corrupt vastly. The plutocrats are well aware of the corrupting power of money and attempt to use it to their own advantage. By degrees the whole country becomes corrupted with the small, tightly knit inner sanctum of rulers increasing their power until it becomes absolute and the people are reduced to becoming their serfs.

CORRUPTION BY TREACHERY AND SUBVERSION

An oak tree attacked by dry rot may give all the outward appearance of health. From a distance and even close up, it resembles all the other oak trees in the neighborhood. The bark has a good texture, there are some leaves, the branches thrust powerfully into the sky. Unknown to the observer the rot has eaten away most of the interior of the tree trunk. A child could push the tree over.

In the same way a society invaded from within can give all the appearance of health: the trains are running, the newspapers are pouring off the presses, military parades are held, air flights are on schedule, the price of bread remains stable, and the government appears to be in the hands of men of responsibility who know what they are doing. France in the years 1936–39 was governed by men of ability. It had the largest army of Europe and therefore of the world. The Maginot line, named after André Maginot, a former minister of war who had been badly wounded during World War I, provided an impregnable defense along the entire border between

France and Germany, but since only "phantom fortresses" dotted the border between France and Belgium and the Maginot line could be easily bypassed, the whole line built at the cost of half a billion dollars was an irrelevance. All this would become known later. Meanwhile French industry had recovered from the Depression, the factories were thriving, and France still retained a large and profitable colonial empire.

In spite of outward prosperity there were some ominous undercurrents. A secret rightist revolutionary organization known as CSAR (Comité Secret d'Action Révolutionnaire) had sprung into existence in the army with the avowed intention of taking over power. Protected by high army officials, having links with Germany and Italy, and largely financed with Italian money, CSAR already had worked out blueprints for transforming France into a fascist state on the model of Mussolini's Italy. The Cagoulards, the "hooded ones," were the terrorist arm of CSAR. Their task was to create turmoil among the public and to assassinate the members of the government at the appropriate time. Another rightist paramilitary organization, the Croix de Feu (the Fiery Cross), largely made up of veterans and led by Colonel François de la Roque, was dedicated to the principle that the French Chamber of Deputies served no purpose whatsoever and needed to be destroyed. The Croix de Feu did in fact attack the Chamber of Deputies and nearly succeeded in destroying it. On the left were the French Communists led by Louis Aragon and other agents trained in Moscow. The Communists were also capable of putting paramilitary forces into the field.

By the beginning of 1938 the lines were clearly drawn: the right against the left. The Spanish Civil War was still going on, and it helped to polarize the conflict between the right and the left. The French government had the resources to control the CSAR, the Croix de Feu, the Communists, and other smaller militant factions like the Action Française, which was dedicated to the restoration of the monarchy. But it had few if any resources against subversion from Hitler's Germany. Huge sums of money were poured into France through a special agency attached to the Chancellery in Berlin, and more money came through the German foreign office. Hitler, a master of corruption, took a deep interest in corrupting France.

Politicians, newspapers, and journalists were bought. *Le Matin,* *Le Temps,* and *Le Figaro,* the leading newspapers, were receiving subventions from Germany. Some newspapers were bought outright, and the Germans were then in a position to choose the board of directors, the editors, and the reporters. The fifth column went about its deadly work with quiet efficiency, and all news from Germany was carefully slanted. The French were presented with a Hitler who was pacific, sweet-tempered, generous to excess, even at a time when the Wehrmacht was moving into Austria. Under the able direction of Otto Abetz all French institutions were being honey-combed with sympathizers of the German dictatorship. The minister for public works, Anatole de Monzie, was arrested and dismissed from office for having secret dealings with fascist Italy, and Loys Aubin, the chief editor of *Le Temps,* was arrested for receiving millions of francs from Germany. Most of the aristocracy favored Hitler, regarding domination by Germany as infinitely favorable to a government of the left. Anatole de Monzie expressed the aristocratic disdain for the left in a famous statement: "I prefer to receive a kick in the behind than a bullet in the head." It was understood that the kick in the behind meant military defeat by Germany and a bullet in the head meant a government of the left in France.

German infiltrators, saboteurs, spies, and fifth columnists penetrated all the places of power in France. The sums of money paid into the politicians' and journalists' bank accounts were staggering. Nothing was left undone. When the government of General de Gaulle finally turned its attention to the Frenchmen who had acted so treacherously in the days before the war, it brought out a list of 2,000 journalists, editors, lawyers, army and naval officers, and members of the Chamber of Deputies, all of them in the highest positions.

On July 14, 1939, the French celebrated the 150th anniversary of the taking of the Bastille with the usual military parade along the Champs-Elysées. It was a beautiful clear day with just enough wind to make military capes billow and set the feathers in the military caps trembling. The tanks rumbled past, the *poilus* marched briskly, the *spahis* in crimson capes rode on horseback, and a company of Grenadier Guards in black busbies and scarlet tunics marched in the procession to emphasize the alliance between Britain and France. Nearly 40,000 troops took part in the procession, and 350 airplanes flew in close formation over the Champs-Elysées, swooping down so that all the chestnut trees waved in the airplanes' wake. In addition to the armada of French airplanes there was a squadron of the Royal Air Force.

The French foreign minister, Georges Bonnet, was asked what he thought about the Bastille Day procession. "It demonstrates the order, discipline and irresistible force of the French Army. From now on how can one fear Germany?"

France resembled the oak tree eaten away by dry rot, outwardly splendid, inwardly ruined.

Hitler had seen to it that the ruin would take place silently, systematically, without force. No one was killed. An army of German agents had entered France quite legally and disbursed large sums of money. A network of German agents had penetrated the government offices. The future leaders of France had been chosen in Berlin on the basis of voluminous reports. "Controlled, planned corruption"—the phrase was Hitler's—had been worked out in such meticulous detail that the Germans had compiled dossiers on 100,000 Frenchmen, and at least half of them had been approached to see whether they were corruptible.

Already in 1932, before he achieved power, Hitler was engrossed in the contemplation of defeating France by massive, prolonged acts of corruption. Then, at the very last moment, he would send German soldiers wearing French uniforms to Paris to take over the General Staff, the ministries and the Chamber of Deputies. Here is Hitler describing to Albert Forster, the *Gauleiter* of Danzig, how he proposed to conquer France:

> When I wage war, Forster, in the midst of peace, troops will suddenly appear, let us say, in Paris. They will wear French uniforms. They will march through the streets in broad daylight. No one will stop them. Everything has been thought out, prepared to the last detail. They will march to the headquarters of the General Staff. They will occupy the ministries, the Chamber of Deputies. Within a few minutes, France, Poland, Austria, Czechoslovakia, will be robbed of their leading men. An army without a general staff! All political leaders out of the way! The confusion will be beyond belief. But I shall long ago have had relations with the men who will form a new government—a government to suit me.
>
> We shall find such men, we shall find them in every country. We shall not need to bribe them. They will come of their own accord. Ambition and delusion, party squabbles and self-seeking arrogance will drive them. Peace will be negotiated before the war has begun. I promise you, gentlemen, that the impossible is always successful. The most unlikely thing is the surest. We shall have enough volunteers, men like our S.A., trustworthy and ready for any sacrifice. We shall send them across the border in peace-time. Gradually. No one shall see in them anything but peaceful travellers. Today, you don't believe me, gentlemen. But I will accomplish it, move by move. Perhaps we

shall land at their flying-fields. We shall be capable of transporting not only men, but arms, by air. No Maginot Line will stop us. Our strategy, Forster, is to destroy the enemy from within, to conquer him through himself.

What interested Hitler even more than military conquest was "to conquer him through himself." He proposed to use the same methods he had used so successfully in his conquest of the German people. "Mental confusion, contradiction of feeling, indecisiveness, panic—these are our weapons," he declared. Armed force would be used on a massive scale, but only as a *coup de grâce* after the enemy had been rendered harmless. First the anesthetic, then the knife. Almost it was as though he found little use for the military except as an occupying force.

Again and again Hitler discussed with his associates the simple ways in which countries could be corrupted, reduced to nothing more than pathetic façades, destroyed from within. "How shall I press my will on my opponent?" he asked, and answered, "By first splitting and paralyzing his will, putting him at loggerheads with himself, throwing him into confusion." He saw himself as a hypnotist who would dominate his victim by sheer willpower, and then when the victim was in a half-conscious state the hypnotist would order him to lie on the floor and pretend to be dead. Hitler conceived of a transmission of the will that was almost physical in its intensity. Invisible poisons would be directed at the enemy's nerve centers, giving him at first a feeling of euphoria, which would be followed by a feeling of total insecurity and confusion once he recognized the extent of the danger confronting him. Finally all that needed to be done was to administer a slight pinprick, and the enemy would beg for mercy. Hitler regarded the instrument of terrorism as indispensable; it had the great virtue of spreading confusion on an ever-widening scale and with the least expenditure of energy.

Hitler had made a profound study of human motives and human fears. He knew to a hair's breadth at what point a man could be corrupted. Just as he organized a vast dossier of information on every influential person in the world, so he organized dossiers on all his important followers. Thousands of people were involved in drawing up these dossiers, and he complained of the cost. But he regarded them as eminently worthwhile because they provided him with the tools of subversion. He needed to know the answers to the following questions: Can he be bribed? Is he vain? What is his sexual life? Is he a homosexual? (He attached extraordinary importance to this question because it opened prospects of blackmail.) Has he anything in the past to conceal? What is his business? What are his hobbies? Does he enjoy travel? Does he take part in sports? "The aims I have in mind," he declared, "can only be achieved by the systematic corruption of the possessing and governing classes." In his view they were the weakest classes because their possessions were of more importance to them than anything else, even the defense and honor of their country. He detected exactly the same attitude of mind in the aristocracy of Germany and in the big German industrialists. Since they would do anything to safeguard their property, he gave them something to do: either submit or be ruined.

It was all very simple, much simpler than Hitler had expected. Corruption paid off; under pressure virtually everyone was corruptible. Thus, very early in the campaign for power, he corrupted his storm troopers by giving them the right to loot. "Enjoy life and enrich yourselves," he said. They could steal whatever property they wanted, amass huge bank accounts, take possession of any automobiles they pleased, raid jewelry stores and liquor stores, and even take over farms and factories, but only on condition that they maintain their absolute loyalty to the Führer. It was a very simple way of ensuring their loyalty, and it had the added advantage of spreading confusion throughout the country. Dr. Hermann Rauschning, who knew Hitler well, wrote that the words "planned corruption" were first used by Hitler in connection with his program of enriching his followers at the expense of the German people.

Although Hitler took full credit for the concept of "planned corruption," he was not the first to use it. It was in fact a very old invention, mentioned by Sun Wu, the ancient Chinese author of *The Rules of War,* who announced that the best way to conquer a country was by employing all possible stratagems short of war and proceeded to explain the many arts of subversion. But to Hitler must be given the credit for employing subversion on a scale hitherto undreamed of. It had been an art; he converted it into a science. It was the subject of his fondest dreams and delighted hopes, the one subject on which he regarded himself as a supreme authority. If he failed, it was not because corruption fails. He failed because there remained in the world an overwhelming number of people who refused to be corrupted.

Subversion is a dangerous weapon that sometimes backfires. Although Hitler firmly believed that all men are corruptible, the statement is simply not true. The very rich are corruptible; so are many officials, lawyers, and journalists. In these four categories we find the largest number of corrupt men. Conversely we find among officials, lawyers, and journalists men who are the declared enemies of corruption in all its forms. When the American government sent its secret CIA agents into Chile, they succeeded in toppling a democratically elected government and instituting a military dictatorship and a reign of terror. But when the same government sent hundreds of agents into India in the hope of toppling Indira Gandhi's Congress government, they proved to be wholly incompetent because no potential military dictators stepped forward to receive the gifts of arms, ammunition, and money that are the rewards of treachery.

Corruption has its limitations, its excesses, its pitfalls. It does not always do what it sets out to do. When it is habitual, it tends to become sterile and unimaginative. When, for example, two powerful but opposing nations attempt to corrupt a smaller nation with gifts of money and arms, the smaller nation is in the happy position of being able to play one corruptor against the other. The two acts of corruption cancel out. Egypt, receiving gifts from the United States and the Soviet Union, preserves a perfect neutrality at the expense of American and Russian taxpayers, who were never consulted about Egyptian neutrality. Corruption sometimes produces stalemate.

There are historical lessons to be learned from the fact that corruption can be neutralized by corruption. Hitler's "planned corruption" may, after all, have been a waste of time and energy. In spite of the thousands upon thousands of questionnaires, in spite of the massive amounts of money expended, it is possible that corrupt Frenchmen had very little influence on the course of events. France fell in military defeat and came to birth again as a result of military victory.

CORRUPTION BY CLASH OF CULTURES

Some forms of corruption do not derive from human malice, treachery, greed, or the desire to dominate. They have their origin in historical accidents or events that happened long ago, and therefore no living person is responsible for them. Areas of dead and decaying cultures appear where civilizations overlap, where the historical associations and psychological needs of one are contrary to the historical associations and psychological needs of the other. In these areas the moral codes break down, ordinary human laws are no longer operative, sudden and apparently inexplicable hatreds flare up, and life becomes nearly valueless. Here is the wasteland, where the survivors find themselves at war with one another and with ghosts.

Out of this wasteland there emerges a character who has grown familiar to us from Dostoyevsky's novels—the nihilist. He believes in nothing, and attaches very little value to his belief. He has no roots, refuses to abide by accepted human values, rejects all authority, worships no god, and regards himself as outside the mainstream of culture. He may believe that he has achieved complete freedom by separating himself from traditional ways of thought, but freedom interests him as little as his own fate or his own ideas. He behaves like Stavrogin, of whom Dostoyevsky wrote: "The prince has no ideas. He has only an aversion to his contemporaries. He does not believe in God and has lost the distinction between good and evil because he has ceased to know people. And so he can kill whenever he chooses to kill." In what he calls "the last deception in an endless series of deceptions" he decides to kill himself, implying that this act too is totally motiveless and without any significance whatever. In fact, as he well knows, his suicide has a profound meaning. Believing and unbelieving, belonging and not belonging, at once in the world and outside the world, Stavrogin is not so much a split personality as a man whose several parts cancel each other out. He kills himself because he is forced to the conclusion that without loyalties and beliefs a man has no reason to live. His death is a sacrifice to his own inhumanity.

The landscape of the wasteland is now familiar to us largely because Dostoyevsky has charted it for us. It is not unlike the landscape of the concentration camps where the most improbable and terrible things take place casually and methodically, causing no surprise. The crematorium chimney is decorated with Christmas lights, the clean white walls of bathrooms conceal the ducts where the poison gases come out, and the scenic railways carry only dead bodies propped up so that they can look out at the painted landscape. The supreme law of the wasteland is "All that is human, generous, decent and loving is here abandoned." In the wasteland everything is permitted but only on condition that it is vulgar, bloody, and irrational.

The wasteland is not so remote from us as we would like to believe. It exists in nearly all large cities, and its boundaries are continually expanding. It appears wherever there are poverty and hopelessness, wherever men find no reasons to go on living. Increasingly, modern industries are commanded by faceless and anonymous boards of directors, who are not accountable for the poverty and hopelessness in the dead areas of modern civilization. They are indifferent to suffering, and it would never occur to them that they are responsible for the shantytowns and decaying tenements where the poor live. They are remote and unassailable. Their loyalty is to their ledgers, not to the living world. The wasteland is the empty space reserved by the boards of directors for everything that does not fit neatly into their account books and therefore comes under the heading Miscellaneous Losses.

While the boards of directors are hopelessly corrupt because they are indifferent to the life-giving processes, the inhabitants of the wasteland are corrupted by poverty, sickness, misery, lack of hope, and lack of faith. A culture representing the interests of finance encounters a culture representing the poor and the underprivileged, and even though there is no apparent communication between them and no words are spoken, the very indifference of the culture of finance helps to make the poor poorer and to undercut the few remaining privileges of the underprivileged. Between Wall Street and Bedford-Stuyvesant, a slum area in New York City, there is no communication. Out of the slums comes a corruption that can kill a whole city.

In the slums there are forces at work that continually tend to increase the virulence of the poisons and to exacerbate tensions beyond any possibility of reducing them. The energy that might more usefully be employed in creating better living conditions is expended in feuds and gang wars, which rarely end in victory but generate more feuds, more gang wars, more deaths. The wasteland offers the spectacle of armed men moving cautiously in the shadows, and it is all one to them who is murdered and who survives, for life has lost all meaning to them. They murder, rape, and inject heroin into their veins, but they do these things mechanically, indifferently, without any hope that they will be happier. Their lives have become devoted to the creation, the perpetuation, and the increase of misery.

Imagine a Puerto Rican youth living in Bedford-Stuyvesant with his mother, brother, and sisters. His father is dead. His mother earns a bare living as a cleaning woman, but she has a heart condition and can work only two or three days a week. Because the apartment consists of only a living room which becomes a bedroom at night, the youth spends as much time as possible in the street. He has no regular source of income but earns enough by running errands to provide himself with cigarettes and to supplement his mother's small income so that the family can live just above the starvation level. He is deeply religious, attends Mass, and is well regarded by the local priest. He is profoundly aware of his Puerto Rican origins although he was born in New York and has never set eyes on the land he regards as his ancestral home.

He joins a street gang out of loneliness and quickly finds himself caught up in elaborate rituals and adventures. The constant, nagging sense of alienation vanishes. He is among people he understands, sharing a common loyalty, a common purpose. The gang gives him a sense of confidence, even of superiority, and he feels that he is better than the Irish policemen, the shopkeepers from Eastern Europe, the blacks in the next street. He has reached the age when *machismo* has become an extremely important element in his life. The gang answers to his human needs, and in the absence of anything else to live for he lives for the gang.

From the moment when he enters the gang profound changes take place in him, although at first he is scarcely aware of them. The gang becomes his fortress, his stronghold, his reason for existence. He sees less and less of his family and goes less and less often to church. To demonstrate its *machismo* the gang wages war against the black gang in the next street. At first the war is conducted according to a well-defined rule: only fists may be used. Later they use knives, then guns, and in the excitement of possessing guns and to bolster their courage they take to drugs. One of the Puerto Rican youths is badly hurt by a bullet fired from a sawed-off shotgun, and soon the limited war becomes an all-out war. Elementary moral safeguards are abandoned, and the gangs become wolf packs.

All this has happened within a very short period, without anyone really being aware that the escalation has become inevitable. Step by step, without intending to do so, the Puerto Rican gang changed from a more or less peaceful organization designed to bolster young egos to a gang of murderers. A similar process has taken place among the blacks. The clash of cultures inevitably ends in death. Boys are killed or maimed for life, and if they are asked why this happened they have only one answer: "We had to fight them." A categorical imperative led them to destroy one another.

Let no one imagine that deaths and maimings are the worst things that happen. The entire neighborhood is affected by it, and each boy's death carries its weight of misery and sorrow. His brothers and friends must inevitably seek revenge or are reduced to psychotic terror. Misery spreads like the circles on the surface of a pond when a stone is thrown into it. Grief hardens, and becomes violence. Two or three generations pass before the wound heals.

New York with its mixed population has witnessed the clash of cultures throughout most of the nineteenth and twentieth centuries. Wave after wave of immigrants, rejecting assimilation, has poured into the city and asserted the right to cultural independence. This would be a valid claim if the cultures could be hermetically sealed from one another; instead they overlap, and the deepest wounds and the most terrible confrontations occur precisely in the overlapping areas. Sometimes three or more cultures overlap in this way:

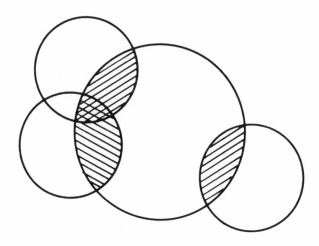

In the dead areas represented by the cross-hatching, profound alterations take place in the cultures. The moral code of each culture is bent and distorted, and men fighting for survival or what they believe to be survival are not inclined to show mercy. Puerto Ricans fighting blacks in Bedford-Stuyvesant are not so much fighting for territory as for a point of honor or because they feel threatened by the mere presence of blacks, and the blacks in their turn are fighting on behalf of their own interpretation of *machismo* and because they too feel threatened. The police are neutral; the Jewish shopkeepers find themselves in the line of fire; a priest counting the offerings of his parishioners is in mortal danger from the roving gangs; drug-traffickers take advantage of the increasing misery to sell their wares; and the area becomes daily more degraded, more corrupt. There are streets in Bedford-Stuyvesant where people live out their lives in very nearly the same kind of degradation that was seen in the Nazi concentration camps, with the added horror of the drug traffic.

There is only one thing that can be done with such areas of corruption: raze them to the ground. Where assimilation is clearly not taking place, where rivalries and confrontations are continually, feverishly occurring, where poverty and theft have reduced habitable buildings to the deadliest of slums, the conditions for a decent society no longer exist.

Societies cannot long endure once corruption sets in. The murderous riots that took place after the assassination of Dr. Martin Luther King were a foretaste of things to come. All over the world we are witnessing the breakdown of the forms of government that are not responsive to human needs, and while half the population lives in misery it is not likely that the poor will consent indefinitely to be ruled by corrupt rulers or to have their children live amid the corruption of slums.

Of the five faces of corruption—old age, conquest, tyranny, treachery, and the clash of cultures—only old age is inescapable. The days of the conquerors may be very nearly over. There exist human remedies against tyranny and treachery, and with forethought the dangerous tensions aroused by the clash of cultures can be prevented from exploding. Even an old and dying culture can sometimes be revived. The problems are not insuperable, but they cannot be solved unless we recognize that all corrupt societies spew out poisons that inevitably corrupt neighboring societies. There are no frontiers of corruption.

In the last pages of *Crime and Punishment* Dostoyevsky relates one of the dreams of his hero, Raskolnikov. He dreams that the whole world has been condemned to a terrible plague. Strange new microbes attack the bodies of men, and these microbes are endowed with intelligence and will, causing men to believe that they alone are in possession of the truth, and so they become mad and kill one another in senseless spite. They form armies, but the armies disintegrate as the soldiers fall on each other, stabbing, biting, and devouring each other, or else they meet in groups, hold debates, agree on what must be done, and swear to remain faithful friends, only to find themselves a moment later at one another's throat, bent on murder. The plague continues, the cities burn down, famine spreads over the land, until finally "all men and all things are involved in destruction."

Dostoyevsky was telling a parable about the contagion of corruption, and it is still applicable in our own time.

The Corrupt
Individual

We have seen that the corruption of society takes place in many different ways as the result of many different factors, some of them accidental, some inherent in the nature of society, all of them deriving directly or indirectly from a certain attitude of mind that can best be characterized as contempt for humanity. Once a man despises other men he has crossed the threshold of corruption. Once a society collectively despises another society, then it too has crossed the threshold of corruption and is already on the way to destroying the other society while at the same time destroying itself through the poison of contempt. We have seen that contempt can be manufactured and instilled in a people by propaganda and that the propaganda of contempt is all too readily available and can be produced on a mass scale. It is conceivable that a society may genuinely despise another society, but an artificially inspired propaganda is equally effective. More often than not a society is corrupted by the poisons it has exuded from its own flesh.

When the body dies, the processes of decay assume an extremely complex form. Since the brain dies first, there is no central organization to direct and govern the rending and dismemberment of the body. The heart, the liver, the kidneys, the nerves, muscles, and flesh break down into their essential components at different rates; and so it is with societies. They die many deaths over a long period of time. They die, and they sometimes go on living.

Although the corrupt individual has much in common with the corrupt society, there are significant differences. His corruption comes about as the result of a single cause—his overwhelming ambition for power at the expense of and to the injury of everyone who stands in his path.

The corruption of the individual is therefore a much simpler affair than the corruption of society. For the most part men corrupt themselves; they need no propaganda; they make their own choices; they know what they are doing as they march to power and trample on everyone in their way; they die their own deaths. A society is propelled by the momentum of its traditions and is charged with the energy of the past. It obeys laws that are not the laws of individuals and rides roughshod over the laws that apply to individuals. A society does not corrupt itself; it is corrupted by ancestral memories and desires, by contradictory forces working within it, by cancers that are not localized but spread throughout the body politic; and the desire for power is not the only force propelling it. Societies are more influenced by the weight and momentum of traditions than by any other cause.

The corrupt individual has advantages denied to a corrupt society. He can move more easily and quickly; he can adapt himself to changing conditions; he can employ many stratagems that cannot be employed by societies. If a man has nimble and quick wits, he can use the laws of the society to his own advantage. If he is a genius, he can corrupt the entire society. Society has provided the corrupt with endless loopholes that permit them, when they are sufficiently knowledgeable, to defy the most elementary laws of the society. A corrupt man is the master of his own destiny; a society is not. He can choose; a society once entangled in the processes of corruption cannot. He can go into hiding; a society cannot. He can, in the words of Ivan Karamazov, "throw in his ticket to God"; a society cannot. He can die or be killed; societies rarely die completely.

Even so, there are general laws of corruption that apply equally to society and to individuals. Both society and individuals before they become fully corrupt can turn back. For both there is a period of confusion, hesitancy, and uncertainty. At such moments they must decide whether they dare to embark on that full-scale corruption which can end only with the abandonment of all traditional moralities and total subjection to criminality. They are most alike in the final fugue state when, having lost their bearings, they become savagely incoherent and surrender to homicidal mania. But even in a nation given over to homicidal mania there usually remains a small nucleus of courageous and levelheaded men who stand apart and remain uncorrupted, ready to shore up the ruins and with almost superhuman effort attempt to restore the nation once the madness has spent itself.

The corrupt man walks alone, gathering more and more power and wealth to himself, leaving a trail of destruction wherever he passes until he finally destroys himself. The corrupt society resembles an armored train full of captured treasure with a drunken driver in the engine cabin. Traveling at full speed, with the last wagons uncoupled to make it lighter, the train hurtles along the tracks and finally leaves the rails to plow through the countryside and create a vast havoc until the boiler explodes and the driver is blown sky-high. Even then it is not beyond the bounds of possibility that skilled technicians can repair the engine and set it back on the rails.

How do we recognize the corrupt man? What are his chief characteristics? How does he maneuver through the many stages that lead ultimately to absolute corruption? What manner of man is he, and would we recognize him if we saw him in the street?

One aspect of him is immediately recognizable: his contempt for his fellow men. Hence his ruthlessness, his celebration of himself at the expense of everyone else, his absorption in his own affairs to the exclusion of all other affairs. Hence, too, his secretiveness, his intense sensitivity to real or imagined slights, for his contempt does not exclude a certain fear. He is necessarily a conspirator who imagines that his fellow men are conspiring against him. This, of course, belongs to a later stage of his development, for it is only when he has advanced into complicated conspiracies that he is forced to assume that he is surrounded by conspirators. Sometimes he may be justified in this belief, but more often those conspirators who appear to be constantly surrounding him are no more than the ghosts he has raised to comfort himself, like the infinitely repeated images of himself he sees in parallel mirrors.

The corrupt man is nearly always rootless, deeply aware of his rootlessness. A military dictator can rule with total despotism only if he is not a native of the land he rules over, for otherwise he could not bring himself to kill so many. The history of military dictators is full of foreigners who seize power and embark on irresponsible adventures leading to the deaths of millions of people whom they acknowledge publicly and falsely as their countrymen. Napoleon was a Corsican, not a Frenchman; Stalin was a Georgian, not a Russian; Hitler was an Austrian, not a German; Lenin had Scandinavian, German, and tribal blood in his veins; General Yahya Khan, President of Pakistan, massacred the Bengalis of East Pakistan all the more easily because he was a Punjabi, not a Bengali. In the military dictator we confront individual corruption in its extreme form, and he can always be counted upon to corrupt the nation he rules. Indeed, he can hardly escape corrupting it, since to remain in power he must continually corrupt everyone around him.

The corrupt man is one in whom the forces of death are stronger than the forces of life. Almost he seems to be in league with death. He is not only contemptuous of human life but puts no value on it; he does not care how many people he kills or destroys on his march to power or to maintain himself in power. Gratuitous brutality, gratuitous murder, are essential elements in the ceremony of corruption. The massacre principle is elevated to the level of a precise art with its capable practitioners and perfectly organized machines accurately shaping the new contours of death. The game is played so mechanically that one wonders why anyone plays it at all.

Once the dignity of the human person is abandoned as an article of faith, massacre becomes eminently practicable. When the Japanese invaded Manchuria in 1931, they brought with them an attitude of mind expressed in the slogan "Burn all, loot all, kill all," where the last two words appear almost as an afterthought. In the eyes of the Japanese the Manchurians and Chinese were no more than vermin. They wanted Manchuria and China for themselves, and there was a certain rationality in the adoption of the massacre principle. Sometimes a rationale is hard to find. When Tamerlane in his memoirs described the massacre of the inhabitants of Delhi, he was inclined to find excuses. There had been a clash in the streets, he had sent some troops into the city to restore order, and the fighting, which at the beginning was scarcely more than a small skirmish, grew to embrace the whole city. He hints at spontaneous combustion. He is not credible. He enjoyed massacres, ordered them at every opportunity, and whenever it was not too dangerous he liked to observe them.

Another formidable agent of destruction was Chang Hsien-chung, a Chinese general who is said to have destroyed thirty million people in the space of a few months. In the early years of the seventeenth

century his armies spread along the Yangtse River and poured into
the rich and populous province of Szechuan. He established his capital at Chengtu, where he proclaimed himself King of the Great
Western Kingdom. The officials and scholars disputed his title, and
were murdered. He gave orders that the merchants should be murdered together with their wives. He ordered the feet of his officers'
wives to be cut off, made a mound of them, and on top of the mound
placed the feet of his favorite concubine. He carefully counted the
ears and feet which his soldiers presented to him after their forays
through the towns and villages of Szechuan. He ordered his soldiers
to kill their own wives so that the army would not be hindered by
camp followers. In this way his armies were able to move swiftly, un-
encumbered by women or baggage trains. Arriving suddenly at a
walled town, they demanded its immediate surrender and threatened that unless it surrendered within an hour, a third of the population would be killed, and if the town held out for another day the
remaining two thirds would be butchered. All the treasure accumulated by Chang Hsien-chung's armies became his personal property.
He wearied of it, piled all his accumulated treasure in a dried river
bed, and drowned it all by diverting a stream over it. Asked why he
did this, he answered that he wanted to deny this treasure to posterity.

Chang Hsien-chung had spent all his life as a soldier, first as a
conscript and then as the leader of a band of peasant rebels. Once
in his early years he was sentenced to death for murder and was
thrown into prison. Vowing vengeance on all those who were in any
way connected with his arrest, imprisonment, and sentence, he murdered them when he escaped from prison. Murder became a habit, a
pastime, a way of life. All settled communities became his prey, all
officials, scholars, and merchants were regarded as natural enemies
to be wiped off the face of the earth, and since he despised women,
they too were expendable. Students from all over Szechuan were
invited to attend the examinations held at Chengtu. As soon as they
arrived in the capital, they were set upon by soldiers and stabbed to
death. Every general and high officer in his armies was ordered to
present a complete list of the people he had murdered; quotas were
arbitrarily laid down, and those who had not murdered a sufficient
number of people were themselves murdered.

Chang Hsien-chung was far more than a bandit chieftain creating
havoc among the peaceful and hard-working farming communities
of Szechuan. He was almost a force of nature, a hurricane or a tor-
nado bursting with destructive energy. In his own eyes, he was an

avenger who had come to earth to carry out the Mandate of Heaven. The mandate was a simple one: "People do not deserve to live; therefore they must be destroyed." As much as was humanly possible for one man, he carried out the mandate he believed had been entrusted to him. In Chengtu he caused to be erected a stone tablet bearing an inscription with twenty-one Chinese characters:

Heaven brought forth innumerable things to support man;
Man has never done one good thing to recompense Heaven.
Kill.   Kill.   Kill.   Kill.   Kill.   Kill.   Kill.

This tablet, which could still be seen sixty years ago, provided the philosophical basis for mass slaughter. Since man was utterly powerless, insignificant, and unworthy of the bounty poured unstintingly on him by Heaven, it was perfectly permissible to dispense with him. Heaven owed him nothing; his life was forfeit because he owed Heaven everything. If all of Szechuan and all of China were suddenly swept clean of people, no harm would have been done and much would have been gained; for then Heaven would reign in absolute purity and all debts would have been paid.

The tablet in Chengtu was clearly an afterthought, an *apologia pro vita sua* after the damage had been done. Chang Hsien-chung was not a scholar and poet; he could not have written the first two lines; and there is no evidence that he ever gave any serious thought to self-justification. Nevertheless there were scholars in his court, and the tablet was erected at his orders, not to justify or to explain but to announce quite simply to future generations what had been done and why it had been done. The puzzling thing is that Chang Hsien-chung troubled to address himself to the future, for he appeared to be determined to destroy it. Few men have come so close to destroying the future or reveled so fiercely in destruction.

The real cause of Chang Hsien-chung's total nihilism is not hard to find. The fact that he was once sentenced to death was a matter of enormous importance to him. In prison, with the knowledge that he was about to be executed, he had vowed revenge on the entire society, which in his view was responsible for his death sentence. Ultimately everyone who came within his power was sentenced to death, for all mankind was implicated. He acted as though every man was his enemy, and he had the power to punish everyone to the full extent of the law, which declared that man was unworthy of Heaven's benevolence.

Not surprisingly, Chang Hsien-chung showed no dignity when

the Manchu armies finally caught up with him. One of his generals, fearing for his life, deserted his master, made contact with the Manchus, and revealed Chang's hiding place. There was a skirmish, and Chang Hsien-chung was wounded by an arrow. He took refuge in a village and was found cowering under a pile of firewood. He was led out and promptly beheaded. The long reign of terror, which devastated Szechuan and reduced its population by half, was over.

Chang Hsien-chung is an extreme example of the man who despises his fellow men so much that he can enjoy killing them by the millions. He was one of those who are absolutely corrupt, so far beyond hope of redemption that Redemption itself shrivels at the mere thought of him. At his death in 1646, he could claim that he had killed more people than anyone before him, for he killed more people than Genghis Khan and Tamerlane combined. Only in our time have there been mass murderers who killed on the same stupendous scale.

Understandably, Chinese historians are inclined to shy away from Chang Hsien-chung. He came at a period when the Ming dynasty was in full decline, when the armies of the imperial government were busy fighting off the Manchus and falling back in helpless disorder. Chinese historians sometimes fail to mention him or else grant him the dubious tribute of a footnote. But the Szechuanese historians remembered him vividly, and the popular prints show him with beetling brows and a ferocious beard, like the god of war. It was remembered that he was born in Shensi of poor parents and that when he was a young man he rallied the peasants and was a competent chieftain of peasant guerrillas. In Szechuan, when he was murdering everyone in sight, he announced to the peasants that they would never again have to pay taxes if they came over to his side. Believing him, they flocked to his banners. They paid no taxes until he needed money; then he murdered them if they did not pay taxes in advance. The historians record that he permitted his soldiers to keep captured horses and captured swords, and that he was sometimes kind to starving peasants, giving them food, clothing, and money. When the Manchu army came at last, the soldiers were greeted as saviors.

The phenomenon of mass slaughter is intimately related to corruption, but corrupt individuals are not necessarily addicted to mass slaughter. They want to dominate at all costs, and they regard power as an end in itself. If power involves the power to kill, they are not disturbed, for killing is the ultimate form of power. They despise the people around them, and killing is therefore all the easier.

Treachery can sometimes be more effective than murder, and the shock of betrayal hurts more than a knife in the back.

Almost by definition the corrupt individual is a traitor to the human race. He is one of those who despises men so much that he feels no loyalty to them. The corrupt are loyal to the corrupt only as long as it serves their advantage. Since loyalty usually demands some kindness and fellow feeling, the corrupt generally reserve their loyalties for their intimates.

It is not easy to select a typical corrupt individual, for there have been so many. They come in all colors, in all sizes, in all epochs. They were rare in Athens during the age of Pericles, but they existed. The most brilliant and glittering specimen was Alcibiades, who resembled, according to the Athenians, one of the half-divine heroes of ancient legends. He was so handsome that people were struck dumb by his beauty; he was so intelligent that Socrates regarded him as one of his best pupils. Only his domineering manner prevented him from being universally loved. On the spur of the moment he would say things so brutal and painful that they would be remembered like festering sores; and he created enemies more easily than he made friends.

He was among the wealthiest men in Athens and therefore despised the poor. Indeed, he despised nearly everyone except Pericles, in whose house he was brought up, and Socrates, who was more than half in love with him. He was given to acts of senseless brutality. Once on the wrestling ground he struck one of his own servants with a staff and killed him. At another time his wrestling opponent got the better of him, and to escape the man's grip Alcibiades bit his hand. It was a deep bite with force in it. "You bite like a woman, Alcibiades," the wrestler said. "No, like a lion!" he retorted.

Throughout his life there was a disproportion between his acts and his interpretations of them. He was quick-witted, insolent, avid for attention. He would go to almost any lengths to ensure that he was the talk of the town. He owned a fine wolfhound with a splendid tail. When he cut off the tail, one of his friends remonstrated with him, saying that everyone in Athens was fond of the hound and they were all sorry. "I did it so that the Athenians would talk about it," Alcibiades laughed, adding, "This way they won't say anything worse about me!"

In 424 B.C., when he was about twenty-five, he fought in the battle of Delium, where his life was saved by Socrates. He studied the military arts and learned to become an exceptional public speaker, famous for his marshaling of arguments and for a trick of pausing in the midst of a speech to gather his thoughts together. His military prowess and his eloquence were admired; not so admirable were his sudden bouts of drunkenness, dissolute living, and exhibitionism. He flouted contemporary morality by appearing in the marketplace in a long, trailing purple gown. On his shield he painted a naked boy holding a thunderbolt on a golden ground, to the bewilderment of the Athenians, who were accustomed to shields of classic simplicity. Out of a fierce pride and to attract attention he once struck the wealthy and powerful landowner Hipponicus across the face, and the next morning he appeared naked at the house of the landowner, begging to be scourged in punishment. The old man not only pardoned him but gave him his daughter Hipparete in marriage with a dowry of ten talents, an enormous sum in those days. When the first child was born, Alcibiades claimed another ten talents for having given Hipponicus a grandchild. He squandered the money in princely fashion, fitted out triremes and gave them to the state, contributed heavily to the war chest, and accumulated dozens of mistresses, making sure that all these extravagances were widely publicized. Once, while still a private citizen, he entered seven chariots in the Olympic games at an expense that might have crippled even the rich and luxury-loving tyrants of Sicily; and no one was permitted to forget that he won the first, second, and fourth prizes.

Socrates was inclined to pardon these excesses, putting the blame on the flatterers who surrounded Alcibiades. "Socrates," says Plutarch, "observed the noble qualities and fine disposition in and under his wealth and high position, and seeing that foreigners and Athenians flattered and caressed him, and might corrupt him, he deliberately set himself to act as a moderator, to prevent the flower from perishing before it bore fruit." Not even Socrates could prevent Alcibiades from following the path of corruption.

The Athenians, who watched Alcibiades with envy, alarm, and a kind of appalled fascination, did not know what to make of him. He seemed to possess a vast appetite for the more terrible aspects of power. "They felt disgust and apprehension and abhorrence at his free living and contempt of law, as things monstrous in themselves, and indicating designs of usurpation," says Plutarch, who adds that the Athenians also found themselves continually making excuses for him. When he wanted to, he could charm them with his sweetness and gentleness, but they had an instinctive fear that his sweetness and gentleness masked fanatic cunning. Above all he wanted to be a "great man," tyrant or dictator, and he allowed nothing to come between himself and his dreams.

In 416 B.C. Athens, or rather the leaders of the Athenian empire, suffered one of those attacks of madness that from time to time afflict great nations. The small rock-girt island of Melos, proudly independent for seven centuries, refused to become part of the Athenian empire or to pay tribute. The island was therefore invested by a naval force, and its capital was surrounded. The islanders might have held out indefinitely but there were traitors in their midst; the city fell; all the males were killed and the women and children were sold into slavery. It comes as no surprise that Alcibiades was the chief instigator of that senseless massacre or that he took one of the captured slave women to be his mistress. He had a child by the woman and took care that the boy received an education. Plutarch says that the Athenians regarded his care for the boy as "an act of humanity." They were discovering virtues in all his vices, and if he performed any ordinary act this too was pronounced a virtue.

The leaders of Athens were enlarging their ambitions. There existed a myth that they had conquered the Persians; in fact, in the early years of the century they had fought off a series of Persian invasions, all of them ill prepared. They were not satisfied with their small empire of Greek islands. They planned to conquer North Africa and Italy and perhaps the entire Mediterranean basin. The stepping-stone to conquest was Sicily. Once again Alcibiades became one of the instigators, summoning the Athenians to arm a vast invasion fleet and offering to be one of its commanders.

One day in May, 415 B.C., shortly after the sack of Melos, with the Athenian fleet amounting to 134 triremes and a host of auxiliary vessels—the largest fleet ever assembled up to that time—about to sail for Sicily, an extraordinary event happened. A band of conspirators ran through Athens in the dead of night mutilating the herms which stood outside most of the houses and official residences and in the public gardens. Originally used as signposts and boundary markers and later used as sculptural decorations, the herms were statues of Hermes, the head mounted on a tapering stone column adorned with male genitals. The band of vandals smashed the faces of the herms, which were regarded as sacred. To the Athenians it was at once evident that only Alcibiades was capable of organizing such an outrageous plot. It was widely rumored that he had recently taken part in a ceremony mocking the sacred Eleusinian mysteries, the equivalent of a ceremony mocking the Mass. But why had he done it? And more especially, why had he done it at this time, on the eve of the invasion of Sicily? It was an act of impiety and of sovereign contempt, a taunting of the manhood of the Athenians. It was such an act as might have been done by a Sicilian as a desperate stratagem to ward off the invasion. So widespread were the mutilations that it would have needed a whole army of conspirators to accomplish them. Strangely, no one had seen a single herm being mutilated.

Although he was under suspicion, Alcibiades was never called to account for this strange deed. He was permitted to leave with the fleet, and it was only some weeks later that an order for his arrest was issued, not because of suspicion that he had mutilated the herms, but because it was believed that he had taken part in the mockery of the Eleusinian mysteries in his own house. A ship was dispatched to bring him to trial from Sicily, where the Athenian fleet was engaged in some trivial skirmishes. Alcibiades meekly allowed himself to be arrested but escaped when the ship put in at Thurii.

Thereafter, except for a brief period when he was invited back to Athens after taking command of a fleet and routing the enemies of Athens, Alcibiades was a wanderer on the face of the earth, traveling from court to court and offering his services to the reigning prince in return for the command of an army or a fleet which could be thrown against Athens. He had no loyalty to anyone, even to the princes he served. He took refuge in the court of King Agis of Sparta, the hereditary enemy of Athens, but had to leave after seducing the king's wife. He passed over to Asia Minor, where he succeeded in inducing the Ionic allies of Athens to revolt, and allied himself with Tissaphernes, the Persian satrap. Everywhere he went, he took on the appropriate coloring, like a chameleon. "At Sparta he was devoted to athletic exercise, was frugal and reserved; in Ionia, luxurious, gay and indolent; in Thrace, always drinking; in Thessaly, ever on horseback; and when he lived with Tissaphernes, the Persian satrap, he exceeded the Persians themselves in pomp and magnificence." A cold, calculating mind was relentlessly at work. People, nations were expendable, so long as he was in power. But power eluded him. He conducted negotiations between Tissaphernes and the Athenians, presenting himself merely as a mediator but in fact taking sides, now arguing on behalf of the Persians, then on behalf of the Athenians, until it became clear that he was using the negotiations to advance himself. He attempted to corrupt everyone he encountered, and his corruptions were organized with singular grace and intelligence. He amassed vast wealth, but a great part of it was stolen in Bithynia by some Thracians who carried it off from his well-guarded fortress during his absence. Reduced to comparative poverty, Alcibiades thought of making his way to Persia to serve in the court of Artaxerxes, the King of Kings. On his way to Persia, he visited the court of Pharnabazus, satrap of Phrygia, where he was entertained and treated with great respect. Spies reported his movements to Athens, to Sparta, to Miletus, to Samos. He was feared, admired, detested, and despised; above all, he was feared, because men saw in him the potential tyrant. While he was staying with his mistress, Timandra, in a small house given to him by Pharnabazus, the Spartans caught up with him. They set fire to the house, surrounded it, waited for him to rush out, and then killed him with javelins and arrows. When he died, he was about forty-six years old.

Alcibiades was a portent, an intimation of things to come. He had the grace of Alexander, the calculated cruelty of Caesar, the detachment of Augustus. The Athenians, watching him closely, observed in him an explosive power that both terrified and fascinated them, and most of all they remembered the strange incident of the mutilation of the herms on the eve of the ill-fated Sicilian expedition. Alcibiades had helped to launch the expedition, but he was far away in another country when the Sicilians at last rose up and destroyed the Athenian fleet and army so completely that Athens from being an empire was reduced to little more than a city. Yet in his own way, by his insolence, his pride, his feverish fanning of the flames, Alcibiades contributed to these terrible events. Plutarch's summing up of his character is relentlessly brief: "Of all men he was the most unscrupulous and the most entirely careless of humanity."

If a man is insanely proud and remains in an insane asylum, he does no harm. He can issue orders to imaginary armies, order the massacre of his enemies, write MINE across large areas of the map, bomb imaginary hospitals and murder imaginary civilians to his heart's content. No one is bothered except the attendant who has to listen to the speeches of the somber man who believes in his "victories." But it is another matter when we find a real general giving the same orders, with bombing planes and armored divisions at his command. The Athenians, recognizing the danger, were able to hold Alcibiades at bay through the greater part of his life. They knew that given the opportunity he would always aim for supreme power without any consideration of the fortunes of ordinary men. His aim was not to better them but to better himself, and not only to better himself; he had an overwhelming desire to exalt himself over all men.

The qualities of such a man were well known and easily recognizable. Unscrupulousness, indifference to humanity, a gift for betrayal, a delight in excess, a capacity for sudden savagery, a flair for grandiloquence, a cold and calculating manner. Seventeen years before he became the dictator of Russia Lenin wrote, "The bitter lesson: to regard all persons without sentiment; to keep a stone in one's sling." Such coldness and remoteness and desire to punish lie at the heart of the mystery of corruption. If one asks, "For God's sake, why must you punish?" there is never any coherent answer. The desire to punish is built into their characters and is as much a part of them as their continual acts of betrayal, their grandiloquence, and their unscrupulousness.

An unchanging pattern can be observed through history—when the people are weak and divided, a tyrant arises to take advantage of their weaknesses and divisiveness. He comes usually from the middle or upper class; he is either a soldier or a lawyer; he moves with extraordinary speed to identify himself with a revolutionary party, takes command of it, and then uses it to enlarge his power over his party and all other parties. He acts decisively and ruthlessly, driving wedges between people and setting them in opposition to one another so that they neutralize each other. He is the master of corruption, and if necessary he will seek to corrupt the whole state to maintain his power. His weapons are the familiar weapons of subversion, treachery, and lies. All tyrants are brothers under the skin. They speak a common language, announce the same laws, employ the same punishments, delude themselves with the same delusions. They learn nothing from the past or from their own failures. They see themselves as "the new men," though they are following principles as old as Cain. Their characters do not change or develop. They act out their roles in much the same way, and they like to embark on dangerous foreign adventures because to do so gives them a feeling of self-importance and also because it distracts the people from worrying about internal affairs. They like to confront the people with the unanswerable slogan "Tyranny or chaos." They shout that the country needs law and order, and they are themselves the most lawless of men.

Aristotle, who carefully examined many tyrannies and added up the years the tyrants remained in power, concluded that tyrannies were "exceedingly short-lived." He admitted, however, that some tyrannies were exceedingly long-lived. The tyrant Orthagoras and his descendants ruled over Sicyon for about a hundred years. In Aristotle's eyes this could be explained by their "exceptional moderation." Most tyrannies ended in blood and misery, with the violent overthrow of the tyrant. Tyrants held on to their power as long as possible because they enjoyed the uses of power in all its forms and felt helpless without it. It pleased them that they could throw away all customary restraints and succumb to the temptations of pride. Herodotus, the confirmed democrat, offers a carefully thought-out argument comparing autocracy with the only tolerable government recognized by him. He called it *isonomy,* which means "equal under the law." He wrote:

> The characteristic vices of an autocrat are envy and pride; envy, because it is a natural human weakness, and pride because excessive wealth and power lead to the delusion that he is something more than a man. These two vices are the root cause of all wickedness: both lead to acts of savage and unnatural violence.
>
> Absolute power ought, by rights, to preclude envy on the principle that the man who possesses it has also at command everything he could wish for; but in fact it is not so, as the behavior of kings to their subjects proves: they are jealous of the best of them merely for continuing to live, and take pleasure in the worst; and no one is readier than a king to listen to tale-bearers. A king, again, is the most inconsistent of men; show him reasonable respect, and he is angry because you do not abase yourself before his majesty; abase yourself, and he hates you for being a superserviceable rogue. But the worst of all remains to be said—he breaks up the structure of ancient tradition and law, forces women to serve his pleasure, and puts men to death without trial.
>
> Contrast with this the rule of the people: first, it has the finest of all names to describe it—*isonomy,* or equality before the law; and, secondly, the people in power do none of the things that monarchs do. Under the government of the people a magistrate is appointed by lot and is held responsible for his conduct in office, and all questions are put up for open debate. For these reasons I propose that we do away with the monarchy, and raise the people to power; for the state and the people are synonymous terms.

Herodotus puts these words into the mouth of Otanes, a wealthy Persian nobleman who came to prominence during the brief interregnum between the death of Cambyses and the elevation of Darius to the throne. It was, on the face of it, an unlikely speech for a Persian nobleman to make, all the more so because Otanes held high rank and was himself in the running to become king of Persia. Nevertheless it is entirely possible that something like this was said, for

Herodotus knew the history of Persia well and had ample sources of information among the Persians themselves.

Herodotus's attack on tyranny is repeated at intervals in his *History*. Inconsistency, arbitrariness, sudden rages, defiance of law and tradition, wantonness and savage executions—these were the characteristics of tyrants. Their inhumanity appalled him; and just as they corrupted the laws, so they corrupted everyone around them. *Isonomy* had the sweetest sound to his ears because it represented the triumph over the evils of tyranny. One would like to think that Otanes, the author of the superb speech against tyranny, remained a man of the people. Instead, according to Herodotus, he reverted to type as one of the leading noblemen in his country when he was appointed a general in the Persian war against Greece. When he attacked the island of Samos and met heavy resistance, he defied the order of Darius "not to kill or capture any Samian" and massacred the entire population.

All through the great funeral speech of Pericles, recorded by Thucydides, we are made aware that tyranny is the uninvited specter at the feast. Pericles presents Athens as the city where men are equal before the law, where all offices are open to men of ability, and where the laws are weighted only when it is a question of protecting the oppressed. He celebrates isonomy as vigorously as Herodotus, and for the same reason. Isonomy is absolutely necessary if men are to live in dignity.

Many Greek historians and philosophers studied the character of the tyrant. They saw the tyrant as the corruptor of the people, the generator of the nightmare. They believed that it was in man's power to destroy the evil once and for all; and while history shows the belief to be unfounded, honor lay in holding to this belief against the evidence.

The American Declaration of Independence was one more, and not the least important, attack on tyranny. One sentence in it derives ultimately from the funeral speech of Pericles. "We hold these truths to be self-evident, that all men are created equal, that they are endowed by their Creator with certain unalienable Rights, that among these are Life, Liberty and the pursuit of Happiness." These are not the rights that commend themselves to tyrants. In the eyes of the Founding Fathers tyranny must be expelled forever from the shores of America.

Unhappily, tyranny is not something that can be legislated away by declarations or acts of parliament. It lurks in the background, always ready to pounce on an unsuspecting people. The criminal mind delights in wielding arbitrary power, and there is never any guarantee that another Chang Hsien-chung or Alcibiades will not arise. In the modern age the techniques of tyranny have advanced to a stage of near-perfection, and it becomes increasingly difficult to remove a tyrant from power. "The price of freedom is eternal vigilance." But against the armed police of a modern dictatorship something more than vigilance is needed. We need the courage that survives torture and degradation, a ferocious dedication, a vast hope, a vast despair.

In our own age it becomes more and more difficult to wage war against corruption. The corrupt tend increasingly to acquire power, and the uncorrupted want more and more to be left alone. This is why it is so necessary to recognize the corrupt individual, the potential tyrant, to observe him closely, and wherever possible to destroy him.

The Nature of
Human Corruption

Let us imagine a policeman who wears a badge, a gun at his hip, a row of bullets round his waist, and carries a small billy club, which he likes to swing on a leather thong. Club, gun, bullets, badge, and uniform reinforce his formidable authority. He can crack a skull open or shoot a man, and a sympathetic judge will not ask too many questions. The populace is a little afraid of him, and he is well aware of the fear he inspires.

Let us imagine he is a normal cop without any psychological hang-ups, generally law-abiding, with a wife and children he adores. He is cordial to his friends and appreciative of small kindnesses. He will show the photographs of his wife and children to complete strangers, delighted when they smile approvingly. At the end of a day's work we see him dropping into a restaurant near the police station. He orders a cup of coffee, and the restaurant owner says the coffee is on the house. It costs very little; there is no need to make a fuss about it; the restaurant owner is eager to be on good terms with the policeman, who accepts the coffee with good grace. Only the faintest, scarcely perceptible shadow has appeared on his conscience, and perhaps there is no shadow at all. If he had not been a policeman, if he had entered the restaurant unarmed and without the billy club, he might still have received the free coffee. The pillars of civilization have not shuddered, and he leaves the restaurant in an equable frame of mind, delighted with the restaurant owner's cordiality and his own response to it.

A few days later, after work, he drops into the restaurant and orders a dinner. His wife has gone to stay with her mother; the marriage is not going very well; he cannot pay the mortgage on his house in the suburbs and obviously needs cheering up. The convivial restaurant keeper listens to his troubles, lends him a hundred dollars, and says the dinner is on the house. He is in an expansive mood, and so at the end of the meal is the policeman. The gift of a meal and the loan of a hundred dollars are not earth-shaking events, and no one has been harmed. Everything has been done in the name of friendship, and the cop and the restaurant keeper are calling each other by their first names.

"You know," says the restaurant keeper, "there have been a lot of burglaries around here. We need people to keep an eye on our shops. If we could have a few more patrols, especially at night, it would make a world of difference. What do you say?"

"It's a good idea, Charlie!"

"Of course it is! We could pay for it, too. I could collect a bit of money in the street to see that we get this extra protection."

So it is arranged that for $250 a week there will be more foot patrols in the street at night, and the police make a concerted effort to see that the burglars keep clear of the street. They have now a substantial stake in the well-being of this particular street. The money is divided among five police officers, and all of them enjoy free meals at the restaurant.

Soon it occurs to them that there is more money to be made by giving special protection to other streets. The shopkeepers are canvassed and they agree, although reluctantly, to pay protection money. A map is prepared, the precinct is divided up into twelve separate areas, ten of them paying $250 a week for special protection and two of them, in the outlying, more poverty-stricken areas, paying $200 a week. The money is beginning to roll in. At first the five policemen did in fact go out on night patrol and offer protection. Gradually they find themselves too busy to fulfill the task; they forget to go out or report in sick; the money comes whether they patrol the streets or not. It is a very happy discovery that money can be obtained by doing nothing at all.

But at this point something very strange and troubling occurs. The five policemen find themselves suffering from a variety of ills. They are living high, but they are guilt-ridden. They must conceal their illicit gains from the Internal Revenue Service and from other policemen in the precinct, and they are becoming increasingly aware of the risks involved, the very real possibility of exposure. In the restaurant, where they take their meals, they observe that they are not always greeted with conviviality. The restaurant keeper still calls them by their first names, but his manner betrays a certain lack of warmth. As for the policemen, they find themselves drinking and gambling the money away, partly in order to get rid of it and partly because they are on edge and learning something about which they had never previously been informed. They are learning to be afraid.

The next step is not an easy one, but it seems inevitable. The possession of money far in excess of their legitimate earnings gives them little pleasure. To deaden the sense of guilt and the risk of exposure they need much greater sums of money. Like a drug addict who must continually increase the dose, they find themselves seeking these vast increments of money as coldbloodedly as previously they hunted for criminals. They make arrangements with the local mafia to turn a blind eye on the trade in hard drugs. There remains one further step. From being protectors of the mafia they become active participants. Money now falls on them in an unending shower, like the gold shower that fell into the lap of Danaë, but so many bribes have to be paid and so many hangers-on have to be placated, that in fact none of them becomes wealthy; and over them all, inevitable as doom, hangs the threat of exposure.

What has happened here is something relatively simple and commonplace. Corruption did not seize them by the throat; it glided into view with an exquisite gentleness. They were scarcely aware that it was engulfing them. The first steps were so easy that they seemed to happen of themselves, and the last steps, though difficult, were accomplished with seeming ease.

Petty corruption, or base corruption, has existed since the beginning of recorded time. The temple guards in Babylonia took bribes to permit the worshipers to see the holy of holies. Every functionary, everyone in a position of power, however small the power, has demanded some favor for himself from those less favored than himself.

It is almost a definition of a government functionary that he is one who takes bribes and will bend toward those who will bring him an advantage. For the most part this is done on so petty a scale that it passes unobserved except by those who make a practice of watching them closely. Vile and despicable as the custom is, it has been sanctified by long tradition. John Donne, the English poet and Dean of Saint Paul's, who explored the nature of sin as brilliantly as he explored the nature of God, wrote about these small corruptions in one of his sermons: "There are some sins so rooted, so rivetted in men, so incorporated, so consubstantiated in the soul, by habitual custom, as that those sins have contracted the nature of Ancient possessions."

But although John Donne accepted the fact that they were probably ineradicable, being part and parcel of human nature, he cast a wary eye on them. Those "ancient possessions" have a corpselike quality about them. That they are habitual does not make them any more desirable, and that they smell of death is as indisputable as human mortality. In his sermon Donne is a little puzzled by these sins that cling so steadfastly to the human animal, like fleas. He wishes they could be brushed away, but even God seems not to bother with them. In the end he comes to regard them as the habitual signs of human corruption, to remind us of our corruptibility.

Mother Courage, the heroine of Bertolt Brecht's play about a woman wandering through the disasters of the Thirty Years' War, surviving by native wit and happy accidents, has another opinion on the matter. When she is in desperate need, she can always, or nearly always, find the right officer or functionary and bribe him. "Thanks be to God they're corruptible!" she exclaims. "They're not wolves, they're human and after money. God is merciful and men are bribable, that's how His will is done on earth as it is in Heaven. Corruption is our only hope. As long as there's corruption, there will be merciful judges and even the innocent may get off!"

Mother Courage is not being in the least ironical. She is not concerned with morality. She is concerned with survival, with the lives of her children, with the facts of life and the world as it is. Her attitude toward corruption is essentially a healthy and heroic one. Implicit in her cry is the age-old condemnation of those miserable functionaries who try to make life so difficult for other people. "Corruption is our only hope." Perhaps; but it is only a hope. If it is to his advantage, the judge will send even the innocent to the gallows. This she knows, and she is prepared for it.

The policeman who aspires to a career in corruption is assuming the role of the judge who condemns the innocent. He becomes a destructive agent, bringing death in ever-widening circles to the city. When he traffics in dope or even when he offers protection to the mafia, he appears to be behaving in a reasonable and purposeful manner, but in fact he is just as destructive of human life as a man who goes out on the street with a submachine gun and shoots at random. By simple and clearly recognizable stages he has come to absolute criminality.

There are three stages by which the policeman becomes the pure criminal. They can be described as Base Corruption, Area of Confusion, and Toward Absolute Corruption. Base Corruption is familiar and commonplace; it demands small services, a cup of coffee, a dinner, a bottle of whiskey. (A city building inspector will look the other way if there is a minor infraction of the rules, and expects to be paid for lowering his eyelids.) Base Corruption becomes addictive; the dose must be increased, but within suitable bounds. The cup of coffee becomes many cups of coffee, the bottle of whiskey becomes a case. The very nature of Base Corruption demands a certain groping for higher things. Inevitably there is some wavering. For days or months the policeman may discover that life is perfectly acceptable without committing the slightest act of corruption. He is not an addict. Corruption has been a very tentative thing, and he tells himself that he can put it away. He goes about his work totally immersed in his humdrum task; he is pleasant toward his superior officer and likes to accompany old ladies across the road, holding out his hand to ward off the approaching traffic. But he knows that simply because he has committed some minor acts of corruption in the past, he is always in danger of committing them again. He lives with the knowledge that the smallest act of corruption conceals within itself the seed of the greatest acts.

At this stage questions of morality scarcely arise. The moral law is abundantly full of loopholes, and sometimes the policeman finds himself dreaming of wealth and power, a life free of the bothersome demands of duty. Dispassionately he observes the world around him, the many men who spend their time enlarging the loopholes of the law. Temptation comes; he succumbs to it; the danger was much less than he imagined. This, of course, is the hidden trap present throughout the first and second stages of corruption; the trap becomes obvious in the third and culminating stage. Danger wears the robe of invisibility; it can be felt obscurely, but is not perceived.

The second stage, the Area of Confusion, has its own inner logic without possessing any outward logicality. The moral issues are at first confused and unresolved. Guilt manifests itself at first ambiguously, later with extraordinary acuteness. There are no pathways through this wilderness; the ground is uncharted; and if by some miracle it were possible to chart the Area of Confusion, it would resemble a maze where the pathways are intended to mislead and only the least likely pathways lead to the hidden center. And just as a man making his way through a maze finds himself frequently coming to a dead end, and then retracing his steps, so the man wandering through the Area of Confusion finds himself frequently going in the direction opposite to the one he intended.

In this area there are pitfalls everywhere, but there are also aids for the traveler. All is not lost in the Area of Confusion. There is always the possibility of returning to the world of Base Corruption, where the pickings are so small that there is a chance that no one will prosecute, for society accepts small-time corruption. There is not simply one point of possible return. There are many points where the traveler can rest long enough to see that the journey is not worth making. He can abandon his journey completely or he can continue onward into the higher reaches of massive corruption. The choice is a conscious one, but it is not easily arrived at. "A man can fall into the heights as well as into the depths," wrote the German poet Friedrich Hölderlin. But the heights are likely to be less well charted than the depths, and to the observer standing in the midst of the Area of Confusion the prospects are not altogether inviting.

There are ancient maps where the words "Here are Tigers" meant only that a traveler might encounter perils hitherto unknown. "Tigers" meant almost unimaginable savageries, scorpions the size of a man, elephants armor-plated like crocodiles. He simply did not know what terrors awaited him. So the man dedicated to a career in corruption skirts the lower reaches of the Area of Confusion in trepidation, takes deep breaths, rests frequently, and carefully observes the behavior of anyone else he finds wandering in the maze. Indeed, he seeks out strangers who have found themselves in this mysterious region for exactly the same reason that he entered it; and these chance encounters are sometimes fraught with strange consequences. He and the stranger may unite their forces—a dangerous expedient given the nature of the journey, which is best made alone.

So perplexing and terrifying is the Area of Confusion that it becomes necessary to chart or at least attempt to chart the territory. There has to be some kind of touchstone, some way to escape from the haunting knowledge that quicksands, unimaginable beasts, and fierce storms lie in wait for the traveler. He makes a rough sketch, keeps notes of his journeys, attempts to record all his separate incursions into the forbidden territory. He notes where the gamekeepers were last seen, their probable hiding places, where he thought he heard wild animals, and where the prisons are. He also notes down as accurately as possible his conversations with chance acquaintances, not only to be able to study them at his leisure and find out who is speaking the truth, but also to retain a record of his own thoughts. Records, which he has rarely kept in the past, suddenly become important. He has embarked on a dangerous errand, and these records help him to recognize his exact position at any given moment.

Meanwhile his prodigious effort to map out the territory and to chart his progress continues. A liar keeps track of his lies for fear of being found out. Similarly, a corrupt man keeps track of his acts of corruption in order to learn where he is, and how far he dares to go, and where it is safe to advance, although he must know there is no safety anywhere in his chosen territory. Hence the voluminous memoranda, diary notes, bankbooks, tape recordings, copies of letters in triplicate, which he leaves behind him or abandons in his journey. District attorneys are constantly surprised by the mass of records left behind by corrupt officials, enabling the prosecutors to trace step by step the subtle and complex paths they have followed.

It is worthwhile to pause briefly to consider the Area of Confusion, because this is the place where the mystery of corruption occurs. Of all the areas the corrupt man passes through it is the most difficult to understand in terms of human behavior. All that happens afterward is predetermined by the experience gained in the Area of Confusion. Here he decides upon the way of life he will follow throughout the foreseeable future, weighing the profit and the loss, reaching the conclusions that were perhaps as inevitable as an article of faith, and as sordid as death.

To understand the Area of Confusion it is useful to suggest a comparison with the mystical Dark Night of the Soul, the long agony experienced by the religious recluse as he waits in fear and trembling for the vision of God. All is aridity and emptiness, torment and misery, a continual turning around a central point offering no consolations, no warmth, no certainty. God has vanished—*Deus absconditus*—and it appears that he will never reveal himself and even takes pleasure in not revealing himself. This landscape, too, has been well charted, and there is considerable similarity in the charts drawn independently by the great mystics to describe a very real and terrifying experience. The Spanish mystics Teresa of Avila, John of the Cross, and Ignatius of Loyola have all described it at length, but the concept is not the invention of the Spaniards. It originated among the early Christian mystics, who compared it to the Wilderness the Children of Israel had to pass through before they reached the Promised Land.

The Dark Night of the Soul is not a night and is not necessarily dark. It is simply a state of soul in which doubts and hesitations prevail, in which the soul is thrown back on its own naked resources and recognizes its own nullity, its unworthiness, its absolute incapacity to see the vision of God. At the same time, according to the mystics who have passed through this wilderness, there is a continual sense of movement, even of expectancy, although all hope has been abandoned.

In the Area of Confusion we observe another Dark Night of the Soul, but in a contrary direction—not toward God and the splendor of created things but toward corruption and death.

We have observed the corrupt man wandering confusedly through an uncharted landscape, bracing himself against the strangeness of the place, uncertain of his bearings, attempting in various ways to maintain himself in an environment that is demonstrably unhealthy, going about his affairs very secretively, taking careful notes and leaving voluminous records behind him. He is continually in movement, cautious, fearful, in a mood of expectancy. Many of his actions derive from a consciousness of guilt, and much labor is expended in attempting to expunge the guilt that confronts him at every turn in the road. But these actions are not entirely negative. Some things have been accomplished: he is gradually reaching a state of mind that permits him to embark on the third stage of his adventure. He has uprooted himself from the familiar world where ordinary people live; he has destroyed one by one the loyalties that attached him to his friends; he is becoming, as he sees it, a free agent to do with his life whatever he pleases. He realizes that what he is searching for at long last is the gate that will permit him to pass into the third stage, which I have called Toward Absolute Corruption. (There is a fourth stage—Absolute Corruption itself—but this is achieved by very few individuals and does not concern us at this moment.)

When and where does the traveler discover the gate? About this gate there is very little mystery: it has been there all the time, clearly visible. Indeed, the whole maze of the Area of Confusion is designed to lead ultimately to the gate; reaching the gate is the final goal of the wanderer in the maze. Only a few, however, are able to pass through. Only after a long and arduous journey, which involves the extinction of human values and loyalties, can the corrupt man pass into the mysterious regions of Toward Absolute Corruption. His passage is sudden and has the intensity of a religious conversion. And just as religious conversion often appears to come unexpectedly without any previous laboring of the spirit, so the sudden passage from the Area of Confusion comes with the same appearance of careless abandon, although in fact it has been prepared over a long period of time.

There may be some who enter a career of corruption for no apparent reason, for a whim, committing an *acte gratuite,* an entirely motiveless act. But human experience suggests that it is usually possible to trace the origin of an apparently motiveless act to an obscure desire for revenge. Baudelaire speaks in *Le Spleen de Paris* of the sudden prodigal courage that allows some people to execute essentially absurd and even mortally dangerous acts, and he observes that they are generally lazy people of marked sensuality, who are otherwise incapable of doing the simplest and most ordinary things. As an example he mentions an inoffensive man much given to waking dreams who took it into his head to set fire to a forest "just to find out whether the fire takes hold as quickly as people say it does." He set fire to ten forests before he was able to convince himself that fire travels at an amazing speed.

Baudelaire tells another story about one of his friends "who lit a cigar near a barrel of gunpowder, just *to see, to find out, to tempt fate,* to force himself to make a show of energy, to play the gambler, to taste the pleasure of anxiety, for nothing, for a whim, out of boredom." No doubt such men exist, but to tempt fate for a whim suggests a desire to do more than tempt fate. People who play Russian roulette are not so much tempting fate as inviting sudden death.

So we may imagine that the Area of Confusion is sometimes bypassed, and there are some men who slip into the mysterious regions beyond easily, almost without thought and certainly without design, "for nothing, for a whim, out of boredom." But most men who pass through the gate leading out of the Area of Confusion have some idea of what they are doing. They know, for example, that they are entering an area even more dangerous than the Area of Confusion, and that they are trafficking with death.

This time the gravitational pull that keeps the corrupt man close to the workaday world is absent. He has passed through the gravitational field into the upper regions; no sense of morality restrains him; he is free to move at his own pace toward an even more rarefied air. By this time all moral issues have been resolved by the simple process of annihilating them. He is now dedicated to corruption on a scale which in earlier years he would have regarded as obscene. This is full-scale corruption on all fronts. He is not content with the small pickings of graft. Whole businesses, whole societies, whole populations are at his mercy. What he wants now, at any price, is power and the wealth to defend this power against all comers.

Largely, of course, it is a question of scale. The small corruptions of the past are no different in quality from the massive corruptions of the present. Lying, thievery, sleight of hand, physical threats, and violence have proved their efficacy. But now the field of operations extends even beyond the reach of his intelligence; and as he climbs higher he enters a region where normal human laws and moralities no longer apply, where crimes are committed "for the good of the cause," where every act is excusable because it brings more power, more wealth, more excitement. He openly exults in his power, assumes the trappings of wealth, commits himself to acts of extraordinary daring. To protect himself he provides himself with a front, a legitimate business concern, a holding company, an alliance with corrupt officials in the government or the city, offering them handouts which they know to be bribes, and thus with every act of self-protection he involves himself more deeply in crime. At the same time, by the very nature of these operations, he finds himself amassing so many bankbooks, promissory notes, ledgers, check stubs, and accounts with credit-card agencies that the police have no difficulty in discovering the full extent of his crimes once they have decided to follow his tracks. He makes little effort to hide his crimes, courts danger, rejoices in near-brushes with the law, partly out of daring, partly out of habit, partly out of boredom. Since the world increasingly seems to him unreal, the possibility of arrest, indictment, imprisonment seems to him equally unreal. His energies are concentrated on his corruptions.

The area called Toward Absolute Corruption might be called the Area of Conspiracy if it were not for the fact that even in the first two stages of corruption, the acts of a corrupt man are conspiratorial. In the third stage, however, he thrives on conspiracies, the more intricate the better. Conspiracy becomes a way of life. But conspiracy has its own laws, and he does not always understand them fully. The first law is that the conspiracy, to be successful, must be contained within a simple, clear-cut framework, and the more complicated it is, the more likely it is to fail. Complexities, however, delight him. He resembles the juggler who has succeeded in keeping three balls in the air and now believes that he can keep ten, twenty, thirty balls in the air. There is almost nothing he cannot do. He has trained himself well, and he finally succeeds with ten balls, and then it becomes more difficult; and while he is amazed at his own prowess, he realizes that the time may come when the balls will simply fall to the ground. Nevertheless he continues to exult in his skill. All might be well if it were not that he himself becomes confused and is so absorbed in his conspiracies that nothing else exists for him.

At this stage there occurs an erosion of the core, an internal disintegration and disorientation, so grave that it is likely to destroy his judgment. Gone now is the penetrating vision, the clear understanding of the forces at work. Even when he was occupying the Area of Confusion the issues were clear, all the more so because he was still weighed down with questions of morality and responsibility toward his family and friends. He was continually weighing the risks. Now, having broken through the barrier of morality, he may discover too late that morality of itself provides the basis for human judgments and that without a moral code to fall back upon a man is at the mercy of his demons. "If there is no God, then everything is permitted," says one of the characters of Dostoyevsky. So, unfettered by morality, he continues his dizzy climb to power, influence, and wealth, permitting himself the supreme luxury of striking out blindly at all his enemies, even his imaginary enemies, and surrendering to every passing impulse.

He knows, of course, that he is in danger, but danger only spurs him to greater and greater feats. He has long passed the stage when he can measure danger accurately and take the appropriate precautions. Danger becomes unreal. It is a ghost he can brush away with his hands or it is the oxygen he needs for his expanding lungs. A kind of prolonged stupefaction sets in, and not only danger but all the ordinary familiar things of daily life become unreal. It is nothing to him to give orders to kill people. In business he watches the total ruin of a competitor with indifference. He may order large-scale executions and send enormous wreaths to the funerals to testify to his grief, his civility, and his wealth. In politics he immures himself in his headquarters, embarks on annihilation campaigns against his enemies, draws up death lists or enemy lists, surrounds himself with criminals who take the greatest pleasure in carrying out his orders, and comes to regard himself as the sole authority, the man in complete command, although he is so remote from the people he governs that his commands have no relation to reality. He has reached the fugue state. He neither knows nor cares what is happening around him. All that remains is an unfettered will, a few well-known gestures, a commanding stance. His intelligence is dead, and his glazed eyes reflect the deadness of his soul.

Once embarked on this course he cannot stop of his own accord. Men who have reached the stage of Absolute Corruption cannot pause for reflection. They repeat the same corrupt acts endlessly, and each time it appears to them that they have invented something new and wonderful. The most insignificant modifications of strategy acquire in their eyes the appearance of brilliant improvisations of a new and unexpected character, and they are almost childish in their gleeful acceptance of their own brilliance. In this they resemble catatonics who raise one foot with immense difficulty and regard their success with stupefaction and amazement.

Finally there comes the catastrophe—that catastrophe to which half-consciously they have been aiming through all their corrupt years, for only in catastrophe lies ultimate security. At last they feel the earth under their feet. They know where they are. The life given to excess is over, and they enter the ordinary humdrum world they have been at such pains to avoid, to subvert, and to eradicate. A policeman knocks on the door, a popular uprising removes the politician from power, imprisonment faces him. The long trajectory comes to a stop beside a police desk and a police sergeant who has only the faintest idea about the life of the accused man. The simplest things—a pair of handcuffs, a little pad of black ink—bring him down to earth.

Here, at the point of catastrophe, surprising things happen. The corrupt man protests his innocence, proclaims that he has done everything for the public good, that his arrest is a huge error that will blacken the pages of history for years to come, that at the very worst he has been too trustful of his subordinates. Guilt, like danger, is brushed away; it is a ghost or a flyspeck. Gradually the enormity of his guilt and the inevitability of punishment sink in. Defenseless, he summons morality to his aid. He has been a good son; he has been faithful to his wife; he has cherished the memory of his parents and been kind to his friends and subordinates. He consoles himself with a catalogue of his virtues, and offers himself to mankind as a person of probity who had been misled by his advisers.

Defeat transforms men into good moralists. The corrupt, when found out, become especially good moralists. They weep unrestrainedly over the sins of the world and picture themselves as humble men who wanted to do good. Thus Hitler portrays himself in a letter written during the last hours of his life as a man who had to fight the greatest war in history because it was forced on him. He writes that he hopes his collection of paintings will embellish the city of Linz and that his relatives will be permitted to live in petit-bourgeois respectability. Similarly, Richard Nixon at the moment of defeat spoke about his hard-working father and saintly mother, blamed his fall on the lack of a suitable power base in Congress, and went on to quote a maudlin passage by Theodore Roosevelt about the blood-stained gladiator in the arena who fights to the bitter end. All these appeals to morality and good intentions are designed to make defeat more palatable. They are ritualistic performances that satisfy only one person, though they are intended for a large audience. So vast is the accumulation of self-serving moralities that there is no room for penitence. The great corruptors remain impenitent to the end.

Nevertheless, the catastrophe has the effect of changing their characters. There is a folding back, a return to moral principles and copybook maxims, a sustained effort to employ morality against the accusers. But this is done by rote, almost mindlessly. Instinctively the corrupt man searches at this last extremity for a point of strength and finds it in the Ten Commandments, which he has consistently disobeyed. He promises to repay. The murders committed by his private army were accidents; a long time has passed since they were committed; the circumstances were difficult to assess. Since the historical record is inaccurate, he will write his own memoirs to prove demonstrably that he committed nothing more than a few minor errors of judgment. But all this is unavailing. The church has recognized for two thousand years that penitence alone absolves the criminal. He must come barefoot to the altar, begging for the mercy he has never given to others, and plead for forgiveness from those he has wronged; and thus by completely humiliating himself he preserves his human dignity. But this happens very rarely, and he is more likely to put a bullet into his skull than to admit his crimes.

The trajectory of the great corruptor is a journey to death. He may have known this from the beginning. He may also have known that corruption is always and inevitably in complicity with death.

One does not simply enter upon a life of corruption. There are stages to be gone through. At each stage critical decisions have to be made. We may illustrate this in the form of a graph showing how a man may pass from one stage to another, the places where he makes the critical decisions, the plateaus he reaches, and the escape routes that lie open to him. It would be better if the graph could be shown in three dimensions, thus demonstrating the ample choices open to him. The graph shows an open, many-sided system: he can go in any direction he pleases. Of the four critical points (A, B, C, D), three present him with the possibility of turning back, but at each successive point the choice becomes more difficult, more cumbersome, more absurd. On these levels there exist no exact measurements. Though the corrupt man may bring himself to believe that he is acting intelligently while he is advancing through the stage of Toward Absolute Corruption, he is really engaged in guesswork, and

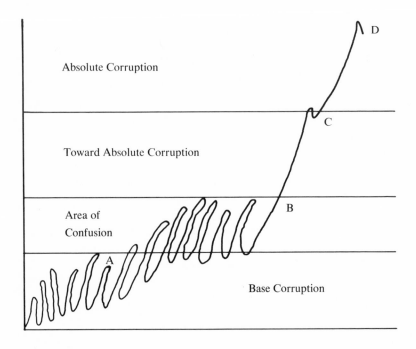

accurate solutions to his problems are not likely to present themselves. At this stage we can expect to find him consulting astrologers or participating in spiritualist séances. He appears to himself to be walking purposefully, with firm strides, but in fact he is simply following the only way open to him; there are no exits from the path of Absolute Corruption. At D, the point of catastrophe, he reverts to simple piety and abruptly blocks out everything that has gone before. How did he reach the point of catastrophe? He does not know and dares not recall.

For the absolutely corrupt man the real world has never had much meaning; now it has no meaning. Even his trial and execution can have no meaning. When he recites his moral maxims after his fall, he is like the dying man who recites the songs he heard in his childhood. He has gone beyond logic and rational observation into a world where logic and rational observation have no place. In a very real sense he has reverted to the stage of his early childhood where everything, even an act of grace after committing an unpardonable crime, is possible.

The corrupt mind is the mind infected with death, with nullity. Death encloses it and spills out of it. Ultimately it finds its salvation only in self-destruction.

The great corrupters are never hard to recognize. They have a curious sameness about them, and as we study them in the pages of history we detect the same stridency, the same inhumanity in all of them. They are generally regarded as "great men" because they have succeeded, at immense cost to their fellow men, in deflecting the course of history. "Great men," wrote E. M. Forster, "produce a desert of uniformity around them, and often a pool of blood, too." One wishes they produced only pools of blood, but they are more likely to produce rivers of blood and untold suffering.

In politics they arrive so often that one wonders why the world has not grown weary of them. They are helpless to conceal their lust for fame and their indifference to their fellow men. They demand attention; they proclaim themselves natural leaders; power is handed over to them; then they sharpen the knives of power and use them for their own purposes. The world takes such men at their own valuation, forgetting that they are mortally dangerous and are bent on destruction.

We speak of great artists, great sculptors, great dancers, great musicians, great actors, and there is no taint of corruption in them. We can no more think of a corrupt Beethoven than we can think of a corrupt sun. But once a man runs for office, corruption trails after him like his shadow. He tells lies in order to be elected, and the harm is done with the first lie. Then, as the lies accumulate, they take on a life of their own, dancing round him like a chorus of devils. He must spend the rest of his life attended by his private chorus.

The politician is fatally addicted to corruption, and there are few politicians who have not felt the breath of corruption on their faces.

In time, like men with decayed and rotting teeth, they become accustomed to their own smell and smilingly announce that they would not have it otherwise. Corruption settles on them like a well-worn garment. They move lightly from petty corruption to that confused area where temptations multiply and fester, and they have no difficulty ascending the steep road leading through the gate of Absolute Corruption. The farther they climb, the greater is their contempt for the people, their condemnation of the people. The poor, the young and the old, those who have the least political acumen and the most to gain from any politician with a streak of decency in him, are abandoned. The protective armor of power groups gathers round him, fences him off from the real world, and provides him with the muscle he needs in order to survive. Power calls to power; the corrupt recognize one another; the bill that is so rewarding to the politician and so disastrous to the people is passed by acclamation; and the politician is on the road to that great position he regards as his right by virtue of his intelligence, his compliance, and his conscience. The road to power is thickly covered with grease, and he slides merrily along it.

In the end, of course, he pays the penalty; history catches up with him; inquiring journalists catch up with him; his constituents catch up with him. Even if they fail to catch up with him in his lifetime, the avenging furies lie in wait for him after his death. Corruption is twice a sin: it is a sin against the flesh and against the spirit. The young Winston Churchill, writing his first and only novel when he was a subaltern in India, commented wisely on the terrible corruption that confronts politicians: "There are sins, sins against the commonwealth of mankind, against the phenomenon of life itself, the stigma of which would cling through death, and for which there was pardon only in annihilation."

The Dialogue with Corruption

The Drunken
Helmsman

Toward the end of his life Plato wrote an autobiographical letter, saying that in his youth he had hoped for a political career but was dissuaded because he soon realized that politics was full of corruption. He remembered particularly an incident that happened in the life of Socrates. The Thirty Tyrants had seized power and issued a warrant for the arrest and execution of a certain Leon of Salamis, an honest citizen. Socrates and four others were ordered to arrest the man and bring him to the executioner. Socrates refused, at great peril to his own life. It was inconceivable to him that he should attempt to save his life by obeying an order that was unjust and immoral and also quite clearly illegal. The Thirty Tyrants were not concerned with justice or legality. They wanted to implicate Socrates in their own crimes; they wanted to use him for their own purposes. He refused to be used. The four others did what they were told to do, and Leon of Salamis was put to death.

The Thirty Tyrants fell from power after conducting a short-lived reign of terror and were themselves hunted down. A new and more representative government emerged. By an unlucky accident this government included some men who detested Socrates and were determined to hound him out of the country. They claimed wrongly that his philosophical skepticism demonstrated that he was profoundly irreligious and that by holding philosophical classes with the youth of Athens he had succeeded in corrupting them. They remembered that among his pupils were Critias, one of the Thirty Tyrants, and Alcibiades, who had elevated corruption to a fine art and brought about the destruction of the Athenian army and the Athenian fleet. In search of scapegoats, they condemned Socrates to death. The philosopher, who detested the actions of Critias and Alcibiades, submitted to the verdict of the judges on the ground that he had no right to disobey the laws of the city. He could have escaped; instead he drank the hemlock. Overwhelmed by shock and misery, Plato abandoned Athens and went to live and teach in Megara.

When Plato wrote that these two incidents—the order to arrest Leon of Salamis and the death of Socrates—led him to decide as a youth to avoid a career in the rough and deadly game of politics, he was being slightly disingenuous. In fact he enjoyed three separate political careers, all of them at the court of the tyrant of Syracuse, whom he served as an adviser. To his credit, he once enraged the tyrant so much that he was sold into slavery. The tyrant died, a new tyrant came to the throne, and Plato, released from slavery, served his successor. For a philosopher intent on discovering the laws of good government, service in the court of Syracuse was of inestimable value. Plato was given an opportunity to watch at close hand the subtle alterations in the character of the tyrant and the even more subtle alterations in the character of the people who suffer under a tyranny. When writing *The Republic,* Plato was expressing ideas that came to him when he was close to the seat of power as well as other ideas that came to him when he was merely theorizing.

As the foundation for his theory of the state, Plato proposes the Ideal or Archetypal State, which is perfect, suffers no change or corruption, and is so far removed from the ordinary state we know, with its government and marketplaces and constant traffic, that it is to us virtually inconceivable. We can imagine an Ideal or Archetypal Chair, but it is much more difficult to imagine an Ideal or Archetypal State. Nevertheless the fiction serves Plato well. In this imaginary state justice rules, the people are content and well cared for, corruption is unthinkable, and the government acts with the willing consent of the governed. The best men rule, and since the worst can have no place in a perfect society, we are led to imagine that everyone in the state has good intentions and is determined to serve the community. This imaginary state is a standard to which all men can repair. Conspiracy, treachery, and all the other ills of society are unheard of. People eat in common, education is open to all, and no one is rich or poor, for all property is held by the community and all wages are the same or very nearly the same. Plato is describing a Golden Age inhabited by people immune to the diseases of the flesh and the spirit, without restlessness and without ambition, for their society has reached a state of perfection.

Plato then describes how the Ideal State gradually becomes corrupted, passing through many stages until it finally evolves into anarchic tyranny, the most corrupt of all forms of society. As he describes the corruptions that bring about the gradual disintegration of the state, Plato pauses at intervals to remind the reader that the process is not irreversible. The state in its downward path to tyranny suffers from a variety of diseases, but each disease can be cured. Tyranny is not inevitable. A corrupt state is corrupt because men have made it so; good men can restore the balance; the duty of men of good will is to ensure that tyranny will not prevail.

Gradually the Ideal State is transformed into a timocracy (*timē* = honor), by which Plato means roughly what we mean by *aristocracy*. The best men rule, but they are beginning to acquire bad habits. They marry the wrong women, produce offspring unworthy of them, take possession of houses and lands that previously belonged to the community, reduce the farmers to serfs, and, in order to maintain their power, transform themselves into a military elite. For the first time armed force emerges as an instrument to suppress the population. Indeed, armed force is used more frequently to suppress the people than to defend the state against a foreign enemy. The military elite encourage hunting and athletics but have no interest in learning and the arts. They are greedy for money, acquire fortunes as rapidly as possible, and hoard everything they have gained. They are parsimonious and avaricious; their greatest pleasure is to gaze at the heaped gold and silver in their private treasuries. Private property, aristocratic privilege, and armed force to suppress the people have made their appearance. An enslaved people confronts its armed rulers.

The second corruption of the state is oligarchy (*oligos* = few), in which the military elite is narrowed down to a few ruling families of immense wealth and prestige, who now openly flaunt their wealth and possessions. The many fall into great poverty, and the oligarchs feel no responsibility toward them. To make ends meet, the poor are reduced to moonlighting. Plato points out that a man with many jobs loses his identity but is all the more ripe for rebellion. With all the power and wealth concentrated in a few hands, and with the poor growing more desperately poor every day, the state is transformed into two states: the very rich and the very poor, who have nothing in common. Inevitably the poor resort to crime, and the rich, in order to increase and preserve their wealth, also resort to crime, but more effectively since they have greater resources. Violence becomes the rule, criminality a way of life. When poor youths are drafted into the army and find themselves living beside the well-fed and effete sons of the aristocracy, their hatred and contempt lead to more violence. A small spark may touch off a conflagration. One of the two states, the rich or the poor, receives help from a foreign state, and the country is drowned in civil war.

Plato points out that the conflict between the rich and the poor is not inevitable. The rich do not have to lend their money to the farmers at usurious rates of interest. If the rich behave with moderation, they can forestall the revolution. If they want all, they will lose all; if they surrender some of their wealth to the common good, they can retain large fortunes. But in general the rich do not behave with moderation, and they are swept aside in a violent upheaval.

The military elite possessed a concept of honor and practiced it; the oligarchs are without honor. The chief incentive of an oligarch is to acquire more and more wealth, and his indifference toward the poor is a mark of his absorbing, lifelong interest in money. He will not give it away, and he will have as little as possible to do with the poor. The poor rise in rebellion, and his wealth is destroyed unless he can escape with it to another country. The democratic revolutionary destroys the oligarch.

The third corruption is democracy (*demos* = people), which is not quite what we mean by *democracy* today. For Plato, who regarded both oligarchy and democracy as undesirable, preferring a state ruled by a philosophical elite, the democratic revolution provides no real answer to the problem. The faults of democracy are just as obvious as the faults of oligarchy. In an ironic passage in *The Republic,* Socrates portrays the oligarch as too fat to be able to fight against the youthful democrat. He says:

> It seems we have found some other things against whose secret entrance into the city the guardians must take every precaution.
> What are they? asked Adeimantus.
> Riches and poverty, for the one produces luxury and idleness and revolution, the other revolution and meanness and villainy besides.

I agree, but Socrates—think about this. How will our city be able to carry on a war if it has no money, especially if it is forced to fight a great and rich city?

To me it is obvious that fighting one city will be rather hard, but fighting two will be easier.

What on earth do you mean?

Don't you agree that our men will be soldier athletes fighting against rich men?

Yes, of course.

Well, Adeimantus, don't you think that one perfectly trained boxer is an easy match for two fat wealthy men who can't box?

That, of course, is the trouble with oligarchs: they are too fat, too luxury-loving, too incompetent. They are too eager to safeguard their possessions and have little inclination to safeguard the state when their possessions are in danger. Oligarchs simply do not care about the fate of democrats, and when the fight is engaged they are likely to be taken off-guard. Oligarchs are usually middle-aged men; democrats have the fire of life in them.

From the Socratic dialogues there emerge certain well-defined attitudes. First, the governors must receive the consent of the governed. There is no room in any state for great riches and great poverty. This has nothing to do with socialism or communism; Plato is merely saying that great wealth without responsibility is as reprehensible and damaging to the state as great poverty. Tyranny is the worst possible kind of state; the best is a state governed by a philosopher-king. Admittedly that ideal state is rarely reached. Plato calculates that tyranny is 729 times worse than the ideal state. Exactly how he arrived at this figure ($729 = 9 \times 9 \times 9$) is unknown, but what he meant is clear.

Plato proposes that neither rulers nor soldiers should be permitted to own property. The reason is, very clearly, that both rulers and soldiers are potentially tyrannical and are capable of doing grave harm to the republic. Their fellow citizens should provide them with all necessities; gold and silver should never pass through their hands; and soldiers, being especially dangerous, should be trained to serve as watchdogs, not as wolves. A corrupt military and a corrupt ruler were regarded by Plato as the worst disasters that could fall upon a people, and when he insists that soldiers and rulers must be removed from the temptations of wealth, he is saying only that it is necessary to safeguard the nation from its leading citizen and from its sworn defenders.

As Plato builds up his portrait of a workable state, we gradually become aware that he is deftly constructing the image of a nation where corruption is virtually impossible, not only because there are built-in safeguards against corrupt forces but because the people are trained to despise and punish corruption in all its forms. He regards the pursuit of wealth as a social disease to be avoided at all costs, and he regards poverty as a crime. The ruler's task is to bring harmony to the nation, to give it direction, and to defend it from its enemies.

What Plato feared above all was the state gone berserk, without a clear-headed ruler, with mutinous intriguers grasping for power, a corrupt state in a murderous drift toward disaster. Into the mouth of Socrates he puts the story of the Drunken Helmsman, for Plato was a storyteller as well as a philosopher:

> Imagine a fleet or a ship in which there is a captain who is taller and stronger than any of the crew, but he is a little deaf and has a similar infirmity in sight, and his knowledge of navigation is not much better. The sailors are quarreling with one another about the steering —everyone thinks he has the right to steer, though he has never learned the art of navigation and cannot tell who taught him or when he learned, and will further assert that it cannot be taught—and they are ready to cut in pieces anyone who says the contrary.
>
> So they cluster around the captain, begging and praying to him to commit the helm to them, and if at any time they do not prevail, but others are preferred to them, they kill the others or throw them overboard, and having first chained up the noble captain's senses with drink or some narcotic drug, they mutiny and take possession of the ship and make free with the stores; thus, eating and drinking, they proceed on their voyage in such a manner as might be expected of them.

Plato's story of the Drunken Helmsman begs many questions, for the helmsman himself—part blind, part deaf, with little knowledge of navigation—is scarcely better than any member of the crew taken at random. The ship, as Socrates describes it, is obviously sailing to its doom, which it will meet not because of any natural disaster but because the mutinous sailors are totally incompetent and mad for power. The ship will not dash itself against rocks; it will not be torn to pieces in a storm; it will sink as a result of all the malicious forces contained in it. Socrates implies clearly that the captain must possess undisputed knowledge and authority, for without these he is always at the mercy of mutinous sailors.

The captain in the story is also at the mercy of his own pride, his deafness, his lack of sight or vision, his stubbornness. He refuses to surrender the helm. Why? Chiefly because of his pride. Traditionally the Greeks regarded pride as the most dangerous of vices, certain to provoke heaven's vengeance. In *The Eumenides* of Aeschylus we read of another shipwreck:

> *He who transgresses through overwhelming pride*
> *Or brings upon himself treasures unjustly acquired,*
> *For him there comes a time of retribution.*
> *He, when he sets sail upon the evil ocean*
> *Is like a ship with the yardarm split asunder.*
> *Though he cry out his voice will not be heard,*
> *He shall struggle in the wild waves,*
> *And the gods shall laugh, seeing him.*
> *Having boasted of enduring fortune,*
> *He will see all things taken from him.*
> *Riding the wavecrest he is tossed like a weak thing,*
> *To perish unwept and unseen.*

The same theme runs through the entire literature of ancient Greece. The proud tyrants bring the whole state down with them when they fall. The Greeks believed that pride provoked the gods into using their most terrible weapons; pride was a fatal disease, like galloping consumption, and there was no cure.

Ultimately the Greeks and especially the Athenians tested all political actions against the enduring concept of sophrosyne: moderation, sobriety, balance. Like the Chinese doctrine of "the mean," sophrosyne involved a general respect for all opinions and a wise adjudicator acting as a moderating influence. It was not a static concept; on this balance all things trembled. Thus, it did not mean striking an average or resolving opposites mechanically, for the Greeks had no trust in mechanical solutions. Above all, sophrosyne involved an act of faith, a belief that moderation was possible in a world that was often chaotic and inexplicable.

In *The Laws* Plato introduces this argument several times, but never more cogently than when it is told by the Athenian Stranger:

Athenian Stranger: Nothing can be clearer than the observation I am about to make.
Megillus: What is it?
Athenian Stranger: That if anyone gives too great a power to anything, too large a sail to a vessel, too much food to the body, too

much authority to the mind, and does not observe the mean, then everything is overthrown and, in the wantonness of excess, runs in the one case to disorders and in the other to injustice, which is the child of excess. I mean to say, my dear friends, that there is no soul of man, young and irresponsible, who will be able to sustain the temptation of arbitrary power—no one who will not, under such circumstances, become filled with folly, the worst of diseases, and be hated by his nearest and dearest friends. . . .

On this level the argument is irrefutable; generations of tyrants have only reinforced it. "The wantonness of excess" feeds on itself, and is fatally involved in its own destruction. By "the wantonness of excess" Plato is describing the same phenomenon Lord Acton was describing when he wrote, "Power tends to expand indefinitely, and will transcend all barriers, abroad and at home, until met by superior force." Power by its very nature tends to be explosive. The only bounds it recognizes are the bounds presented by other powers.

The Greeks were fascinated by the machinery of tyranny, for they had ample opportunities, especially in the Ionian states, to watch it in operation. In *The Politics* Aristotle describes the methods employed by the tyrants to remain in power. All outstanding people are removed; all clubs for social and cultural activities are disbanded; schools are frowned upon and closely watched for any signs of disloyalty. Ideally the tyrant will keep everyone in the city within view, and he will require them to spend a good deal of time at the palace gates, waiting to receive his largesse or merely hoping to catch a glimpse of him. He spends vast sums of money on espionage, and deliberately causes disturbances, setting friend against friend, class against class, rich men against rich men. In this way he weakens all opposition, but he may forget that in the process he is weakening the state. "Also," says Aristotle, "it is in the interest of the tyrant to keep his people poor, so that they will be in no position to purchase arms and also because they will be too busy trying to make ends meet to think about revolution." To enslave them further he embarks on huge public works. Aristotle offers the examples of the pyramids of Egypt, the temple of Olympian Zeus, and the even vaster temple built at the orders of Polycrates of Samos. Alternatively the people can be kept poor by taxation or they can be forced to join the army, which has the added advantage of keeping them busy. The ultimate aim, says Aristotle, is to produce a subject people who (*a*) are mindless, (*b*) do not trust each other, and (*c*) are quite incompetent to do anything at all. The tyrant then finds himself ruling majestically over a nation of halfwits.

Scorn and irony are not weapons usually employed by Aristotle, but they appear in his description of the corrupt and debased subjects of an active tyranny. Mindless, powerless, and lacking in confidence, and thus totally deprived of the means of revolution, the people are effectively silenced. Aristotle adds that a tyrant, unlike a monarch, cannot afford the luxury of having friends. He must be very circumspect in his dealing with young women and youths; if he rapes them, there will be such a storm of indignation that he may find himself in grave danger. He should be circumspect not only in his sexual behavior but in his other behaviors as well. "I know of some tyrants," Aristotle writes, "who begin the day drinking and continue to drink for days on end, for the express purpose of permitting others to observe how supremely happy and fortunate they are. In such matters moderation is best, and at the very least a tyrant should avoid getting drunk in public."

According to Aristotle a tyrant is a caricature of a monarch, for while the monarch rules with magnificent self-assurance, at ease with all, filling his court with the best men of his kingdom, and never in any fear of them but using them to the best advantage, the tyrant is reduced to living fearfully, without friends, with no intelligent people to talk to, and more at ease with foreigners than with his own people. By definition he is a man who is terribly afraid.

Aristotle's own inclination was toward monarchical government, perhaps because he had served in the court of King Philip of Macedon as the tutor of the future Alexander the Great. Yet he was the first to write about democracy with a clear understanding that it involved a paradox: "to rule and to be ruled."

About the year 425 B.C. an anonymous pamphleteer, known to history as the Old Oligarch because no other name was more suitable, denounced democracy in terms that have a familiar ring today. "If you really desire good legislation," he wrote, "then you must have truly intelligent people making laws on behalf of all the others, and thus the better class will curb and chastise the lower orders. The better class will sit and discuss matters on behalf of the state, and they won't permit any crack-brained fellow to appear at the council or to speak at the assembly." He laments the fact that the poor in a democracy are allowed to have a voice in the government. "The truth is that the poor, the low-born, and the common people are receiving more consideration than persons of quality. Of course, this should not come as a surprise. Evidently this is the keystone of democracy." The Old Oligarch positively quivers with fear at these multitudes who decide their own fate without the benefit of advice from the rich. He thunders: "Among the people you will find the utmost ignorance, disorder and rascality—most of it traceable to poverty!"

The Old Oligarch rages like a man possessed with an overwhelming resentment against the poor. He is a rich man and desperately wants to preserve his wealth and privileges. He recounts how the Athenians built beautiful bathhouses and in the normal course of events only the beautiful people would be allowed in them, but nowadays all the common people flock to the bathhouses. Heavy taxes have been levied on the rich. "Unfair! Unfair!" he cries. "They are showing too much favoritism to the poor!" He takes some comfort from the fact that the poor remain uneducated in the finer arts of music and gymnastics, adding that in any case the cultivation of these arts is quite beyond their powers.

The Old Oligarch, prepared to defend oligarchy at all costs or to revive it by force if necessary, was far from being a spent force. He remained on the stage, impenitent and corrupt, determined to retain his special privileges even if it meant forming an alliance with the enemy. Treachery, as the Athenians learned only too frequently, was one of the occupational diseases of oligarchs.

But there was another disease, equally terrible, that could be found sometimes among all classes: an anarchic fury arising from the lust for power. Quite suddenly, and almost inexplicably, men began to lie, to deceive, to invent fantastic stratagems, and to make agreements they had no intention of carrying out. They invented a new language: if a man acted wildly, he was called a "real man"; a fanatical party member who committed crimes on behalf of his party was called a "loyal party follower." Criminality became a part, almost the major part, of politics. Corrupted by power, uninhibited by moral scruples, the leaders threw themselves into situations that could not possibly be resolved except by bloodshed. Thucydides relates that this phenomenon occurred for the first time in history in Corcyra, when a certain Peithias, the leader of the democrats, had five rich men arrested for cutting vine poles in the sanctuaries of Zeus and Alcinous. They were found guilty, each was fined a gold stater, and that might have been the end of the matter, but the oligarchs refused to pay, rushed to the senate house, stabbed Peithias to death, and killed sixty of his followers. The cutting of the vine poles led to a civil war fought with astonishing brutality and viciousness on both sides.

By murdering Peithias the five rich men had made the war inevitable. People were caught between the oligarchs and the democrats. Every murderous stratagem was employed. Fathers slew their sons; suppliants were carried bodily out of the temples where they had sought sanctuary and were killed; new forms of killing appeared; and it was as though blind rage had gripped everyone on the island. Finally the oligarchs were cornered in a large building, and soldiers of the popular party climbed on the roof and poured arrows down at the huddled masses of doomed men. Then the dead bodies were flung crosswise on wagons like lumber and carried out of the city.

Thucydides describes these events coldly, without pathos, remarking that these things, first observed in Corcyra, happened throughout the Peloponnesian War. At the heart of the mystery, according to Thucydides, lies the lust for power and advantage, but he is puzzled that it should take such intricate forms and be so destructive of morality. His severely logical mind attempts to grapple with the problem of anarchic murder as he grapples with the problem of the terrible plagues that from time to time devastated Greece, but he finds plagues and murders equally inexplicable. How could the cutting of the vine poles lead to so much murder? He does not know. He merely records that these things happened, and he observes that they are likely to happen again and again through history.

In 201 B.C., two hundred years after the death of Thucydides, there was born in the Greek city of Megapolis in Arcadia another historian who also took part in the wars he described. Polybius lacked the incisiveness of Thucydides. He had neither the brilliance nor the severely logical mind, nor did he write so well. But while Thucydides believed that history endlessly repeats itself, Polybius believed that it moves forward under the force of destiny toward great consummations and has a purpose independent of man's power to alter it. The task he gave himself was to write in Greek a history of the Roman conquest of the world.

He was widely traveled, knew everyone in the Roman government, and was on especially good terms with the younger Scipio. He was present in 146 B.C. when Carthage was utterly destroyed by Scipio's huge annihilating army. In the same year he saw the destruction of Corinth. He was therefore in an admirable position to write about the wars, for there was scarcely any battle described by him that he had not observed with his own eyes or learned about from survivors or the sons of survivors. The Greeks loved him because he interceded on their behalf with the Romans, and to this day in some Greek cities there survive monuments erected to honor

Polybius as a savior and protector. We see him wearing the short, kilted dress of a Roman; he was a Greek who became a Roman with all the ardor of a convert.

Polybius was well aware that nations die; he had seen so many of them dying. When he stood with Scipio before the ruins of Carthage, he knew that he was witnessing a great culminating disaster that would forever after be remembered. He watched Scipio closely and heard him saying, "It is all so beautiful, and yet I have a foreboding that the same fate is reserved for my country."

Carthage, in Polybius's view, had succumbed to the iron force of Roman discipline. But the Carthaginians themselves, by their avid delight in luxury, contributed to their own ruin; wealth and power corrupted them. Like Scipio, Polybius had little doubt that a similar fate might be reserved for the Romans. He wrote:

> That all existing things are subject to decay and change is a truth that scarcely needs proof; for the force of nature is sufficient to force this conviction on us. There being two agencies by which every kind of state is liable to decay, the one external and the other the growth of the state itself, we can lay down no fixed rule about the former, but the latter is a regular process. . . .
>
> When a state has weathered many great perils and subsequently attains to supremacy and uncontested sovereignty, it is evident that under the influence of long established prosperity life will become more extravagant and citizens more fierce in their rivalry concerning office and other objects than they ought to be. As these defects go on increasing, the beginning of the change for the worse will be due to love of office and the disgrace entailed by obscurity as well as extravagance and purse-proud display; and for this change the populace will be responsible when on the one hand they think they have a grievance against certain people who have shown themselves grasping, and when on the other hand they are puffed up by the flattery of others who aspire to office. For now, stirred to fury and swayed by passion in all their counsels, they will no longer consent to obey or even to be the equals of the ruling caste, but will demand the lion's share for themselves. When this happens, the state will change its name to the highest sounding of all, freedom and democracy, but will change its nature to the worst thing of all—mob rule.

Polybius speaks in the authentic tones of the aristocrat: contemptuous of the people, certain that in all governments there are men swayed by avarice and pride, who work against the best interests of all and eventually weaken the state. Like Aristotle, he sees the state continually changing its form, but always repeating the changing pattern. Monarchy is followed by tyranny, which gives place to aristocracy, which degenerates into oligarchy. This in turn gives place to democracy. Finally the grandchildren of the democrats, "who have become so accustomed to freedom that they no longer value it," grow violent, give themselves up to murder and rapine, and out of this chaotic reign of terror there once more rises a monarch, thus completing the cycle of political revolution.

In the eyes of Polybius a benevolent monarchy is clearly the most desirable political system. Thereafter there is only a continuous process of decay until democratic "license and lawlessness" bring about mob rule, the inevitable result of the excesses of oligarchy. The hourglass is turned upside down and the sand begins to fall again.

For Polybius the rather mechanical cycles described by the Greek philosophers are not quite sufficient; he adds another element— *fatum,* fate, destiny. The concept is Roman, tragic, vivid with a new excitement and new dangers. For the first time pity and fear appear on the stage like presiding goddesses. Polybius sees the Romans as the instruments of disembodied fate. As they reach out toward the mastery of the world, they are no longer in full command of themselves. Fate has them by the throat. Mastery of the world, but what then? What was the purpose of it all? There was no answer except that destiny, having reserved a singular fortune for the Romans in their time, may have reserved still greater fortune for them in a later time. Always there was the haunting fear that destiny might change her mind and suddenly, in the twinkling of an eye, the empire, which had been built up over so long a time and at so great an expense of treasure and human lives, might perish of its own triumphs, its own corruptions.

The Roman Triumph

Historians of the Roman Empire have long disputed the precise moment when it began to fall into a decline, forgetting that there were many declines and many resurrections. Like the Chinese Empire, the Roman Empire was so large, so pervasive, so deeply rooted along the seaboard of the Mediterranean and the continent of Europe that it seemed to possess the gift of endurance amounting to immortality; and it was so ponderous that it could weather with little effect cataclysms that would have destroyed small nations. The Roman Empire sometimes suffered a mortal blow at the heart: Rome was sacked, her treasures were carried away, and her people were massacred, but the empire went on living. It never completely died, and to this day many of the outward forms of the Roman imperial court survive in the spiritual empire of the Roman Church.

There are civilizations that do not completely die, that no amount of corruption has been able to dissolve. Both the Chinese and the Roman empires remained virtually invulnerable, dying many deaths but always reviving in time to attend their own funeral ceremonies.

They have defied history and time. Like huge ships that have been wrecked and then patched up and sent out to sea again, sunk and then dredged up, thrown off course, struck by lightning, and hurled into the paths of hurricanes, they continue to plow the seas and are recognizably the same ships that were seen centuries ago. The ancient architects who designed them gave them an essential stability that no amount of damage could alter. They were not designed for speed, but for longevity.

Nevertheless, historians are justified in seeking to discover the precise moment when the Roman Empire began to decline and fall, even though in an absolute sense no decline and fall took place. When Edward Gibbon roundly asserted that the emperor Septimius Severus may "justly be regarded as the principal author of the decline of the Roman Empire," he was saying something that needed to be said. He had observed a sudden faltering in the cardiogram, a spasm that boded ill for the patient. With the emergence of Septimius Severus the Roman Empire suffered one of its hardest and most dangerous blows.

A small, spidery, snub-nosed man with a delicately curled beard, Septimius Severus came to power during the confused period following the death of Marcus Aurelius. A professional soldier in command of the Army of the Danube, he advanced on Rome, captured the city, disarmed the Praetorian Guard, replacing it with his own Illyrian and Thracian guards, and thereafter ruled the empire as professional soldiers always rule—by edict, by murder, by martial law. From the day in A.D. 193 when he entered Rome in full armor to the other day eighteen years later when he lay dying in York with his sons around him, saying, "Do not quarrel among yourselves, heap money on your soldiers, and despise everyone else," he remained a military dictator. He did not solve problems; he obliterated them. He murdered sixty senators, and would have murdered more if he had not grown weary of murdering them. He fought countless rebellions; plundered Spain, North Africa, and the Near East; and died in Britain while attempting to add Scotland to his empire. He militarized the whole Roman imperial structure until it became one vast parade ground.

There is very little good to be said of Septimius Severus: he was cruel, vindictive, avaricious, totally ruthless. He amassed the largest fortune ever acquired by a Roman emperor, and he did this by confiscating the property of all those he proscribed or sentenced to death. He vastly increased the size of the army, and used it for private vengeance as well as for amassing triumphal honors. He assumed the titles Parthicus, Arabicus, and Adiabenicus in honor of his victories in Persia, Arabia, and Adiabene. He made war, says Aelius Spartianus, because he was possessed by a thirst for glory, not for reasons of necessity—*gloriae cupiditate non aliqua necessitate*. His victories served no purpose except to exalt the fame of the emperor.

Under Trajan, Hadrian, and Marcus Aurelius, the wars served the purposes of the Roman Empire; the frontiers were strengthened, the frontier kingdoms subdued or pacified. Septimius Severus had no rational plan for preserving the empire; he made war on the slightest provocation and sometimes for no reason at all. Merciless to his enemies, he was just as merciless to the Roman people. In a speech to the Senate, which he despised, he declared that the severity of Sulla, Marius, and Augustus had proved to be a safer policy than the clemency of Pompey and Julius Caesar, which brought about their downfall. Thereafter severity became his watchword.

Inevitably there was widespread cynicism among the population. Dio Cassius, an intimate of the emperor and the chronicler of his reign, describes what happened when news of still another war was brought to the crowd attending the chariot races:

> An enormous crowd had assembled to watch the last chariot races before the Saturnalia in the Circus Maximus. When the six-chariot races were over, there was a demand for silence and a sudden clapping of hands. Then came some shouting and prayers for the welfare of the country. Then the people began to cry for help to the goddess Roma, addressing her as "Queen" and "Immortal," and shouting: "How long are we to endure such things? How long are we to go on waging wars?" After shouting further things of this kind, they finally ended, as suddenly as they had begun, with the cry: "So much for that" and turned their attention to the races.

It is a peculiarly modern picture, and we should have no illusions about the same thing happening in modern times, when television and radio serve the same purpose as the ancient circuses. The circuses dulled men's minds with a continuous program of free entertainment and murderous brutality paid for by a grateful emperor who expected and received the blind obedience of his subjects. They went through the motions of invoking the goddess of Rome when they heard of a new war, complained a little, and then gave their undivided attention to the races. The circuses were the opium of the people.

Septimius Severus was an African, born in Leptis Magna in

Libya. He had no roots in Rome, no sympathy for Roman aspirations, and to the end of his life spoke Latin with a pronounced accent. The empire, which he had seized by force, existed to be looted, and he set up an administrative body with vast powers to safeguard and catalogue the treasures acquired by his agents, who were known as *procuratores privatarum rerum.* No other emperor had ever set up an administrative body to acquire loot for his personal use.

Originally Septimius Severus had no intention of following a military career. His family was rich; he was well provided for; and he had planned to become a lawyer after studying in Athens. He was intelligent and quick to grasp ideas, and Dio Cassius says "he was not a man to leave anything human or divine uninvestigated." He became a magistrate, then a senator, then an army officer, who distinguished himself by the suddenness and secrecy of his attacks on the enemy. The soldiers adored him, for he provided them with booty, raised their pay, and later, when he became emperor, permitted them to take their wives with them when they were campaigning. The army became his private weapon and the instrument that led him to supreme power. Thereafter the empire was ruled by martial law.

Under him the body politic withered and died. Through the eyes of Dio Cassius we can watch the familiar processes of corruption taking place. For the first time we begin to hear of large-scale murder by drugs. "During this period," wrote Dio Cassius, "there were many people not only in Rome but throughout the empire who died at the hands of criminals possessing deadly drugs smeared on tiny needles. These criminals could be hired to infect people with their poisons." Traditional morality broke down. The emperor married Julia Domna, the daughter of the high priest of Emesa in Syria, and under the protection of the empress the magical religions of the Near East flourished in Rome as never before. Roman hymns gave way to the incantations of Syrian priestesses; new religions proliferated; and the emperor protected the priests of the Syrian sun god against the priests of Jupiter. He had no interest in religion; his chief aim was to please his soldiers, who embraced the Syrian cults, and the women of his court, who were all votaries of the new temples erected in Rome in honor of the Syrian gods.

The orientalization of Rome was proceeding apace; the ancient moralities succumbed to oriental license. No one dared to protest. There was no Cicero to inveigh against the destruction of public order and the travesty of military rule. Corruption became a way of life. During the reign of Hadrian, Pliny had spoken of "the boundless majesty of the Roman peace"—*pacis Romanae immensa maiestas*. Among the endless wars of Septimius Severus this boundless majesty became a casualty.

The emperor begged his two sons not to quarrel, but they started squabbling the moment he was dead. Caracalla killed his younger brother Geta, and assumed the purple. He was foolish and witless—*stultus et demens*—but like his father he enjoyed killing for private profit and for the sake of the triumphal processions that inevitably took place after his foreign wars. He fought against the Alemanni, whose name first appears in history during his reign, and assumed the title of Alemannicus. He went on to acquire other titles: Germanicus, Parthicus, Arabicus. Someone suggested that he should also have called himself Geticus Maximus, for his greatest victory was the killing of his brother in cold blood.

Septimius Severus was a hard-bitten soldier; his son merely played at soldiering. Septimius Severus was the authentic conqueror, but Caracalla was the authentic profligate only too eager to waste his substance. Once, when his mother wondered whether there was any money left in the treasury, he put his hand on his sword and answered, "Never fear, mother, there will be money as long as we have this!" The treasury could always be replenished at the point of a sword. That, indeed, was what swords were for. But they could also be used to destroy tyrants, and after a reign of six years Caracalla was cut down by one of his own veterans. No one knew or cared why he was struck down. It may have been a private quarrel; it may have been a conspiracy; it may have been a general desire by the army to rid itself of an incompetent emperor.

The Arab historian Ibn Khaldun observed in the fourteenth century that in three or at most four generations a ruling family goes to seed. There appears to be a law of nature that the son of a conqueror will be a profligate and the grandson a weakling. Heliogabalus, the successor of Caracalla, was a monster of effeminacy. He was about thirteen when he came to the throne. The historian Herodian describes his triumphal entry into Rome amid a rabble of women, eunuchs, and priests. The boy was dressed in the silken robes worn by the priests of the sun god of Emesa; his cheeks were painted; his eyebrows were darkened; there were ropes of pearls round his neck; and he wore a jeweled tiara. He had a fondness for walking on carpets of roses, lilies, and hyacinths, and he fed his dogs on gooseliver, his horses on grapes. The Romans of the republic would have died of horror at the sight of that simpering youth parading in the costume of an emperor. Four years later his soldiers rose against him, discovered him cowering in a latrine, stabbed him to death, and dragged his body round the Circus Maximus, to the delirious delight of the mob.

When Alexianus, his cousin, also a Syrian, came to the throne, he assumed the name of Marcus Aurelius Severus Alexander. He was quiet, studious, intelligent, and eclectically religious, for in his private chapel he kept statues of Orpheus, Apollonius of Tyana, Abraham, and Jesus, and worshiped all of them in turn. He had some of the makings of a good emperor, studied Plato's *Republic,* surrounded himself with excellent advisers, and during his campaigns shared the food of his soldiers. After waging war against Parthia, he claimed the inevitable triumph, which was remarkable for the fact that his chariot was not drawn by four snow-white horses but by four elephants and also because the emperor, instead of riding in the chariot, chose to walk on foot in front of the captured elephants. There was some humility in this gesture, and he seemed to be walking surefootedly into history when, during a campaign in Germany, he was struck down at the age of twenty-nine by Maximin, a former member of his bodyguard who wanted to be emperor. During the following fifteen years, from A.D. 238 to 253, some thirty usurpers claimed the throne and all were murdered, for the most part by their own bodyguards.

"Corrumpere et corrumpi saeculum vocatur," wrote Tacitus in his *Germania.* "They call it the spirit of the age to corrupt and to be corrupted." He was writing about A.D. 100, when the Romans were seriously concerned with the inroads of the barbarian Germans. In the eyes of Tacitus the Germans had remained uncorrupted in their tribal organizations, while the Romans had given themselves up to corruption on a stupendous scale. Tacitus could not have guessed that Rome would see thirty usurpers in a period of fifteen years.

Among Roman historians it was the custom to say that corruption entered with the empire while the Roman Republic had remained virtually untainted. In fact the seeds of corruption were planted very early, at the end of the First Carthaginian War in 241 B.C. With victory came the frenzied desire for excitement, the hankering after luxuries, the decay of religion. The close bonds that once united the people and their rulers were broken by the war. Enormous power was exercised by a few wealthy families. Corruption settled on the city and gradually corroded the Roman way of life. As unheard-of luxuries poured into the city, the Romans began that long feud with themselves that left the city and its growing empire strangely unstable. When it was strongest militarily, it was weakest morally. It seemed to be enjoying one victory after another, but beneath the surface there can be detected a curious uncertainty, a failure of nerve. What did they want? The whole world? But they scarcely knew what to do with the conquered territories. In the age of Augustus Caesar, when at last most of the known world was being governed by the Romans and Caesar himself was being portrayed as a man of the utmost beneficence, to be compared with Plato's philosopher-king, Livy concluded that Rome had become a cesspool and all her previous history proved only that she was beyond redemption. He wrote in the introduction of his *History of Rome from the Foundation:*

> Contemporary history displays our nation suicidally eating up its own mighty resources. Let it be noted how the moral rot started, how standards were gradually sapped, then crumbled more and more ominously, and finally began to collapse into utter ruin. That is the stage we have now reached. Our defects are unendurable to us—and so are their cures. From unlimited self-indulgence has come a longing to pursue vicious extravagance to the point of personal and universal annihilation.

Livy was saying that his entire *History* was largely a recital of the causes that brought about Rome's decay and inevitable extinction. But we should be on our guard. The fashionable pessimism of the time demanded such statements. The realization that Rome was in grave danger from a simultaneous collapse at the center and along the wide-ranging frontiers haunted the Romans, and they spoke of these things quite openly, without self-consciousness, and also with familiarity. Livy's opening statement should not be taken too seriously. Rome survived its fashionable pessimism, its incessant corruption, its endless wars. Like a huge flat-bottomed ship, it could never capsize. Cruel, heartless, and arrogant, the Roman rulers dominated the stage, oppressing the Roman people almost as much as they oppressed the conquered tribes.

In theory the Roman Empire was ruled by the Senate and the Roman people—*Senatus populusque Romanus*. The Senate took comfort from its ancient traditions; the people obeyed; the emperor ruled. It was a method of government that satisfied no one except the emperor. The Senate was corrupt because it was permitted to be corrupt within the limits of the small residual powers entrusted to it. The people were corrupted with bread and circuses, and the emperor was corrupted by his arbitrary power, his courtiers, and his Praetorian Guard. Corruption became woven into the fabric of the empire.

Nevertheless, there were traditional limits to some forms of corruption. Extortionate proconsuls ruling the provinces of the empire might suddenly find themselves confronted with an imperial tribune possessing the power to examine their accounts and their conduct. In theory the tribune represented the Roman people; in fact he represented the emperor, who needed the assurance that the empire was not being endangered by too many corrupt governors. Extortion was permitted; large-scale extortion was practiced; gross extortion was sometimes punished. Pliny prosecuted Marius Priscus, proconsul of Africa, in A.D. 100. The trial took place in the Senate in the presence of the emperor Trajan and lasted three full days from dawn to dusk. Pliny was assisted by the historian Tacitus. The Senate was crowded; the emperor enjoyed himself, and from time to time sent word to Pliny to spare his voice and his breath, for he was shouting and engaging in great rhetorical flourishes. Unmoved by the emperor's pleas, Pliny continued to attack his adversary, and there was no stopping him. He was a senator, entitled to wear red shoes and the broad, purple stripe down the front of his robe, and he was as ambitious for fame as his friend Tacitus. It was a memorable occasion, for Trajan was one of the few tolerable emperors, and he was in good company with Pliny and Tacitus.

The crimes of the proconsuls usually included much more than extortion. They stole on a vast scale, murdered, raped, terrorized, had everyone at their mercy. No house, no temple, no statue was safe from them. Gaius Verres, proconsul of Sicily, regarded the whole island as his private territory. Cicero accused him of almost every crime under the sun, and there was enough substance in his charges to bring about a verdict of guilty in the Senate. Verres is reported to have said, "In the first year I shall make my fortune, in the second I shall reward my friends in Rome, in the third year I shall raise enough money to pay off the judges." He was sent into exile and was later murdered at the orders of Mark Antony, who wanted his great art collection. At Antony's orders, Cicero also was killed in the general proscriptions. It was an act of vengeance, for Cicero had very justly accused Antony of unspeakable crimes. Cicero's head and hand were nailed to the rostrum in Rome, and Antony's wife stuck a needle through the tongue that had spoken so loud and so eloquently.

Cicero saw himself as a bastion against the general corruption that in his lifetime always threatened to engulf Rome. Conspiracies abounded: the rich played the game of power without thought of the consequences. One of the most dangerous conspiracies was brought about by Lucius Catilina, of a well-known patrician family. Pale, with glaring eyes, an abrupt manner, and a strange habit of walking slowly and then breaking into a run before walking slowly again, he commanded a secret society of young desperadoes who drank from bowls filled with human blood and wine as they swore to follow him. Catilina was more than half-mad. His plan was to capture Rome by a sudden assault, by massacre, by setting fire to half the city. He was completely ruthless; so were his young followers. According to Sallust, they practiced every imaginable vice, used well-born women as their couriers, and were perfectly prepared to drown Rome in blood so long as they were given high positions, wealth, and large estates.

Cicero got wind of the conspiracy in November of 63 B.C., shortly after Catilina slipped out of the city to join forces with some Gallic allies. In a speech delivered at this time Cicero spoke of "that intolerable plague which will break forth wherever it can find room, and even now is threatening the Roman people. Soon it will descend on the suburbs and inspire madness in the army, fear in the Senate, conspiracy in the Forum, bring soldiers to the Campus Martius and devastation to the whole country."

The threat was a real one, for Catilina was capable of anything. Nothing came of the conspiracy, because Cicero was able to round up the chief conspirators in Rome and Catilina was defeated in a hard-fought battle by a Roman army not long afterward. For a brief moment the Romans had seen the flames of the furnace.

If Rome had been put to the flames and her inhabitants massacred, many of the people in the conquered territories would have regarded it as a just punishment. The Roman armies conducted the most frightful massacres by design, by habit, by nonchalance. It was not enough to burn a city, to kill all the males, to destroy the crops, to drive off the farm animals. Julius Caesar proudly claimed that his unprovoked attack on the Helvetii cost them more than a quarter of a million lives, many of them noncombatants. He reveled in his cruelty. In 55 B.C. a large German tribe, with its baggage wagons, women, and children, was attempting to cross the Rhine. Caesar heard of it and sent his cavalry against them. Some of the Germans fled; others were hunted down; others hurled themselves into the fast-flowing river and were drowned. The tribe was wiped out. Caesar's dispatches describing these events reached Rome and were crowned with laurel wreaths in honor of his victory.

Cato the Younger thought the massacre an indelible stain on the honor of the republic and said publicly that divine retribution must surely be on its way. He suggested that to atone for such an infamous act of treachery the least the Romans could do was to hand Caesar over to the Germans. It was a brave speech, and a very dangerous one, for thereafter Caesar vowed vengeance and hounded Cato at every opportunity. Nine years later, in 46 B.C., Caesar advanced on Numidia, imposed his own undivided rule, and formed a new province, Africa Nova. Cato, defending Utica, the capital of the province, realized that the republic was doomed and that Caesar would take all power in his hands and rule with unimaginable severity. The mild-mannered Cato, who wanted to save lives, confronted the terrible Caesar, who thought the sacrifice of a quarter of a million lives merely added to his glory. Knowing the fate in store for him, Cato stabbed himself to death after a night spent quietly reading Plato. He was, says Plutarch, "the only free and only undefeated man." In fact, he was a doomed man, defeated by an enemy who was still far away, and he was free only to kill himself.

Caesar's victory over the Romans and the Roman Empire was complete. The republic perished, and Caesar became the first emperor, although he never used the title. In the autumn of 46 B.C. he gave himself four triumphs in celebration of his victories over Gaul, Egypt, Pontus, and Africa.

The Roman triumph was a long-established institution designed to reward victorious generals. Its origins are obscure, perhaps dating from the time when Etruscan kings ruled over Rome. The triumph was more than a victory parade, for it involved, even though only momentarily, the apotheosis of the general in the temple of Jupiter Capitolinus. There, standing alone, wearing the *toga palmata,* his cheeks painted bright red, the general solemnly laid the laurels of victory on the lap of the god regarded as the sovereign ruler of the Roman people, and at that moment he entered into communion with the god.

In the procession, chained prisoners marched in front of the *triumphator*'s chariot, which was usually drawn by four white horses. Behind him marched his private household, his guards, secretaries, armor bearers and personal aides; then came the victorious army, and rounding up the procession came the Roman senators. Vanquished kings stumbled in front of the conqueror, and sometimes huge painted canvases were displayed showing the conqueror in his triumphs on the battlefield. The booty was piled high on carts, and there would be signs announcing the total number of captured gold and silver vessels. Sometimes under the empire a clown rode beside the *triumphator* on his chariot, whispering in his ear, "Remember thou art mortal!" More often the *triumphator* was accompanied by his own children. But from the very beginning it appears that clowns and buffoons were permitted to gambol beside the chariot. The procession, which often took a whole morning to wind its way from the Porta Triumphalis around the Palatine and so up to the Capitoline hill, was at once a fiesta, a military parade, a celebration of a general's glory, and a preparation for the ritual sacrifice of prisoners, who might or might not be taken to the Mamertine prison carved out of the Capitoline cliffs and there strangled.

Whenever there was an important victory, the Romans staged a triumphal procession. The highest honor that could be paid to a Roman was to grant him a triumph.

These great, glittering processional triumphs served as a barometer of the degree of corruption. The more triumphs, the greater the corruption. Under the mad emperors triumphs proliferated, and there came a time when the emperors would demand the honor of a triumph even when they could claim no military victories. Nero gave himself a triumph for winning innumerable prizes at the Olympic Games. Aurelian led tigers, giraffes, elk, and elephants in his triumphal procession. Inevitably, the triumphs, once singularly powerful evocations of military power, became *divertissements*. The triumph itself became corrupted.

The Romans were well aware of the corruption of their empire and wrote about it soberly, without much subtlety, and rather hopelessly, as though it were something to be deplored even though it was inevitable. The practiced moralizers of the republic had warned against luxury as the single most dangerous consequence of conquest. But luxury came to Rome like a galleon with all its sails flying, openly, without the least attempt at disguise. Rich nobles flaunted their solid silver coaches and gold-embossed horse-trappings. They took to wearing silks, and Ammianus Marcellinus, in a passage beloved by Gibbon, who translated it, described how they liked to parade in their silks in such a way that the outer garment floated in the wind, revealing the undergarments patterned with figures of wild beasts. Conspicuous consumption became the delight of the Roman nobles, who wasted their substance without thought of the future. Effete nobles complained when flies settled on the silken folds of their gilded umbrellas, and they talked about "mounting an invasion like Alexander's" when they were setting out in their painted ships to spend a leisurely weekend in their country villas. Trimalchio in Petronius's *Satyricon* quotes self-consciously a poem in honor of the general corruption of the times:

> *The walls of Rome crumble in the abyss of pleasure.*
> *To satiate your bellies caged peacocks are served,*
> *Arrayed in gold plumage like Babylonian tapestries.*
> *Numidian guinea-fowl, capons, all perish for thee,*
> *And even the wandering stork, the welcome traveler,*
> *Model of filial piety, slender of leg,*
> *Randy-voiced exile from winter, spring's harbinger,*
> *Finds his last nest in your gluttonous stewpot.*
> *What is the priceless pearl of India to you,*
> *That your wife, all decked in the sea's treasures,*
> *Must hurl herself onto a stranger's bed?*
> *And what of green emeralds, those glassy baubles,*
> *Or the fire of the ruby: unless their chastity*
> *Shines from their depths? And what of our brides*
> *Who saunter into our public places nearly naked,*
> *In garments of woven wind sumptuously adorned?*

Silks and jewels, peacocks, guinea fowl, all the foods and treasures of the earth poured into Rome to satisfy the insatiable desire of the Romans for luxury. In economic terms it did little harm; psychologically it was destructive. Self-indulgence became a way of life. Like Trimalchio, the Syrian freedman who acquired a fortune and spent the rest of his life devising the most amusing means of squandering it, the Roman noblemen saw no reason to spend their wealth responsibly. What is most saddening is the growing sense of irresponsibility in the empire. Tiberius, the coldest of emperors, despised the Romans and felt no responsibility toward them. Bored with life, bored with luxury, bored with his catamites, he looked down at the impassive sea from the high crags of Capri where he made his home and announced plaintively, "After me, let fire destroy the earth!"

The Roman Empire declined but did not fall. It was eaten away by the corruptions inherent in all empires, and chiefly by luxury and irresponsibility. While the empire was being built there was a sense of direction and responsibility, a belief that all the Mediterranean lands should come under a single rule and obey a common law, but once the goal had been attained, the Romans wearied of their responsibilities and wasted their energies in squandering their inheritance. They thought the empire had been given to them for their pleasure. Augustine believed it had been given to them as a sacred charge and they therefore possessed a duty toward all the people of the empire, a duty they failed to fulfill because it was too burdensome and demanded a devotion they were incapable of giving. Long before the empire had reached its greatest extent, the Romans were bored by it.

The Mandate
of Heaven

While Greek and Roman historians and philosophers concerned themselves with the nature of corruption and the many forms it assumed, they rarely came to any final conclusions or decided what should be done about it. They observed that the tyrannical state was the most corrupt of all, the most likely to come to an abrupt and bloody end, and afterward came democracy, which was also unstable and fraught with dangers. History, in their view, moved in cycles. Timocracy was followed by oligarchy, which in turn was inevitably followed by tyranny. Sometimes the pattern changed with slight modifications in the nature of the emerging forms of government, but these slight modifications only reinforced the general pattern. The historians of Greece and Rome dwelt at length on the character of the tyrant, for they were well acquainted with tyranny. In the normal course of events the tyrant succumbed to the inevitable punishment reserved for men with overweening pride and destroyed himself, or invited destruction, by his own excesses.

In China, where the cyclical theory of history did not prevail, there arose an entirely different attitude toward the corruption of the state and the corruption of tyrannical rulers. When the emperor became tyrannical, ruling in a purely arbitrary fashion and out of touch with the people, it was believed that the Mandate of Heaven had been removed from him, and at such times it was the right and duty of the people to overthrow him and even to destroy him. Exactly how the Mandate of Heaven was received by the emperor was a matter of some discussion, but there was very little discussion about the removal of the Mandate, for there came a time when everyone could see with his own eyes that the emperor had been abandoned by the heavenly powers. Heaven (*t'ien*) was the supreme deity, a mysterious presence who reigned over the universe, the repository of the moral law and the energizer of all things. The Chinese represented it by a pure circle of uncorruptible jade.

The Mandate of Heaven was never a patent of divine right, irrevocable and eternal; it was granted to the emperor in trust and he retained it only so long as he ruled virtuously, in conformity with the wisdom of the ancient sage-kings. When he failed, he lost all the prerogatives of kingship. He became no-man, an outlaw, and it was accounted a virtuous act to kill him. With his death a new dynasty arose. Armed with this invisible Mandate, the new dynasty endured until in its turn it lost the protective blessing of Heaven.

A Chinese emperor's powers differed markedly from those of his European counterpart. He was regarded as both human and divine; he possessed absolute power, and at the same time it was understood that he ruled with the consent of the governed. He was called the Son of Heaven, and these words precisely conveyed his special relationship with Heaven. At great ceremonies which took place at the Altar of Heaven and at the Altar of Earth, he became the vehicle through which Heaven poured out its blessings on the entire community of the Chinese people. He therefore stood at the point of intersection between Heaven and the people. Implicit in the argument was a theory of divine energy which poured continuously from Heaven as long as the emperor remained a worthy vehicle of the heavenly beneficence. If the empire was ravaged by wars, droughts, plagues, or floods, this was a sure sign of Heaven's displeasure, and it was incumbent on the emperor to assume full responsibility for these catastrophes. On such occasions the emperor assumed the role of scapegoat. There survives a remarkable number of decrees in which the emperor castigates himself for his shortcomings and failures, announcing that he had brought on various disasters by his lack of virtue, and apologizing humbly to the people for his errors. Sometimes he was able to weather the storm; his apologies were accepted; Heaven relented; a good harvest excused all faults; and the Son of Heaven resumed his rule in the full knowledge that Heaven supported him, encouraged him, and delighted in him.

The concept of the Son of Heaven ruling under a mandate that could be revoked at Heaven's pleasure goes back to the earliest classical writings, and there is some evidence that it was acceptable doctrine in the Shang dynasty (ca. 1766–ca. 1122 B.C.). Embedded in the *Li Chi,* the book of rituals compiled in the Han dynasty (206 B.C.–A.D. 220), there are many passages that were written centuries earlier. Here the unknown author describes the age of Great Disorder, which is contrasted with the age of Grand Unity, on which Heaven's blessings flow:

> When the soil is worn out, the grass and trees on it do not grow well. When water is often troubled, the fish and tortoises in it do not become large. When the energy of nature is decayed, its production of things does not proceed freely. In an age of disorder, ceremonies are forgotten and neglected, and music becomes licentious.
>
> In such a period musical notes become melancholy but without gravity, or joyous without repose. There is remissness in ceremonies, and the violation of them is easy. One falls into such a state of dissoluteness that he forgets the virtue properly belonging to his nature. In such matters he is capable of treachery and villainy; in small matters he becomes greedy and covetous. There is a diminution in him of the enduring, genial forces of nature, and an extinction of the virtue of satisfaction and harmony.

In the eyes of the Chinese, nature herself was implicated in the age of Great Disorder that comes at the end of all dynasties. Heaven removes the virtue from the earth as well as from men. Storms of unparalleled intensity arise, the crops are ravaged by blight, ominous portents appear in the sky, while simultaneously men come out in open rebellion, the strong overpower the weak, the clever deceive the ignorant, the sick, the aged, and the young go untended, "and there is no place for the orphans and the solitary." Deception becomes the rule, and the people abandon themselves to sexual license. The unknown author lists the familiar symptoms of decay, adding that if only men will observe the rituals and perform the appropriate music, the age of Great Disorder will come to an end, for "music induces an end to anger and ritual will put an end to strife."

In China extraordinary importance was attached to music and

ritual. It was not in the least that music and ritual appeased the heavenly powers; they were themselves heavenly. They purged the world of its despairs and corruptions, for music was the harmony of Heaven and earth, and all things were set in order by ritual. Not only the emperor but all men had it in their power to restore virtue to the empire; and if the emperor bore the chief responsibility, lesser mortals also bore their share. Sometimes the will of Heaven was indistinguishable from the popular will, man walking in concert with Heaven, no longer the servant or the slave. Deep down in the Chinese consciousness was the belief, rarely expressed directly but nevertheless generally accepted, that man had long ago formed an alliance with the heavenly powers. In the chapter called "The Great Declaration" which appears in the *Shu Ching,* the Confucian book of history, there is a remarkable fragment that may derive from an ancient ritual song of a long-forgotten dynasty: "The people are the stars. Among the stars are some that love the wind, some the rain; the course of the sun and moon brings winter and summer; the wandering of the moon among the stars brings wind and rain."

This poetic fragment hints at mysteries that are never resolved, but we learn more about these mysteries later in "The Great Declaration" when we read, "Heaven sees as our people see; Heaven hears as our people hear." Heaven therefore was sometimes very close to earth and to the human heart.

It has been necessary to make this excursus to emphasize that the Chinese attitude toward man differed profoundly from the Judeo-Christian attitude toward man. In ancient China no offerings were burned on the altar to appease a vengeful god; no commandments were inscribed on holy tablets; there was no sense of guilt. When an age of Great Disorder came, it was because, for some unforeseeable and totally inexplicable reason, the economy of earth and man was out of phase with the economy of Heaven. It was as though quite suddenly the two linked machines were operating at different speeds and were out of kilter. The overthrow of the emperor and the beginning of a new dynasty brought the machines into harmony again.

Nevertheless, the Chinese were painfully aware of the symptoms of decay, which they associated with a lazy and incompetent emperor, an excess of luxury at court, licentiousness, overweening ambition, heavy taxes, poverty among the people, and natural disasters. An age of Great Disorder was immediately recognizable, and no one had the slightest difficulty in prophesying the outcome. The pattern was established; similar things were recorded in the ancient annals;

the end was always the same. History, as they say, repeats itself. The strong founding father of the dynasty came to power against formidable odds, set the country on a new path, and filled his people with a new vigor. His sons and grandsons, born to luxury and intrigue, dissipated their vigor in licentiousness and useless wars but succeeded in keeping the country prosperous. Only a few courtiers surrounded them. In later generations the number of courtiers increased, a new ruling class was established, the capital blossomed with palaces, the emperor amused himself with gigantic building projects, and there were continual wars on the frontiers, which had to be paid for out of higher taxes. The peasants starved, the irrigation dikes filled up, the exactions of local officials increased, floods and famines ravaged the land, bandits concealed themselves in the mountains and the marshes, and the frontier forts were neglected or abandoned, allowing the enemy to approach the capital, while the provincial armies renounced the oath of loyalty to the throne, made peace with the invaders, or turned to banditry. This is the familiar pattern common to the West and the East, but there was one essential difference. In the East there was no cycle of timocracy, oligarchy, democracy, tyranny. The throne was restored, or, rather, according to an accepted tradition, the throne remained inviolable, for only the incumbent was changed. With the coming of the new emperor the floods abated, the parched land brought forth crops, the enemy retired behind the frontier, the wound was healed.

In the Chinese imagination the natural disasters were not so much the consequences of misrule and incompetence at the center as manifestations of disharmony. Nature, emperor, and man were in disarray; the same poison flowed through all of them. Heaven, aided by bandit chieftains, sucked out the poisons and restored them to health.

The reign of Wang Mang (A.D. 9–23), the first and last emperor of the Hsin dynasty, was one of the shortest in the history of China, and one of the most tragic. The course of his reign, which briefly interrupted the Han dynasty, seems to reflect in miniature the rise and fall of an entire dynasty lasting hundreds of years. He had no right whatever to the throne. A nephew of the empress dowager Yüan, he ingratiated himself in court circles by his flattery, his successful intrigues, his affectation of profound scholarship, and his feigned modesty; he refused to occupy important offices when they were offered him, saying he was unworthy of such high honors. All the time he was quietly seeking the highest office of all. He was determined to become the emperor. He poisoned the boy-emperor, placed a two-year-old infant on the throne, and became regent. He was a master of propaganda. Soon, from all over the empire there came news of mysterious and wonderful portents announcing the coming of a new and brilliant emperor equal to the ancient sage-kings, and perhaps even greater. Altogether there were twelve portents including a three-colored horse, a tablet of dappled jade, a stone tortoise, a silk charter embossed with copper seals, and "the stone of a dark dragon." Wang Mang professed to be awed by these messages from Heaven and quite unable to accept the Mandate of Heaven, while convincing himself that he had a mandate to depose the two-year-old emperor and to assume the title Acting Emperor. Finally it was announced that a gold casket found in the temple of the founder of the Han dynasty contained a document prophesying that Wang Mang would ascend the throne. The implication was that the prophecy had been made by the founder of the dynasty some two hundred years earlier.

Wang Mang was adept at falsifying documents. In the walls of Confucius's house were found ancient Confucian texts in what was called "old character writing." These were edited and published, incorporating newly written passages highly favorable to Wang Mang. Deception became a habit, then a master. In time Wang Mang came to believe in the frauds so assiduously practiced upon the public.

Under Wang Mang a new kind of state emerged: everything was owned by the new emperor. All the gold of the empire found its way into the imperial treasury. He established monopolies of salt, wine, and iron tools. He devalued the currency, levied heavy taxes on hunters, fishermen, silk-workers, artisans, and professional men, and he acquired enormous revenues through his "equalization offices," which were designed in theory to buy cheap goods in times of plenty for resale at the original price in times of scarcity, thus preventing excessive price fluctuations and safeguarding the poor. In fact the "equalization offices" bought cheaply and sold dearly to the consternation of the peasants who thought they were being protected. In an imperial edict announced the year he founded his new dynasty, Wang Mang decreed that "all the land belongs to the nation, all slaves whether male or female are attached to the land, and neither land nor slaves may be sold." By "the nation" he meant "the emperor." With this decree he became the sole possessor of all the land and all the slaves.

The historian Pan Ku, who wrote at length about Wang Mang in his great work *The History of the Former Han Dynasty,* resembles Plutarch writing about Alcibiades. He is appalled and fascinated; sometimes he appears to nod his head in disbelief. Yet he has collected and assembled the documents and presents them to us fairly. The new emperor threw the whole nation into turmoil. New laws poured out in an endless stream. The result was that the court grew rich beyond men's dreams of riches and everyone else became poor. Farmers and merchants were reduced to beggary and landless peasants took to banditry. While the peasants starved, the horses and dogs of the courtiers were fed on beans and grain. Thus, wrote Pan Ku, "both the rich and poor committed crimes."

In the flood of edicts, decrees, laws, and pronouncements issued by Wang Mang, we detect the hand of a scholar continually amusing himself as he quotes Confucius for his own purposes. He was fascinated by complex court rituals and spent a disproportionate amount of time developing new and ever more complex rituals. He was a short man, sturdily built, with a wide mouth, a receding chin, large brilliant eyes, and a deep, rasping voice. Because he was short he wore thick soles, and his clothes were padded with felt to make him appear stouter. During audiences he held a mica fan to his face, so that he could see and not be seen. He had a vile temper, ordered executions on the slightest provocation, consulted his astrologers as often as he consulted the Confucian classics, and waged war against the tribesmen on the frontier so ineptly that he lost all of his possessions in Chinese Turkestan. To raise money for his wars he levied a tax amounting to four fifths of the private wealth remaining in the country.

It soon became apparent that the Mandate of Heaven was being withdrawn from him. Earthquakes, bad harvests, uprisings, an eclipse of the sun, desertions from his army, and the inroads of the Hsiung Nu tribesmen on the frontier, all suggested that something had gone profoundly wrong. Wang Mang thought everything was going well. When one of his commissioners reported that the common people had been impoverished by the laws and by thieving officials and were threatening to rise up against him, he fell into a rage and dismissed the commissioner from his court. Another official who pronounced that the people deserved to be executed and that this was an appropriate time for executing them was promptly promoted. Punitive expeditions were sent out. Pan Ku says that China lost half its population during Wang Mang's short reign. Presumably they died of starvation and of mass executions, and many must have fled across the borders.

In A.D. 18 the Red Eyebrows, one of the numerous bands of rebellious peasants, became strong enough to defy the emperor's forces. They were so named because they painted their eyebrows red to make them more fearsome and also because red was the color of the Han dynasty. Wang Mang's Hsin dynasty had adopted yellow as its official color. Five years later the Red Eyebrows were winning victories over the imperial army and Wang Mang was addressing Heaven: "Since thou hast given me thy Mandate, why dost thou not annihilate these robber bands? If I, thy servant Mang, have in any way offended thee, then strike me dead with a thunderbolt!" Then he struck his heart with his palm, wept, and prostrated himself on the Altar of Heaven.

In October, A.D. 23, the Red Eyebrows fought their way into Ch'ang-an, the capital, and went in search of the emperor. One of the court women revealed his hiding place in a tower rising from the middle of a lake. The attackers took their time, and it was not until the late afternoon that they climbed up the tower steps and found the emperor and some members of his court. They cut him down with their swords, hacked off his head, and carved what remained into small pieces. It is related that in the excitement of cutting up the emperor many people were killed.

Thus died Emperor Wang Mang, who usurped the throne of China and who, as Pan Ku says, "lacked benevolence and had a talent for flattery and doing evil things." According to the historian, he committed almost every crime known to man. He was murderous, deceitful, tyrannical, and vicious; he scorned the will of Heaven and violently oppressed the people, exhausted all the possibilities of crime and spread his poison among all the people, even among the barbarians who lived beyond the frontiers. "He injured every living person and his crimes reached even to rotting bones."

He was the arch-corruptor who defiled everything he touched, a cancer that spread through the whole of China. The small, ugly, owl-eyed man who wore bright yellow robes to emphasize his descent from the legendary Yellow Emperor possessed no gift for ruling, only a supreme gift for corruption. Pan Ku tells us at length about those strange calculated hesitations by which Wang Mang reached out for the throne, and how once he occupied the throne a great calm settled on him and he launched immediately into a vast program of expropriation and self-glorification, always justifying himself by an appeal to the Confucian classics. His cold-bloodedness, his breathtaking hypocrisy, and his total indifference to the effect on the people of the decrees he issued in such profusion marked him as a tyrant of a new and unfamiliar kind. No one quite like him had ever ruled before. The wonder was that Heaven permitted him to reign for so long. In the end, cornered in his tower, wearing his robes of office with all the appropriate seals, pendants, aprons, and ceremonial weapons, he called for the divining board, placed himself in the proper position for receiving Heaven's decrees as announced by the board, and said: "Heaven begat the virtue that is in me. The Han troops—what can they do to me?" They were his last recorded words. Characteristically, he had borrowed even these words from the Confucian classics.

When a man falls in China from a great height, they say of him that he is a dragon who has flown too high and whose breath has been cut off. Wang Mang is so described by Pan Ku, who adds that it was not really necessary to compare him with a dragon, for he was more like a stain, or a croak. His death was appropriate to his life.

The traditional Chinese attitude toward the tyrant differed markedly from the attitude fostered in the West, where the divine right of kings, even arbitrary and tyrannical kings, became accepted doctrine. The theory of the Mandate of Heaven involved an invitation to rebellion when the emperor proved to be incompetent or fiercely exacting, when the emperor was himself in rebellion against Heaven. But in the West, too, there arose voices proclaiming that the tyrant was in rebellion against God. John of Salisbury, the learned secretary of Thomas à Becket, wrote in his *Polycraticus,* or *Statesman's Book:*

> The Prince is in a way the image of the Divinity; the tyrant is the image of violence which is in revolt against God, and of perversity, the daughter of Hell. As the image of Divinity, the Prince ought to be loved, venerated and obeyed; as the image of diabolical perversity the tyrant ought in most cases to be put to death.

John of Salisbury was not simply weaving these ideas from the smoke of a scholar's lamp. He was the greatest scholar of his age, but he was also a man who lived in the thick of affairs, and he was standing close to Becket in Canterbury Cathedral when the armed men advanced and hacked the archbishop to death.

The Chinese were well aware of the dangers of corruption in government, and very early in their history they did something about it. If the emperor was corrupt, then inevitably Heaven pointed an accusing finger at him and divested him of his powers, and just as inevitably the rebel forces overthrew him. But corruption among government officials could be almost as dangerous as the corruption of an emperor. At all costs it was necessary to find incorruptible men to rule the country.

The method employed was an examination system of considerable subtlety, demanding of the candidate a rigorous training in the Confucian classics, the power to express himself keenly, and a sense of style that could be detected in the quality of his handwriting. It also demanded the capacity for sustained effort, for the examinations were held over a period of many days with the candidates locked in cells under close observation. A man who survived these examinations and achieved high marks would, it was believed, combine learning, administrative ability, a humble manner, and a sense of responsibility to his country. An embryo examination system appears to have been in existence in the time of Confucius. We learn that the Han emperor Wen Ti, who in his lifetime was regarded almost as a saint, presided over the examinations and set the questions. This was in 165 B.C. The practice continued throughout the Han dynasty and survived up to the time of the Revolution of 1911. In the West no comparable examination system for entry into the civil service existed until well into the eighteenth century.

The Chinese examination system went through many changes, but the essential elements remained. The examination was a test of character as well as of learning; in theory, it was open to any promising scholar, and the poorest had the same chance as the richest. The examiners never knew the real names and origins of the candidates, and elaborate efforts were made to see that the examinations were conducted impartially, without fear or favor. In practice, the very poor were nearly always excluded; unlike the middle classes and the rich, they could not afford tutors to help their sons prepare for the examinations. Although there were always abuses, a scholarly youth possessed of a fine-drawn intelligence could expect to be seriously considered for the coveted degree of *chin-shih* if he also possessed the stamina to survive the examinations. We hear of students who were so determined to acquire the degree that they took the examination time after time until they had long passed middle age. We hear, too, of some students who were so distressed at the prospect of failing that they hanged themselves in their cells.

Although abuses occurred, the system was designed to reduce them to the utmost extent. Many of the lists of successful candidates have survived and have been closely examined. Thus we learn that during the Sung dynasty, when the system was at its height, more than half of the successful candidates came from families in which no previous member had entered the civil service for three generations. Once he had entered the civil service, a scholar could sometimes rise to high position very quickly, depending on his abilities. The emperor and the Board of Rites, which presided over the examinations, were on the lookout for men of pronounced ability, those rare individuals who possessed the Confucian virtues to a remarkable degree. Anyone who ranked at the top of the list in the final examination could expect to become eventually the governor of a province, a minister, or a close adviser to the emperor.

In this way the examination system succeeded in recruiting the most talented men in the country for government service. There were quotas limiting the number of students from each county and province, so that all the geographical areas of China could be represented. Once given a high position, the scholar would usually find himself appointed to a region far from his birthplace. It was felt that he would serve least well in his own province, where he might be tempted to indulge in favoritism. Moved about from place to place, he never acquired deep roots; and this too was part of the deliberate design. Censors were appointed to enquire into the conduct of all officials, and any imperfections were reported to the emperor. Traditionally the censors had the right of direct access to the emperor, they could report on any matter that came to their attention, even those matters that displeased the emperor, and they were empowered to remove high officials for acts of corruption. But a censor who wrote a memorial against an imperial favorite was in mortal danger. The tradition of the honest and incorruptible censor who risked his life for justice survived in Chinese governments down to the twentieth century.

The Chinese saw clearly that what was needed was a stable officialdom made up of the best talents of the country, men who had been through a rigorous course of intellectual training and were capable of acting justly and forthrightly. There were checks and balances. The scholars were the real rulers of the country, and except for the emperor no one in the imperial family or in his court was permitted to exercise political power. In this way it was hoped to make corruption virtually impossible. So stable was the government that from A.D. 960, when Chao K'uang-yin usurped the throne and founded the Sung dynasty, until 1911, the Chinese continued to be ruled by scholars. A dynasty would fall to a foreign invader, but the scholars had made themselves indispensable and continued to rule. Under the Yüan and Manchu dynasties the tradition of scholarly officialdom remained unimpaired.

What was most remarkable about the Chinese system of government was the implicit condemnation of corruption at all levels, from petty corruption to the fierce corruption that comes about when a tyrant occupies the seat of power. After the Sung dynasty no usurper arose to impose arbitrary rule on China; no subject ever succeeded in usurping the imperial prerogative. Members of the imperial family connived and intrigued for the throne, poisoned or murdered one another, or plotted with the help of the army to remove a reigning emperor. It scarcely mattered. The real power was securely in the hands of the scholar-officials.

The Chinese had discovered very early in their long history a truth that has escaped the West until recent times. They learned that competitive examination encouraged a continual flow of talent into the government. The more rigorous the examination, the more likely they were to obtain the best minds. The proving ground was a small cell, ten feet high and five feet square, where the candidate was confined throughout the examination, which usually lasted for three days. There was a chair, a table, paper, brush, an ink slab; nothing else. The candidate was fed through a hole in the door. All candidates, having surrendered their own clothes, wore identical, simple gowns. All were equal. For those who succeeded in the examinations there opened unparalleled opportunities for advancement, and for those who failed there was always the hope that at the next examination they would succeed. In those wooden cells, each marked by a single Chinese character, in total silence and monastic seclusion, the young scholars endured a trial of intellectual strength that was heroic in its proportions. An elaborate system of watch towers and patrols prevented any surreptitious communication. If a candidate died during the examination he could not be removed through the door, which was sealed; instead, a hole was cut through the wall large enough to permit the guards to drag his body out. Inflexible rigor was the badge the scholars wore proudly to the end of their days.

To this day in many of the provincial capitals of China the ruins of the examination halls can still be seen. In Peking, where there were 8,500 cells, the halls survived until 1913, when they were razed to clear the area for the new Houses of Parliament. They were never built, and the area became a rubbish heap.

In this way there perished a remarkable experiment in government which had existed for considerably more than two thousand years. Throughout this period the scholars contributed to the stability of government and provided a bastion against corruption and dictatorship.

In the early third century B.C., the poet Ch'u Yüan, who was a member of the royal house, found himself asking pointed questions about accepted traditions and mythologies in a poem called *The Heavenly Questions.* He professed to be puzzled about the body of Nu Wa, who had a snake's tail instead of legs, and about why the archer Yi was boiled and eaten by his own son. He was also puzzled by the Mandate of Heaven: "When the high heavenly god bestows his mandate, how does it become known? When dominion over the whole world has been granted to him, how can it be taken away and bestowed on someone else?"

Like so many metaphysical questions, these were virtually unanswerable. The theory of the Mandate of Heaven originated in a dim and distant past, and was as old as China. To a quite extraordinary extent it answered the needs of the Chinese people, who delighted in the knowledge that the emperor was the Son of Heaven but wanted the assurance that he could be removed if he became tyrannical. The theory of the Mandate of Heaven supplied the necessary authority for rebellion when the emperor became intolerable.

For the emperor, too, the theory offered the rewards of a heavenly ancestry and the standing of Heaven's earthly representative, the vehicle through whom Heaven's commands were communicated to the people. On the day of the winter solstice an extraordinary ceremony took place at the Altar of Heaven. Here, shortly before dawn, the emperor, wearing ceremonial clothes, with a black silk cap and blue silk boots, offered sacrifices, listened to the music summoning Heaven into his presence, and performed nine prostrations before the Tablet of Heaven. This tablet, two feet long and six inches wide, bore the characters *Huang T'ien Shang Ti* (Sovereign Heaven, Lord on High), written in gold letters on a vermilion ground. On lower levels of the altar dancers performed a ritual dance invoking Heaven's blessings, and the ministers of the court occupied positions ordained by tradition. In the predawn darkness, barely dispelled by high lanterns and the glowing incense of censers, the kneeling emperor called upon Heaven to protect and bless the people, and it was believed that he received divine assurances. This ceremony before the Altar of Heaven was the supreme ritual act performed by the emperor. Here, as he knelt in the exact center of an immense marble circle, he became the mediator between earth and Heaven.

Originally the ceremony took place on T'ai Shan, the holy mountain, with the emperor in complete seclusion, alone with the Alone. No one else was permitted to see the ceremony, which took place on a small altar. By the time of the Han dynasty the traditional ceremony usually took place on an altar in the suburbs to the south of the capital city, reached in a short drive from the imperial palace. The emperor made the journey in silence, while the people remained in their houses forbidden to look upon his august presence. Thereafter the ceremony became more complex, with so many vases full of offerings on the marble altar that there was scarcely room to move about. But the essential design of the ceremony remained unaltered: while the emperor lay prostrate before the tablet, Heaven opened to pour down blessings and to speak the comforting words heard only by the emperor, signifying that all was well.

During Sung times we know that the Altar of Heaven was a circular stone platform only twenty-one yards in diameter. When the Emperor Ch'ien Lung replaced the existing altar in Peking in 1755, he made the altar much larger and more imposing than it had ever been before. Of the purest, gleaming white marble, the new Altar of Heaven was seventy yards in diameter on the topmost level and resembled nothing so much as a brilliant dancing floor for the gods. With its steps and gateways it had a breathtaking simplicity and majesty, which it retains to this day.

On December 23, 1914, Yüan Shih-k'ai, president of the Republic of China, performed the ceremony for the last time. Since he was calling down blessings for the republic, not for the empire, he rejected the yellow, dragon-embroidered robe of the emperor for a red robe bearing the insignia of the republic. The offerings to the sun, the moon, the pole star, the constellations, the clouds, the winds, the rains, and the thunder were abandoned as being touched with superstition and unworthy of the republic. There were no horn lanterns, no dragon-entwined standards, no dancers with peacock feathers. Instead of taking place at night, the ceremony took place in broad daylight for the benefit of photographers and movie cameras. The prayers were shortened; only a few offerings were made; the president prostrated himself perfunctorily and seemed glad and relieved when it was over. Afraid of being assassinated on that vast open space, he kept looking anxiously in the direction of his armed guards and the regiment of policemen who had taken up their stations around the altar. In the past, the emperor had ridden back to

Peking in a palanquin. Yüan Shih-k'ai rode back to the Forbidden City in an armored car with guns bristling from the windows.

The ceremony that took place on that brisk winter morning was the final corruption of an act of worship that had been in existence for forty centuries. The ancient concept of Heaven had become meaningless; no one any longer knew how to worship it, or cared to worship it. The actors went through their paces in an atmosphere of vulgarity and fear, for the ceremony had lost its significance and they were merely pretending to play their roles. They acted without conviction, looking questioningly at one another, not knowing what to do with their hands or their faces, unable to comprehend a mystery that had outlived its time. The corrupted version of the worship of Heaven was a travesty. What had been a great and mysterious occasion became a public nuisance.

So it is with all ceremonies; they die, as men die; they suffer from the attrition of old age; and the ceremony is corrupt from the moment when the chief participant no longer believes in it. As long as there is faith, the ceremony endures.

One day Confucius was asked by Tzu-kung, one of his favorite disciples, what was most needed in good government. Confucius answered, "Enough food, enough weapons, and the people's faith in their ruler." Then Tzu-kung asked, "If it cannot be helped, and one of them must be given up, which should be the first to go?" Confucius replied, "Weapons." Then Tzu-kung asked, "If you have to choose between the remaining two, which of them should go first?" Confucius replied, "Food, for we must all die one day. But if the people no longer have faith in their ruler, they cannot stand."

This faith, this understanding of good government, provided China with one of its most enduring possessions. There, stated very briefly, was the whole art of government beyond the reach of corruptions.

While in theory and to some extent in practice China was ruled according to the Confucian canon, other influences were also at work. The Legalists, a group of scholars who drew their teaching ultimately from Confucius but bent it to more stringent purposes, attempted to describe a much more rigorous use of kingly power. They gave all power to the king and his ministers, and only the power of obedience to the people. They accused Confucius of undermining respect for constituted authority by asking too many questions. Lord Shang, one of the Legalists, believed that since the people intensely disliked war, the government possessed a perfect method for making them go to war. The method was to make their lives so miserable that they would welcome war as a release from their sufferings. Han Fei Tzu, another Legalist, was not quite so harsh and obdurate as Lord Shang but could on occasion show himself as the defender of the totalitarian state. Because he was especially concerned with the survival of the state, he drew up a list of forty-seven errors in government, which he called "Portents of Ruin." I quote some of them here because they suggest a careful analysis of the political situation on the eve of the Han dynasty and because they provide evidence that the Chinese were well aware that corruption has many faces.

If the ruler is fond of palatial decorations, raised kiosks, and embanked pools, is immersed in the pleasures of possessing chariots, clothes, and antiques, and thus tires everyone out and exhausts the public treasury, then ruin is possible.

If positions and offices can be sought through influential personages, and if rank and bounty can be obtained by means of bribes, then ruin is possible.

If the ruler is easygoing and accomplishes nothing, if he is tenderhearted and lacking in decision, and if he wavers in his judgments and has no settled opinion, then ruin is possible.

If the ruler is greedy, insatiable, attracted to profit, fond of gain, then ruin is possible.

If the ruler is contemptuous of his chief lieutenants, impolite to his uncles and brothers, overworks the people, and slaughters the innocent, then ruin is possible.

If the ruler is fond of twisting laws according to his wishes, mixes private and public affairs, alters laws and prohibitions at random, and frequently issues orders and commands, then ruin is possible.

If the ruler is narrow-minded, quick-tempered, imprudent, emotional, and if when he is provoked he becomes blind with rage, then ruin is possible.

If the ruler's words are eloquent but illegal, his mind sagacious but tactless, and if he is versatile but performs his duties not in accordance with the laws and regulations, then ruin is possible.

Han Fei Tzu's catalogue of portents was essentially an examination of the disturbing elements in a ruler's character. He was painting a portrait of the ruler who has lost the Mandate of Heaven. And, strangely, we have the feeling that we are reading, not about the rulers of the period of the Warring States (403–222 B.C.), but of the dictators and presidents of the present time.

Ibn Khaldun and
Machiavelli

Historically the first philosopher to enquire deeply into the nature of corruption in society was Ibn Khaldun (1332–1406), whose wandering life was largely spent in the northern littoral of Africa at a time when kingdoms and sultanates were crumbling. He had ample opportunity to watch the processes of corruption in operation. The great forward wave of Islam, which had reached across the Middle East, into India and Central Asia, and across North Africa and Spain, was beginning to turn; and he was one of those who watched the turning of the tide and attempted to explain to himself why it happened.

Since he wrote a fairly candid autobiography we know a good deal about him, his likes and dislikes, his beliefs, his habits, his odd quirks, his many griefs. What emerges is the figure of a man robed in white, heavy-set, dark-featured, with black penetrating eyes, one who knew most of the joys and miseries men are heir to. He lost his whole family in a shipwreck; he talked with Tamerlane, the most powerful man in the world, as though they were on an equal footing; and he connived and plotted for political power through the greater part of his early life until he renounced all hope of power and settled down to become a jurist in Cairo. In him were combined two natures: that of a courtier who had exceedingly sharp knowledge of the ways in which kings are corrupted and that of a jurist who upheld the law against all corrupters.

Ibn Khaldun—or, to give him his full name, Abu Zayd ibn Muhammad ibn Muhammad ibn Khaldun—was born in Tunis of a family that descended from a Yemenite clan that took part in the march across North Africa and settled in Spain. Among his ancestors was a certain Umar ibn Khaldun, scientist and philosopher, who died in Seville in 1058. Around the middle of the thirteenth century, when the Christians were advancing into southern Spain, the family fled to Tunis, where one of Ibn Khaldun's grandfathers became a gatekeeper in the palace and another grandfather was a highly placed fiscal official. His father, who was a scholar, died of the Black Plague in 1348, when the boy was sixteen. It was a time of terrible upheavals, for the plague coincided with attacks on Tunis by the army of Fez. The rulers of Tunis were conquered by the rulers of Fez, returned to power, were conquered again, and finally conquered their conquerors. They were Muslims fighting Muslims, and they gave very little quarter to one another. Ibn Khaldun was one of the survivors. To the end of his life, he thought of himself as a survivor, one of those who feel that in some mysterious way they are protected by divine providence.

Ibn Khaldun was a turncoat. He could have stayed in Tunis but chose instead to enter the court of the ruler of Fez, where he became a member of the ruler's circle of scholars, wrote poetry and a book on elementary mathematics, and busied himself with the rather fashionable occupation of making abridgments of scholarly works. He was something of a dilettante, wasting his life away, hoping one day to receive a high position at court. When the sultan, Abu Inan, invited him to accept the post of recorder of petitions—a comparatively humble post, far less important than the one he expected—he indignantly rejected it. Abu Inan kept a close watch on his disobedient courtier, learned that he was in communication with Tunis, and threw him into prison. Ibn Khaldun remained in prison for nearly two years and was released only when Abu Inan died. Ibn Khaldun was then twenty-six years old.

Thus far, his life had been an empty one, with little to show for it, and in the following years it would become even more empty and meaningless. Abu Inan's death brought about a power vacuum; a succession of ministers intrigued on behalf of a succession of sultans, who were no more than figureheads. Ibn Khaldun played a leading role in these intrigues, and the only amusing passages in his great *Prolegomena* recount the miseries of intriguers who have failed, why they failed, and what they might have done in order to succeed. He evidently enjoyed the game and was well aware of its dangers.

Finally in 1359, when he was thirty-seven years old, he achieved his ambition and became secretary of state of Sultan Abu Salim. It was an important, a towering position; he enjoyed his power, his new-found wealth, the deference paid him wherever he went, and he noted modestly that he performed his tasks to the admiration of everyone. When he engaged in intrigues, they were no longer the petty intrigues of his youth; he was corresponding with kings; he was gradually extending his influence throughout North Africa and Spain. When Sultan Muhammad V of Granada was toppled from power and took refuge in Fez, Ibn Khaldun saw the advantages of returning him to power and actively assisted him in regaining his throne, thus ensuring that the sultan would be eternally grateful to him. For two years Ibn Khaldun enjoyed his power at Fez, but after a palace revolution Sultan Abu Salim was forced to run for his life. Characteristically, Ibn Khaldun found himself on the winning side, but no longer powerful. He had been very close to the sultan, and there was some doubt about his loyalty to the new masters of Fez. He was offered minor positions, rejected them indignantly, and at the first opportunity left Fez for Granada, where Sultan Muhammad V received him warmly.

These were dangerous times for sultans. Sultan Abu Salim was caught and butchered to death; Sultan Muhammad V sat uneasily on his throne, being little more than a tributary to Pedro I, the Cruel, King of Castille and León, whose army included a regiment of Moorish knights supplied by the sultan of Granada according to the terms of the treaty between them. Thus, if the sultan was attacked, he would find himself confronting his own best soldiers. But he was not without weapons. He ruled with guile and intelligence, ably assisted by his vizier, Ibn al-Khatib, and he was fairly successful in flattering Pedro I into acting kindly toward him. Ibn Khaldun possessed the gift of flattery to the highest degree and was accordingly sent to the court of Pedro the Cruel with costly gifts. Pedro was enchanted with him, offered him a high position, spoke of returning to him the ancient family estates in southern Spain, and begged him to remain in Seville. Of course it would be necessary for him to change his faith. Ibn Khaldun appears to have rejected Pedro's offers, not because he found anything wrong with them, but because it was impossible for him to become the most powerful figure in the land. When it was time to return to Granada, Pedro gave him a splendid mule with trappings of gold lace.

There followed eight or nine years of precarious living. In Granada, though he retained the affections of the sultan, he was soon on bad terms with the vizier, who recognized that Ibn Khaldun would eventually become a rival. Ibn Khaldun returned to Africa, joining one sultan after another, always intriguing, always attempting to seize power, and looking forward to the day when a sultan would invite him to be vizier and meet him with processions and perfumes, while the people came out into the streets to welcome him and touch his hand. But although from time to time he accepted high positions, he was never able to hold office for long, not because of any defect in his character but because there were continual palace revolutions and because the positions he wanted were also wanted by others. When Ibn al-Khatib was exiled from Granada and living in Fez, Ibn Khaldun went to Spain, but nothing came of his attempt to restore his fortunes in Granada. It was a time of religious fanaticism. Ibn al-Khatib was one of the greatest scholars of his time, and one of his essays fell into the hands of his enemies. He was accused of atheism, thrown into prison, condemned to death, and strangled in his cell. There remained one further punishment, for his body was burned and the ashes were scattered to the winds.

Thoroughly frightened, weary of politics, Ibn Khaldun began to seek a place of retirement. Like Ibn al-Khatib he was a poet—he felt he wrote poetry best when he was occupying great positions—and he had developed an intense interest in mysticism. He was forty-five, and he had spent a quarter of a century in a tumultuous world of petty kingdoms that were constantly quarreling and constantly falling. He took service under Sultan Abu Hamu, who ruled from his capital at Tlemcen. It was a minor post; his pride was affronted. Besides, the sultan distrusted him. To keep him away from the court the sultan sent him on a mission to seek the loyalty of the tribes in the hinterland southwest of Tlemcen. Instead Ibn Khaldun traveled east, having secretly arranged to place himself under the protection of an old friend, Muhammad ibn Arif, the chief of the tribe known as the Banu Arif, who gave him a small house in Qal'at Ibn Salamah, a castle and village in the province of Oran, deep in the interior. Here he began to write in comfort and silence his history of the world, completing the lengthy *Prolegomena,* which runs to more than 1,400 pages in the English translation, in only five months.

The *Prolegomena* was intended as the theoretical foundation for a vast history of the Western Arabs, and perhaps, for he was not yet sure what form his history would take, it would include the Eastern Arabs as well. Only part of the *Prolegomena* is concerned directly with history. Ibn Khaldun had an encyclopedic mind, and it pleased him to theorize about the nature of poetry, prophecy, necromancy, the various kinds of Arabic script, and a hundred other matters. But again and again, like a man obsessed, he returns to the subject of the state, the changes it goes through, the sources of its inevitable corruption. Ibn Khaldun dismisses altogether the "great man" conception of history, perhaps because he had already seen too many "great men." His theme is the state as a living organism, which is born, suffers, and dies, worked on by social forces that shape its course, and itself working on the social forces. He was the first to establish that social transformations follow natural laws.

He lived at the end of an epoch when Arabic civilization had run its course and was in full decay. How had it happened? What strange impulse had led to this scattering of forces? Why, amid so much wealth and splendor, had a great culture gone to seed? The overriding question was whether the process was irreversible. Could it be delayed? What could a man do to change it? For him these were urgent and deeply personal problems, and he wanted answers. He knew the world of power, had briefly enjoyed it, but had never quite understood it. He also knew the world of the Banu Arif, the tribesmen who lived in the shadow of the Atlas Mountains, still vigorous and untouched by the diseases of society; and there gradually unfolded before him "the secret which has eluded everyone else," the knowledge that at the heart of the mystery was the tribal vigor which he called *asabiyya.*

As Ibn Khaldun uses the word, it has no exact equivalent in English. It means the group solidarity arising out of the love men feel for their own. The word derives from *asaba,* "to surround, to fortify," used of families that are close-knit in time of suffering and danger. Ibn Khaldun gives it an active meaning, so that it signifies a vital force, almost tangible. Contained within *asabiyya* is a kind of primitive energy that is not necessarily beneficial, for it can be terribly destructive. When the Arabs immediately after the death of Muhammad swept out of Arabia to conquer half the known world, slicing through the well-guarded frontiers of the Byzantine and Persian empires as though they were butter, it was this tribal vigor that gave them the strength and the daring to accomplish the impossible. Sometimes, when he writes about these tribesmen, Ibn Khaldun cannot conceal his detestation. They are the destroyers of civilizations, the enemies of the arts, "of all people the least fit to rule." They put ancient cities to the flames and think nothing of it. They ride roughshod over the carefully tended estates of great landowners and stable their horses in palaces. Barbarians though they are, they are admirable in their grace and beauty. It is precisely this tribal vigor that is needed in civilizations, but, alas, it withers away once the tribesmen have settled down to become city dwellers.

Asabiyya is the key word in Ibn Khaldun's philosophy. He accepts the fact that it cannot be measured, but he insists that it is clearly recognizable even if it cannot be submitted to precise analysis. Like the word *love* in Christian doctrine its meanings tend to dissolve into fragments, but the concept is not very far from the words in the gospel: "Greater love hath no man than this, that a man lay down his life for his friends." Just as this text has been used by Christians to exalt war, so Ibn Khaldun uses *asabiyya* to exalt the primitive fury of the Arabs when they came out of Arabia even though he had reservations about their destructiveness, for he was himself a city dweller who enjoyed peace, luxury, and books above all things. The Arabs despised peace and luxury and held only one book, the Koran, in honor.

But soon enough, and much sooner than the Arabs expected, this *asabiyya* began to wither away. They conquered great cities and found themselves seduced into luxury. The primitive energy was sapped. At first the ruling dynasty attempted to rule modestly in keeping with its feeling of solidarity with the people. Taxes were collected, the military establishment was properly maintained, property was safeguarded, the ruler moved humbly among his people. But this lasted for only a little while. Some defect in the human character, or perhaps some defect in the characters of rulers, prevented them from enjoying their humble role. Coteries and cliques arose in the court, and the ruler found himself increasingly surrounded by court officials who stood between him and his people, and in addition the members of his own family surrounded him in the hope of receiving the perquisites they felt to be their due. An aristocracy was formed. Gatekeepers were appointed. The palace guard kept everyone at a distance. The process of corruption was beginning, for, once the ruler had removed himself from the people, the original *asabiyya* was destroyed, and only by a miracle could it have been restored.

Ibn Khaldun observes the processes of corruption with jaded eyes. He knows them only too well. He knows the precise moment when the first gatekeeper is appointed, and then the second, and then the third. He knows how quickly the protective ring around the ruler tightens until it threatens the ruler's very life. He observes, too, that there is a period of apparent harmony when the ruler enjoys the fruits of his authority and is tolerated by the people. This is the period when he grants himself immense estates, builds monuments in his own honor, gives costly presents to foreign ambassadors, lays the foundation stones for new palaces and new cities, and is continually inspecting his troops and studying the books of the tax collectors. This is the period of munificence and imperial grandeur. It is also, Ibn Khaldun observes, the last stage during which the ruler is in complete authority. Although it appears to be high noon, it is close to sunset.

There follows a period that Ibn Khaldun characterizes as one of "contentment and peacefulness." He hints at a faintly perceptible diminution of the ruler's powers as he looks back to the time of his forefathers and extols the ancient virtues and traditions. Indeed, he is so much at peace with himself and so attached to traditions that he seems to belong to the past, to be inseparable from the past. This withdrawal into an imaginary past is the first sign that corruption is setting in.

In what Ibn Khaldun calls the fifth stage, corruption is seen advancing like an army with banners. The palace is rotting with luxury, the ruler surrenders himself to mindless pleasures, bestows expensive gifts on his favorites, offers them powers and positions beyond their abilities, listens only to them, and almost succumbs to them. Traditions are flouted. The traditional friends and clients of the ruler are brutally attacked and destroyed, because the new favorites have no understanding of the role played by traditional alliances; and this abrupt reversal, this rejection of the past, is the signal for all the horrors that come later as the ruler becomes more and more isolated from the people, from the army, from the bureaucracy, and ultimately from the favorites, who plot against him and destroy him. Money intended for the army is thrown away in private pleasures and benefactions. Because he refuses access to his person to those who are most trustworthy, the ruler becomes the plaything of the favorites, and it never occurs to him that there is growing resentment among the people. He goes down to his doom like a mindless cripple.

Ibn Khaldun watches this play of forces like a man observing a chess game. Unfortunately it is always the same chess game. At the end the king is left alone on the board with only a few pawns guarding him. Checkmate. Night falls. The palace is destroyed.

The fascination lies in watching the game at close quarters, for Ibn Khaldun knows intimately the subtle maneuvers of corruption. He is speaking of Berber princedoms, but the same lesson applies to dynastic empires, which rise and fall in the same way. The process is quite irreversible. In what may be the most tragic words written by a historian, he writes:

> Several rulers, men of great prudence in government, seeing the accidents which have led to the decay of their empires, have sought to cure the state and restore it to normal health. They think that this decay is the result of incapacity or negligence in their predecessors. They are wrong. These accidents are inherent in empires and cannot be cured.

Although the ultimate corruption of a society is an irreversible process brought about by the inevitable corruption of the ruler, Ibn Khaldun notes that there is sometimes a temporary reprieve, and even an appearance of glowing good health. There occurs a *restoratio,* an attempt to revive the lost authority and the lost *asabiyya:*

> Sometimes, at the end of a dynasty, it suddenly shows such strength that we think its decay is halted; it lights up brilliantly just before it is extinguished, but this is merely the last flicker of a candle that is going out, leaping up in a sudden blaze and giving the impression that it is just starting to burn when in fact it is at its last gasp.

Ibn Khaldun attached very little importance to this last flare-up of a dying empire. He observes that it happens, but gives no examples. In fact, it happens very often, and it appears to be part of the ceremony of the decline and fall of every great civilization. Aware of death, aware that the process is about to fail, the organism asserts itself with all its accumulative strength to reach heights never reached in the past; for a brief while there is a feeling of well-being, almost of euphoria; every talent is brought to bear at the right place and the right time; works of great genius and courage are evolved; and then quite suddenly, having exhausted its strength, the civilization falls into a kind of stupor and disintegrates.

Such things have happened altogether too often to permit the suspicion that they are accidental. The Chinese Empire appeared to disintegrate during the last months of the reign of Ming Huang, in 756, but it was never so brilliant as on the eve of the emperor's downfall. Florence appeared to be at the height of her prosperity and artistic power in 1490. In that year an inscription was written above the frescoes of Domenico Ghirlandaio in the Church of Santa Maria Novella, proclaiming that Florence was "glorious in her riches, her victories, her arts and her monuments, and in full enjoyment of her prosperity, health, and peace." Francesco Guicciardini in the opening pages of his great *History of Italy* announces that "a sovereign peace and tranquillity reigned on every side." Two years later, following the death of Lorenzo de' Medici, Florence began to decline. In 1945 Britain stood at the height of her power and glory, proud of her long, exhausting, and steadfast struggle against German tyranny. The small island off the coast of Europe had proved to be the rock of freedom for the Western democracies. With raw courage and willpower she held off the invaders until her bombing planes were ready to exact a terrible revenge. Never in her history had she acted with greater dignity than in the five years of war. Two years after the war ended Britain lost India, her empire was in decay, and she retained only a vestige of her former power.

Many other examples of this last, splendid outpouring of energy could be cited. It is almost a general rule that nations do not decline gradually. Instead they fall abruptly from their greatest heights.

Something very similar occurs when we examine the changing phases in the development of an artistic movement from the powerful, clear-cut beginnings to the luxurious flowering and the autumnal decay, followed by a sudden renaissance and a final decline. The same phases can be observed in nearly all the arts. What is true of ancient Chinese bronzes is equally true of Buddhist sculptures from their earliest beginnings in Gandhara to the last brilliant, decadent images of the Pala-Sena dynasties, and of Greek sculpture from the archaic beginnings to the Hellenistic ending. The last brief renaissance appears as a desperate fight for survival, a supreme gathering of forces, a spiritual and artistic explosion before the long night descends.

When Ibn Khaldun said, "These accidents are inherent in nature and cannot be cured," he was saying that the stages of decline are invariable, immutable, and infallible. They can be predicted with fair accuracy, given the nature of the country, the ruler, and his court. Is there then no hope? No, he answers, there is no hope at all. Once a nation has been corrupted there is no turning back. The acids have eaten into the nation's face and its former beauty can never be restored.

And yet, and yet, as Ibn Khaldun points out, there are exceptions to all rules, because God can at will pour his energy into the dying and restore them to life. It is all in God's hands. He alone has the power to heal nations and to stanch their wounds. Sometimes it occurs to Ibn Khaldun that the examples he has chosen from the Arab states on the western shores of the Mediterranean are not entirely representative. Great civilizations in the East have proved to be more enduring, riding triumphantly through storms that would ravage lesser states. Egypt, Persia, Syria, and Iraq bend to their conquerors but are not destroyed. Their roots are deep and fecund. Even though the trunk and branches have been blasted away, the tree grows again on the same spot. Thus, in a sense, Ibn Khaldun admits that his theory of the corruption of the state applies chiefly to small states and not to great empires.

Nevertheless, his diagnosis is a valuable one, for he laid bare for the first time the concept of *asabiyya,* the vital cohesive force which joins people together in defense of their liberties, and he examined with remarkable subtlety how this cohesive force breaks down in the face of the temptations suffered by a ruler. What he says about the Arab states on the shores of the western Mediterranean can be applied to modern governments; his description of the ultimate isolation of the ruler and his indifference to everything except his wealth and the favors he showers on his courtiers applies equally to the last stages of the Nixon administration. In the eyes of Ibn Khaldun corruption is a complex process following clearly defined stages that can be charted almost mathematically. The process is strangely inhuman, for it rides roughshod over the individual courage of men. Once the disease has set in, no man or group of men can prevent it unless, in the words of the Koran, "God brings forth a new creation."

After writing his great work in the shadow of the desert stronghold of Qal'at Ibn Salamah, Ibn Khaldun retired to Cairo, where he spent the last twenty-five years of his life as a teacher, a judge, and a courtier under the Mameluke sovereigns. Cairo was then, as it is now, the center of Arab intelligence, and he felt more at home there than he had ever felt in provincial Fez. He journeyed to Mecca, to Jerusalem, to Damascus. Tamerlane had established his camp outside the walls of Damascus and was preparing to sack the city. Ibn Khaldun was one of those who favored surrender; he was lowered over the walls and taken to the invader's camp. Tamerlane, who knew of his fame, engaged him in long discussions concerning the countries of the West, hoping to pry out their weaknesses. Ibn Khaldun was too experienced a courtier to fall into the trap and did his best to paint the West in powerful colors. Tamerlane suggested that Ibn Khaldun might usefully write a guidebook in such a way that anyone reading the book would have the feeling of traveling through the West. This, too, was a trap. Ibn Khaldun wrote the book within a few days, but what he wrote remains unknown, for the manuscript is lost. He appears to have convinced Tamerlane that nothing was to be gained by attacking Egypt. After spending thirty-five days in the camp he was allowed to return to Cairo.

He lived on for five more years, serving as a judge, adding some marginal notes to his historical work, and finishing the last chapters of his autobiography. He died in Cairo on March 16, 1406, at the age of seventy-three. He was one of the world's greatest historians and the father of modern political science.

Some sixty-three years after the death of Ibn Khaldun, another eminent political scientist was born. Niccolò Machiavelli was born in Florence on May 3, 1469, the son of a respectable burgher in straitened circumstances. Quick-witted, with bright eyes, thin, pursed lips, a pointed nose, and a long, narrow face, he devoted his life to the study of political power in all its forms, seeking always to discover the thrust of it, and finding its most exemplary form in the person of the tyrant who was never afraid of using power for his own purposes. The word *Machiavellian* has come to suggest all that is most treacherous, cruel, and hateful in the conduct of a tyrant; this use of the word is entirely justified.

Machiavelli became an intimate friend of Cesare Borgia and studied the prince at close quarters when he was attempting the conquest of the Romagna, learning unforgettable lessons in the art of treachery. He relates in *The Prince* how Cesare Borgia deliberately sought out a certain Remirro d'Orco, known for his cruelty, gave him supreme authority and license to murder as many people as he pleased, and then, when it became clear that the people were outraged by this man's cruelty, Cesare Borgia had him cut in half and thrown down on the public square at Cesena with a blood-stained knife beside him, thus claiming the credit due to a man who avenged cruelty. This was an object lesson in the behavior of tyrants.

And there were many more. At Sinigaglia, in the winter of 1502, Cesare Borgia invited his enemies to meet him under a sacred truce and then strangled them. Shortly afterward, in the small hours of the night, he summoned Machiavelli to tell him about the successful ruse "with the most serene air in the world." Cesare Borgia was enjoying one of the happiest moments of his life. He gave exact details of what had happened, showered effusive compliments on Machiavelli, and spoke of his love for Florence. Since he had no love for Florence, this should have been enough to awaken suspicion. Machiavelli enjoyed ruses and took it all in good part. In *The Prince* Machiavelli, writing about Cesare Borgia, who is the hero of the book, says: "Reviewing all his actions, I find nothing to blame. On the contrary I feel bound to venerate him as an example to be followed by all those who rise to power with the aid of fortune and men's arms."

Machiavelli wrote at great length on the subject of corruption, but he spoke from the enemy's camp. Corrupt himself, admiring the corrupt, he saw no sign of corruption in the bloodthirsty princes who, according to the Florentine historian Francesco Guicciardini, were corrupt to the core and in danger of bringing all Italy down with them. In Machiavelli's eyes the princes possessed *virtu,* by which he meant an exquisite and all-encompassing skill and power of domination. Opposed to the prince were the people, riddled by factions, acting capriciously, the mere dupes of demagogues, capable of the wildest excesses in the name of the liberty they never understood. Machiavelli proclaimed himself on the side of the tyrant and the dictator, "who alone know how to rule."

But Machiavelli was deeply troubled by corruption. Livy's *History of Rome* had taught him the virtues of the Roman Republic, and in his *Discourses on the First Decade of Titus Livius,* he continually seeks correspondences between the history of the Italian states and the history of that ancient republic in which men lived virtuously and were rewarded with domination over most of the known world. It appears that *virtu* is largely military prowess and feats of arms in alliance with *fortuna,* another concept that was dear to him; and corruption (*corruzióne*) is simply the absence of *virtu* and *fortuna.* The words *virtu, fortuna, corruzióne,* and *necessità* dance across the pages in a stately pavane that gradually grows terribly confused as the dancers fall out of step and collide with one another, for each word changes meaning and even becomes its opposite. Machiavelli, in the service of tyranny, is the practiced obfuscator. He speaks of "honorable frauds," "generous cruelties," "glorious crimes." Having in the famous seventh chapter of *The Prince* absolved Cesare Borgia of all his crimes, he goes on in the eighth chapter to tell the story of Oliverotto da Fermo, who asked his uncle and guardian if he could enter the city "to show his splendor," and, permission granted, at once set out with a hundred knights under his command to exterminate his uncle and his uncle's party and take over the city. "Experience has proved in our time that the princes who have achieved great deeds," says Machiavelli mischievously, "are those who have held good faith of little account, and have known how to bewilder men's brains by cunning, and in the end have succeeded better than those whose actions have been ruled by honor."

But, of course, there are exceptions to these rules of conduct. The princes who succeed by ruses also fall by ruses. One day Oliverotto da Fermo rode to Sinigaglia believing that he was about to be received in friendship by Cesare Borgia but instead was strangled. He had ruled over Fermo for only a year.

As Machiavelli enlarges on the great princes of his time, applauding their tyrannies, we become aware that *virtu* sometimes means *corruzióne*. The princes are the proud ones who dare all on a single throw of the dice and care nothing for the consequences. In his biography of Castruccio Castracani, that violent red-headed youth who made himself for a while the master of northern Italy by the simple process of indiscriminate slaughter, Machiavelli remembers or invents some words of Castruccio, which tell us all we need to know about the origins of tyranny: "Men ought to try all things and be terrified at nothing, for it is clear that God Almighty is a lover of courage, because he has made valiant men the ministers of his judgments and corrected the poor-spirited by them."

As we read the works of Machiavelli, we find ourselves gradually drawn into the corrupt world of the princes. Machiavelli knows them well, studies them minutely, and offers them his benediction. They have come to earth as ministers of God's judgment, like avenging angels. As for the poor-spirited, they are merely the playthings of the prince, who is urged to commit his cruelties all at once for maximum effect and to grant benefits to the people little by little, thus demonstrating his extended beneficence.

The Prince is a useful work, but not for the purpose the author intended. It shows us how the prince's mind works: his self-absorption, his delight in conspiracies, his need to live dangerously, his sense of awesome destiny, and his continual fear of losing his power. Even today *The Prince* provides a useful warning, for the essential elements of tyranny have not changed over the centuries.

As for corruption as he understands it, Machiavelli is inclined to make sweeping generalizations. France, Italy, and Spain are "the corruptions of the world"; Germany, of which he knew almost nothing, is "entirely free of corruption"; Genoa is a city where "liberty and tyranny, civil order and corruption, justice and license live side by side." Every city, it appears, has its forms of corruptions, but the worst are in Florence. In his *Florentine History* he describes how a great number of citizens marched to the Signoria in 1372, when the city was being torn apart by party factions. There, "out of love for their country," they delivered a long speech, which clearly represents Machiavelli's deepest convictions and has no relation to any speech actually delivered. Corruption, in Machiavelli's view, arose out of party factions and the ambitions of party leaders.

> The common corruption of all the cities of Italy, magnificent Signors, has corrupted and still corrupts our city; because from the time that this province escaped from the power of the Empire, its cities, not being subject to any powerful influence that might restrain them, administered their affairs not like free men but like factions. From this have arisen all the other evils and disorders. In the first place there is found among the citizens neither union nor friendship except among those who are privy to some wickedness committed either against their country or against private persons. And because in all men the fear of God and religion appear to be extinguished, oaths and pledges are lasting only as long as it is expedient; men observe them only to permit themselves to deceive more easily; and the more easily and securely the deceit succeeds, so much the more glory and applause is acquired. By this means bad men receive the praise due to virtue, and good men are blamed as fools.
>
> Indeed, in the cities of Italy all that is corruptible and which can corrupt others is heaped together. The young are idle, the old lascivious, and both sexes and every age are full of disgusting habits, which good laws, marred by bad practice, do not remedy. Hence comes the avarice observed in the citizens and the appetite not for true glory but for shameful honors, whence come hatreds, enmities, quarrels and factions resulting in deaths, banishments, afflictions for the good and advancement for the bad. Because the good, trusting in their innocence, do not seek (as the wicked do) for those who will defend and honor them by extraordinary measures, and so they come to ruin undefended and unhonored.
>
> From these circumstances grow both the love and power of parties. Bad men follow them from avarice and ambition, and necessity compels the good to follow the same course. And what is yet more pernicious is to observe how the movers and leaders of these parties justify their base designs with pious words; they have the name of liberty constantly on their lips, though by their actions they prove they are the

greatest enemies of liberty. The prize they desire from victory is not the glory of having liberated the city, but the satisfaction of having overcome the others and of usurping the government; and having succeeded in this, there is nothing so unjust, so cruel, or avaricious that they dare not do.

Machiavelli accuses the party factions of doing for gain what the princes do for glory. The wheel turns full circle. He sees the mob and the revolutionary leaders wearing the face of the prince. The long catalogue of crimes committed by the factions—ignorance, debauchery, private murder, private conspiracies, hypocrisy, irreligion, lip service to liberty, indolence, and greed—is the familiar catalogue of the crimes committed by the prince. Spewing out all his hatred, he rages against the factions because they lack the inestimable gift of *virtu,* which belongs to the prince alone. He has found his enemy—the people of Florence.

Though he wrote out of hatred and malice, Machiavelli was a profound observer of the corruption around him. He never addressed himself to the problem of why states sink into corruption, or how they can sometimes renew themselves, or even what precisely was the nature of corruption; he preferred to study the frauds and deceits practiced by the princes and the factions, and to extract from them what lessons he could, however immoral and however distasteful. He liked to shock, and one can almost see his wintry smile of approval as he tells of some particularly unsavory action by one of his beloved princes. Sometimes he will rather negligently hint that he is describing these things so that people will learn to put an end to them, but the core of cynicism remains. He had no feeling for the people, no love for them, no understanding of them. He had a peculiar and morbid fascination for corruption.

Being totally irreligious, Machiavelli announced in his *Discourses* that there is only one way in which princes can remain uncorrupted, and that is "by maintaining in their uncorrupted form the ceremonies of their religion and holding them always in veneration." In the same chapter he proves to his own satisfaction that the papal court has destroyed all piety and religion in Italy. Long ago Aristotle had spoken of the need for the tyrant to observe the outward forms of religion so that the people would be less afraid of suffering injustice at his hands and less disposed to conspire against him because they would feel that the gods were fighting at his side. Machiavelli had read Aristotle's chapters on tyranny but had failed to learn the appropriate lesson that all tyrannies were bad, corrupt, insecure, and murderous. He rejoiced in tyranny because in his imagination he reveled in the tyrant's power.

Machiavelli died suddenly and mysteriously on June 21, 1527, at the age of fifty-eight, shortly after completing his *Florentine History*. This book ends with the death of Lorenzo de' Medici, who "put an end to the internal wars of Italy and by his wisdom and authority established peace" and whose death was followed remorselessly by "the flowering of the poisonous seeds which in a little time ruined Italy and still today keep her in desolation."

Between Ibn Khaldun and Machiavelli there is a wide gulf. Both portray corruption, but with what a difference! Ibn Khaldun probes from outside, reasonably and intelligently, observing the behavior of the corrupt with a kind of compassion, attempting always to understand the circumstances that have brought them to their tragic plight. He sees them in human terms, victims of a social law that pronounces their inevitable doom. Machiavelli, knowing that they are doomed, exults in their brief triumphs, their splendid progresses, their easy murders. In his portrait of the prince he gave us, without intending to do so, a portrait of the completely corrupt ruler.

The Romantic Agony

We think of the age of Lorenzo de' Medici as one of those rare periods when the arts flourished and civilization advanced with all its banners flying, but even in those days there were men who wondered whether civilization could endure in a world given over to tyrannies. Constantinople had fallen, and no one knew which city would fall next. The Catholic Church provided the mortar that held Europe together, but already the mortar was crumbling. Soon Luther would come to deliver the church from the corruption and tyranny of Rome, but even before Luther the spiritual empire of the papacy was in mortal danger. Pope Alexander VI, living in grotesque luxury and fathering a brood of vicious children, showed that the papacy was capable of every infamy. Savonarola had predicted that the end was not far off and that all of Italy would dissolve in corruption.

The Florentine humanists, living under the protection of three generations of Medicis, thought that learning, intelligence, and art provided civilization with its proper safeguards. Neither Cosimo nor

Piero nor Lorenzo was a prince in the Machiavellian sense, for all three had a deep sense of responsibility to the people and ruled with generosity and humanity. Although Machiavelli railed against the Florentine factions, there existed an intense feeling of community, a close-knit *asabiyya*. Florence would endure, if any city endured. All the ingredients that make for strength were present—except one. Faith, purpose, homogeneity, the flowering of the arts, prosperous industries, capable artisans, all these were present. What was lacking was a ruler who could take the place of Lorenzo. The Medicis became the grand dukes of Tuscany, a succession of mediocrities alternately puffed up with their distinguished lineage and cowering out of sight like the last of them, the Grand Duke Gian Gastone, a fat buffoon who surrounded himself with dissolute boys and gravely addressed them by the names of his ministers. He spent the last thirteen years of his life in his dressing gown and the last eight years in bed.

Lorenzo was a human force, a poet, banker, administrator, adventurer, patron of the arts, stage designer, huntsman, collector of all strange and beautiful things. He was the Renaissance man raised to the pitch of perfection. His nose was broken and the nostrils flattened, his mouth was hard, and his heavy chin weighed down a face already burdened with heavy cheekbones. He had great physical strength, but this was mostly in the upper part of his body, for he suffered atrociously from gout in his legs and moved with some difficulty, with the stateliness and dignity of the half-lame. He was pale, like all the Medicis, and there was about him the wariness of those who cannot see clearly. He wore his power lightly and preferred above all things riding his horses, writing poems, and engaging in philosophical discussions with his friends.

Machiavelli dedicated *The Prince* to Lorenzo's ineffective grandson, perhaps in the hope that the book would shock him into becoming effective. No comparable book was written in honor of Lorenzo. The nearest we have to such a book is *The Oration on the Dignity of Man* by Pico della Mirandola, friend of Lorenzo and one of the most learned members of the Florentine Academy. His elegant speech takes the form of a sustained celebration of the dignity of man in his uncorrupted state, bearing "the image of the Almightiest" within himself. He celebrated the dignity of man, free and untrammeled, no longer at the mercy of the weather, or sickness, or death. Pico had no hesitation in proclaiming that man has the power to reach out and dominate the whole universe; he has the intellect, the skill of hand, the depth of sight to grasp whatever he desires to grasp. This is real power, not the shoddy little power of a prince who tricks another into entering his city and then strangles him. Uncorrupted man, with God's blessing, advances across the fields of the universe as though he were walking down a country lane.

Pico, the slight and slender youth of Botticelli's portrait, with steady gray eyes and yellow hair, wrote with wonderful clarity about man's place in the universe. Why is man given life? God answers, "So that there will be someone to reckon up the reason of so great a work, to love its beauty, and to wonder at its greatness." God proclaims his abiding trust in man's infinite possibilities, saying:

> I have set thee at the center of the world, that from there thou mayest more conveniently look around and see whatsoever is in the world. I have made thee neither heavenly nor earthly, neither mortal nor immortal; and like a judge appointed for being honorable thou art made the moulder and maker of thyself; thou mayest knead thyself into whatever shape thou desirest. Thou mayest sink into a beast, or be born anew to a divine likeness. The brutes bring forth from the mother's body what they will carry with them as long as they live; the higher spirits are from the beginning, or soon after, what they will be for ever. To thee alone is given a growth and development depending on thine own free will. Thou bearest in thee the germs of a universal life.

Pico della Mirandola states the case for man's earthly triumph and spiritual victory. Implicit in the argument is the portrait of uncorrupted man, untouched by tyranny, able to develop in perfect freedom and perfect beauty. Michelangelo's *David* is the sculptural counterpart of this vision, which owes much to the earlier visionary writings of the mysterious Dionysius the Areopagite and the more familiar Nicholas of Cusa. *Thou mayest sink into a beast, or be born anew to a divine likeness.*

In the Renaissance it sometimes seemed that the day of the beast was over and there would come into existence the new man whose splendid powers endowed him with a divine likeness. Men talked like this in the court of Lorenzo de' Medici, where Christian humanism went hand in hand with Socratic dialogue. In the person of Leonardo da Vinci there was a hint of the special glory and the latent powers reserved for man. But neither Lorenzo nor Leonardo had followers worthy of him; and soon it became evident that man's imperfections, his cruelty and vindictiveness, his lust for power, and his joy in self-degradation were at least as great as his desire to be free. Never again after the Florentine Renaissance were men to speak with such assurance of man's perfectibility, the belief that he was in measurable distance of divinity.

Throughout the history of Christianity, there had been a core of belief that man was not doomed to be everlastingly corrupt. Goodness would triumph in life, as at the Last Judgment. How in the face of human error this would be brought about no one seemed to know. Evil existed; corruption existed; the tyrants practiced evil and were rewarded with God's plenty. Many Christian theologians wrestled strenuously with the problem of good and evil and came to varying conclusions. Augustine wrestled more strenuously than most and concluded that the universe is demonstrably filled with evil and the wicked fruits of man's perverted will but nevertheless all is good because God is present, and evil is where God is not. There are moments when the logic vanishes from Augustine's arguments, but he is not dealing with logic. He is trying to discover the inscrutable purposes of the divine will as distinguished from the only too comprehensible purposes of the human will. There is a remarkable passage in his *Confessions* where he attempts to find a place for corruption in the divine economy:

> All which is corrupted is deprived of good. But if they be deprived of all good, they will cease to be. For if they be, and cannot be at all corrupted, they will become better, because they shall remain incorruptible. And what more monstrous than to assert that those things which have lost all their goodness are made better? Therefore, if they shall be deprived of all good, they shall no longer be. So long therefore, as they are, they are good; therefore whatsoever is, is good. That evil, then, which I sought whence it was, is not any substance; for were it a substance, it would be good. For either it would be an incorruptible substance, and so a chief good, or a corruptible substance, which unless it were good it could not be corrupted. I perceived therefore, and it was made clear to me, that Thou didst make all things good, nor is there any substance at all which is not made by Thee; and because all that Thou hast made are not equal, therefore all things are; because individually they are good, and altogether very good, because our God made all things very good.

Since for Augustine evil is merely the absence of good (*privatio boni*), he has very little difficulty in proving that corruption has only a marginal place in the divine economy, which is entirely good and incorruptible. His tortuous argument, however, conceals a curious fascination with corruption, however much and however often it is wished away. His conclusion in favor of God's eternal goodness would have been more convincing if he had arrived at it with less difficulty.

Christian ethic since the time of Paul has been concerned with sin rather than with conduct. Since, according to Paul, "by one man sin entered the world, and death by sin; and so death passed upon all men, for that all have sinned," it followed that all men were equally tainted by sin, which could be washed away only by God's unpredictable grace. The absolute sin had been committed in the long-distant and legendary past. The sins of the present time were as nothing compared with the primordial sin committed by the first parents of the human race. In the eyes of Augustine, the earthly corruption was merely a passing phase and earth itself merely a temporary passageway to death. The earthly city was insubstantial; only the city of God was permanent.

To medieval churchmen the problems of tyranny and of man's abasement of man were therefore of no overwhelming importance. "Render unto Caesar" provided a useful argument to anyone who proclaimed that Caesar was too murderous, too avaricious, or too incompetent. The church was satisfied as long as the ruler accepted its spiritual empire. It protected him, demanded that his subjects display proper humility, and forbade rebellion. To Augustine the corruptions of society had no meaning, for every society by definition was hopelessly corrupt.

In the workaday world men still concerned themselves with achieving an uncorrupted society. The essayist Michel de Montaigne, looking out on the sixteenth-century world from his ivory tower, was inclined to see corruption as a disease affecting everyone. "The corruptions of our age are made up of the individual corruptions of each of us," he wrote. "Those who are influential to do so contribute injustice, cruelty, avarice, and tyranny, while the weaker sort contribute folly, futilities, and idleness." Since the blame was spread thinly throughout the human family, the cure, if one could be found, would have to be spread just as thinly. It was not in Montaigne's view a matter of overwhelming importance: the corruptions of one age were probably the same as the corruptions of all other ages; and with a friendly wave he passed on to other things.

After Ibn Khaldun, Giambattista Vico (1668–1744) was the next to enquire seriously into the nature of corruption as an inevitable part of the historical process. In Vico's *Scienza Nuova* a window clatters open; men are seen to be what they are, themselves the creators of the societies they live in, and bearing within themselves the past, the present, and the future, as though an eternal history were implanted in each one of them. Vico's respect for the human creature as an incarnation of history possesses an almost fanatic intensity. But while men are free to create their own history, they are subject in Vico's view to the laws of growth, maturity, and decline. "Men first feel necessity, then look for utility, next attend to comfort, and later amuse themselves with pleasure, thence grow dissolute in luxury, and finally go mad and waste their substance."

But this is not the end of the matter, for out of this final corruption arises a new barbarism; the cycle is repeated, but in such a manner that it is at once an advance and a return. Vico's theory of the *ricorso* (re-run) is central to his idea of history: a society advances to the limits of its abilities and eventually collapses from its inherent vices, only to be renewed by a new, primitive, more brutal society. Thus the Middle Ages in Europe were a *ricorso* of the early primitive society of ancient Rome, and the developing history of Europe may expect to follow the same pattern that Rome pursued to its decline. The concept of *asabiyya* seems to hover nearby. Of the power and force of primitive societies and of their extreme sophistication, Vico had no doubt, and he studied them minutely. He was fascinated by Homer, who represented in his mind the full power of primitive Greek society, and so inevitably his book contains a full chapter on Homer as the portrayer of a rich and spacious society.

Vico's *Scienza Nuova,* published in 1725, when he was fifty-seven, is a very odd book indeed. He was a jurist, a philosopher, a philologist, a historian, a sociologist, and a professor of Latin eloquence, and sometimes these disciplines got in the way of each other. He had the scholastic temper, throwing out ideas pell-mell and then seeking justification for them in the classics. He was a dazzling and erratic philologist, who enjoyed bending history to his own purposes.

Vico also liked to tell stories. One of the best of them concerns Emperor Conrad III, who conquered Weinsberg in Germany and thereupon dictated the terms of surrender. He ordered that the men must remain in the city, but the women were permitted to leave with whatever they could carry on their backs. The city gates were opened and the women streamed out, carrying their men and children on their backs; and the victorious emperor and the army, which was ready to rush in and massacre the men, watched in stupefaction as the women brought their men and children to safety. Just as Vico cherished his theory of the *ricorso,* which gave new life to a civilization after it perished, so he enjoyed a story of a reprieve from danger, a new birth, a new hope. Societies passed from being crude to being severe, then benign, then delicate, then dissolute: this was the law of history; but in the eternal history they were no more than waves rising and falling, one society following after another, each demonstrating its human gifts.

Charles Louis, Baron de Montesquieu, who was Vico's contemporary, was considerably less optimistic. He could not see civilizations as from the sovereign heights, simultaneously advancing and retreating. In his eyes history moved with astonishing subtlety, remote and fragile, like delicately colored balloons hovering in the air or floating in the wind. While Vico would have been perfectly happy in the thirteenth century, Montesquieu was essentially a man of his time, of the Enlightenment, amused, indifferent, patient, believing that all problems could be solved by reason and the application of good will and intelligence. He was a superbly civilized man, and knew much more about the history of remote regions like Persia and China than Vico did. He wrote smoothly; Vico wrote abruptly, with passionate heat. Montesquieu was rich and happy in his life; Vico died miserably.

Because he was a reasonable man, Montesquieu detested tyranny. "When the savages of Louisiana want fruit, they cut the whole tree down and so gather the fruit," he wrote. *"That* is tyrannical government." Or again: "All men are equal under a republican government, and they are equal under a tyrannical government. In the first case they are equal because they have everything, and in the second because they have nothing." Vico, clinging to the cyclical theory, saw the corruptive process at work in the general decline of every civilization, while Montesquieu saw it working wherever the central authority exceeded its just powers. Vico saw corruption as a function of time while Montesquieu saw it happening at a certain place and at a given moment, brought about by the avarice, pride, and malignity of persons in the government or simply by their carelessness and indifference. Vico saw it in terms of the great wave of history, while Montesquieu saw it in terms of human personality and the human addiction to intrigue.

In Montesquieu's *Considerations on the Causes of the Greatness of the Romans and of Their Decadence* and even more in *On the Spirit of the Laws,* we observe a temperate, probing mind that never permits itself to become confused. Montesquieu had something of Ibn Khaldun's temper, and if he knew less about the workings of a royal court, for he was never a courtier, he knew more about more kinds of government. His polished sentences conceal his passion. He employed irony to emphasize a hatred he had mastered but could not entirely conceal. He devoted many pages to corruption, and some of the most barbed passages are directed against the corrupt court at Versailles, where the Bourbon kings disported themselves like absolute monarchs and spent their time superintending endless ceremonies that were totally meaningless, because they affected only the small and ineffective inner world of the court. Here is Montesquieu's verdict on the monarchy in his time:

> The monarchy is corrupted when the King, restoring all power to himself, summons the government to his capital, his capital to his court, and his court to his own person.
>
> The principle of monarchy is corrupted when the first dignities become the marks of the first servitudes, when the respect of the people is withdrawn from the great ministers, and when the vile instruments of arbitrary power are placed in their hands.
>
> It is even more corrupted when honor is placed in contradiction with honors, and a man can be at once full of dignities and covered with infamy.
>
> It is corrupted when the King abandons justice for severity, when like the Roman emperors he places the head of the Medusa on his breastplate, and when he assumes that menacing and terrible look displayed by Commodus in his statues.
>
> The principle of monarchy is corrupted when singularly mean-spirited people take pride in their servitude and come to believe that while they owe everything to their King, they owe nothing to their country.

Montesquieu's observations on tyranny are equally harsh and precise. "Tyrannical governments endlessly corrupt themselves, because they are corrupted by their very nature," he says. The sole remedy is to destroy the tyrant and to root out the last vestige of corruption, for every tyranny is doomed to die of an "interior vice." Under a tyranny all good laws become bad laws, for they are used by the tyrant against the people. Montesquieu had a high opinion of democracy, but he observed that "when the laws cease to be observed in a democracy, then the state is lost already, for such things come about only when the republic is corrupted." He regarded strict observance of the law as the foundation of a democracy, while a tyranny always mocked the laws. The worst crime of a tyranny, he believed, is that it destroys men's courage.

During the reigns of Louis XIV and Louis XV, Montesquieu had ample opportunity to study a decaying monarchy that was not far removed from a tyranny. It was the world described by the duc de Saint-Simon, strangely cold and remote, with the aristocracy performing a stately dance round the king, while in the outer darkness the people were given over to a permanent misery. The king ruled impersonally, scarcely aware of the misery around him; and even if he had been aware of it, he would not have lifted a finger to assuage it. Louis XIV destroyed his people in his wars and siphoned off the public treasury for his private amusements. He destroyed the aristocracy by the simple process of removing them from Paris and from their estates to the Palace of Versailles to dance attendance upon him; it was a form of imprisonment. We see them in attitudes of supplication, or attending his *levées,* or beggaring themselves to wear the fine uniforms that accompanied their high offices —those offices where nothing was demanded of them except that they appear in their finery, bow low, praise the king's majesty, and intrigue maliciously. *Le Roi Soleil,* grown fat and ludicrous, surrounded by his mistresses and his bastards, and never permitting a new idea to enter his head, lived out his last years in an excruciating torpor. At last, after a reign of seventy-two years, having outlived his son, his grandson, and his eldest great-grandson, he died half-eaten away by gangrene. At the autopsy it was discovered that he had a stomach twice the size of the stomach of an ordinary man. There was something symbolic about that ancient corpse: the huge stomach and the black limbs rotted with gangrene.

He died in 1715, three days short of his seventy-seventh birthday, and was succeeded by a five-year-old boy, Louis XV, who was even more remote from reality than his great-grandfather had been. Grown to manhood, Louis XV was merely a smaller and less interesting version of Louis XIV. He, too, was self-indulgent to the highest degree and totally incompetent as a ruler. He lost the French possessions in Canada and India but succeeded without much difficulty in conquering Corsica, thus opening the way to the later conquest of France by Napoleon. At night, wrapped in a black cloak, he would sometimes emerge from the Palace of Versailles and make his way to the Deer Park, a private brothel populated by kitchen wenches. He oppressed the French dreadfully, but it was during his reign that there appeared the greatest galaxy of intelligence Europe had seen since the days of Lorenzo de' Medici.

Laplace, Lavoisier, Diderot, Voltaire, Condorcet, D'Alembert, D'Holbach, Buffon, Marmontel, Rousseau, Jaucourt were all superbly intelligent men who were capable of raising reasonableness to the height of genius. Reason they admired, but reasonableness was their *forte.* Most of them contributed to Diderot's great *Encyclopédie,* which ultimately comprised thirty-five huge volumes intended to convey everything that was known up to that time about philosophy, science, and literature. For nearly twenty-five years (1748–72) Diderot labored on this stupendous undertaking, writing many of the articles himself, quarreling ferociously with the printer, who attempted to censor the work, at odds with the king and the church, at war with obscurantism and ignorance wherever he found it. Denis Diderot was one of those men who create the atmosphere in which great works arise and then write them. His *Encyclopédie* was a revolutionary work of vast scope that helped to precipitate the French Revolution. Unhappily, this was not the revolution the *Encyclopédistes* wanted. They believed that reasonable changes could be brought about swiftly, intelligently, even passionately. They did not believe in destroying the government and leaving the people so weak that they would inevitably welcome the next emperor who came along.

Even in the early years of the reign of Louis XV there were portents of the coming disaster. All those things that formerly protected and comforted man seemed to have vanished or to be about to vanish. Progress, Reason, Logic, even Style were already becoming suspect; the church no longer answered to the pressing needs of the people; the king was lost in the maze of galleries at Versailles. The *Encyclopédistes* made it their task to erect a reasonable intellectual foundation for the new emerging society, little realizing that the French Revolution would have no use for reasonableness or intellect or foundations. It soared under its own energy, capricious and murderous, commanded by a succession of drunken helmsmen. Diderot died four years before the revolution broke out, and like Voltaire and Rousseau, who both died in 1778, he was spared the prospect of seeing his hopes shattered in the horrors of the guillotine and the September massacres.

One of Diderot's greatest works, *Rameau's Nephew,* written during the 1760s, takes the form of a dialogue between a philosopher of the Enlightenment and a youthful romantic nihilist. The philosopher is concerned with reasonableness, dignity, human kindness, while Rameau's nephew lives for survival at any cost. He will play the sycophant, steal, debauch women, sell his wife to the highest bidder, pour flattery on the rich for the sake of a meal, and lick their boots for the sheer joy of seeing them squirm with pleasure. He is a marvelous mimic and regards the whole world as an absurd pantomime in which he is one of the principal actors. Diderot even supplies a portrait of him: powdered hair, black brows, unusually bright eyes, clean-cut sculptured mouth, square jaw, prominent belly. Corrupt, intelligent, merciless, Rameau's nephew has come to a profound conclusion: there is very little difference between the gardener who clips the leaves of a tree with his shears and the worms who perform the same service by feeding on the leaves. Who is the philosopher to say that the worms are not equal to the gardener?

Rameau's nephew is the remote ancestor of Dostoyevsky's "man from under the floorboards." The philosopher attempts to argue intelligently against an adversary who proclaims that all men are insects. *Farceur,* seducer, immoralist, unscrupulous in all his dealings with the world, Rameau's nephew is a figure seen with extraordinary clarity and power. Goethe translated the short novel from the French manuscript; Hegel went into raptures over it; Karl Marx rejoiced in it. Today we are less inclined to see virtues in Rameau's nephew: he was one of those who lit the fires of the French Revolution for their own amusement and in order to add excitement to their barren lives. In this dialogue we see the Enlightenment dissolving into the shadows and flames of romanticism.

Yet even during the revolution there were men who continued the dialogue on behalf of the Enlightenment. The marquis de Condorcet, Perpetual Secretary of the Academy of Sciences, welcomed the revolution with open arms and helped draft the Declaration of the Rights of Man. Elected to the Convention, he mapped out a plan for universal education that was later followed by Napoleon, and he fought for a revolution that was humane, reasonable, and passionately devoted to the progress of equality and the perfection of man. Robespierre attacked him and he went into hiding in the attic of a house close to the Luxembourg prison. In this attic, in mortal fear of arrest, he wrote his long essay on the perfectibility of man. At last, to spare the woman in whose house he was hiding, he slipped away to Fontenay-aux-Roses, where he concealed himself in a quarry until, exhausted by starvation, he made his way to a local inn, where he was recognized. He was thrown into prison and died a few days later of apoplexy or poison. He was one of the few revolutionaries who were not corrupted and who maintained their human dignity.

Rameau's Nephew cast its long shadow over romanticism. The insect-*farceur* with the power of mimicry and the cynical laughter, superb trickster selling his soul to the highest bidder, sensualist and adroit student, became a romantic hero; in various disguises he is the central figure of a hundred romantic novels. Diderot did not invent him; he grew out of the times. Werther and Faust continue the tradition. In 1787 Gabriel Sénac de Meilhan published in London an essay on morals with a famous lamentation: "Impotence, admira-

tion of the past, the self-love that comes from age and the insensitiv-
ity of a withered soul, and finally the lust for money—all these seem
to portray the sexagenarian character of the century." Rameau's
nephew was an answer to the world's weariness and corruption; he
was corruption concentrated and personified, wearing an actor's
mask.

In Goethe's *Faust* Mephistopheles is the arch-corrupter, and he,
too, wears the actor's mask. Faust, discontented with his studious,
ascetic life, clutching at the prospects Mephistopheles opens to him,
is scarcely less a corrupter as he pits his intelligence against the
flawed intelligence of his devil. He sells his soul at a price so high
that Mephistopheles quails before his effrontery, and Faust half-
convinces himself that he has the better part of the bargain. Faust
wears his humanity well, but Mephistopheles, in his scarlet gown
with a cock's feather rising from his hat and a thin, finely wrought
sword at his waist, imperial chamberlain rather than devil incarnate, wears the actor's manner. The subtle negotiations for Faust's
soul are conducted as in a comedy of manners concerned with the
negotiations for the price of seducing a virgin; we have sympathy
for the virgin and little sympathy for the negotiators. Faust is
damned, but it is a heroic damnation; his humanity cries out to the
world's beauty, and he is prepared to die for it:

> *If I should say to the passing moment:*
> *Stay awhile, thou art so fair!*
> *Then mayest thou cast me into fetters,*
> *And I will willingly go down to Hell.*
> *Then may the death knell toll,*
> *And thou art free of thy services.*
> *The clock may stop and the hands fall away,*
> *And time will exist no more for me!*

At such moments Faust lacks the Faustian spirit; his humanity
redeems him. It is precisely this humanity which is lacking in Rameau's nephew.

Romanticism introduced the *isolato,* the man alone with himself,
terrified by the crushing immensity around him. The hierarchical
mold was destroyed in the French Revolution, and no one would
ever be able to put it together again. Men looked back in wonder
at the stable, peaceful societies of the past, and sometimes they
wondered whether in fact those societies had ever existed. Sometimes men took courage from the fact that now at last all the ancient

subterfuges had been discarded, and no longer were men at the mercy of mythologies and dreams. In time the romantic movement would invent its own mythologies and dreams, but the single over-whelming fact was that man was alone, no mythologies could save him, no dreams could provide a refuge, no kingdoms could assure him a fixed place in society, no economy would assure him of a livelihood, no God would protect him. It was not only that he was alone and crushed by his loneliness; he was in a world where every man's hand was against him.

The emergence of the *isolato,* who first appears in a sketchy form in the middle years of the eighteenth century, about the time of the death of Montesquieu, and acquires shape and substance during the French Revolution, was a phenomenon of extraordinary impor-tance in the development of Western civilization. What men had been dreading for centuries had come to pass. By freeing himself of customs, traditions, and divine sanctions, the *isolato* freed himself from morality. He could do as he pleased, reach out beyond all boundaries, assert his individuality against his real and imagined enemies, give himself up to spleen and melancholy, and embrace every irrational whim as though it was the substance of revealed truth. Everything was permissible to him. He had lost the sense of community, and he had lost something even more precious—a sense of direction. Also, he had become dangerous to himself. He was a destructive agent, capable of improbable acts of heroism and daz-zling feats of suicide.

In Stendhal's novel *The Red and the Black,* Julien Sorel fires two pistol shots at Madame de Renal, his beloved, while she is praying in church on a Sunday morning. He is committing an act of bravado designed to bring him to the guillotine; it is an illogical, absurd, satisfying, and highly romantic act. Above all, it gives Julien Sorel a sense of his own significance. In his own way he is accomplishing a destiny, for in his own eyes he is now no longer an *isolato*: he is a hero.

The worst feature of the romantic movement was that it elevated the pursuit of the irrational to a fine art. The romantic hero was a rebel without a cause open to all the corrupting influences. Ques-tions of conscience did not arise. Julien Sorel was not in the least remorseful for killing Madame de Renal. Napoleon, gazing down at the dead on the battlefield, declared, "What do a million dead mat-ter to me?" Man, who had so recently stood at the center of the universe, now appeared to be moving toward its farthest boundaries, lost to sight. He was becoming cannon fodder, an utterly unimportant statistic that could be marched onto a battlefield and mowed down at the pleasure of Napoleon. The romantic movement, which began by celebrating the freedom and independence of the individual from the claims of the church and the state and all the mythologies that had crowded around them for centuries, threw the individual back on himself; he discovered that he was more vulnerable than he had ever expected to be, at the mercy of even more demanding and cruel masters.

The devaluation of man in the nineteenth century was due to many causes—the rise of industrialism, the successes of colonialism, the invention of the machine gun, the vast extension of the secret police, which grew especially strong in France, Germany, and Russia. Each played a role in diminishing man's freedom of action, and war became more murderous than ever. Each contributed to corruption. Man became more faceless, more anonymous. Prince Louis Napoleon became Emperor Napoleon III and quickly developed techniques of repression that were carefully studied by the dictators who came later. Among his chief inventions were the wide boulevards of Paris, designed for the purpose of ensuring unrestricted fields of fire in the event of an uprising. The devaluation of man was accomplished at considerable expense and at a relentless pace. It was as though in the middle years of the nineteenth century the grand design that would culminate in the Russian slave labor camps and the German extermination camps was already being sketched out on the drawing board. The totalitarian state was already emerging. Caesarism, the instrument of perpetual punishment, formless and shapeless except for the clearly outlined figure of Caesar himself, brilliantly lit and visible to all, was an absurd and irrational solution to the problems of governing a modern industrial state, for it responded to the extraordinary complexity of modern society by imposing a criminal simplicity. A population already alienated by industry was to be further alienated by the presence of Big Brother. All this could be seen dimly in the strange, tottering empire of Napoleon III, whose police spies infested all the towns and cities under his rule. He won easy battles in Italy and imagined himself a great conqueror, thus placing himself in the same rank as his uncle, Napoleon I. Napoleon III met his Waterloo at Sedan and became a prisoner of the Germans, who set about building an empire even larger and more centralized than the French Empire; and Caesarism, born again in France, triumphed in Germany under the kaisers.

The poet Heinrich Heine was one of those who foresaw that

Caesarism would later assume a form unknown to the Caesars of his day. He wrote in 1842:

Perhaps there will be only one flock and one shepherd with an iron staff and a flock of human sheep all shorn alike and bleating alike! Wild, gloomy times are roaring toward us, and the prophet who wishes to write the new Apocalypse would have to invent entirely new beasts, and they would be so terrible that the ancient animal symbols of St. John would be like gentle doves and cupids. The gods are veiling their faces out of pity for the faces of men, their foster children for so long, and perhaps they do so out of apprehension over their own fate. The future smells of Russian leather, blood, godlessness, and many whippings. I should advise our grandchildren to be born with very thick skins on their backs.

The future that Heine saw prophetically was a peculiar form of Caesarism that had already been sketched by his friend Karl Marx, who called it Communism. *The Communist Manifesto,* published obscurely in London in 1848, was as full of specters, graves, and sudden terrors as any Gothic novel. Like *The Rime of the Ancient Mariner,* it reveled in the portrayal of doom and destruction. In the high romantic manner, individuals confront an implacable destiny single-handedly and are utterly cast down. In *The Communist Manifesto* the whole world is confronted with an implacable destiny demanding the abolition of property, classes, and national boundaries. All will be one, united in a common freedom. Marx insisted that the goal was the utmost freedom. "In place of the old bourgeois society, with its classes and class antagonisms, we shall have an association, in which the free development of each is the condition for the free development of all."

Karl Marx's vision of the ultimate utopian society derived from ancient sources. The sweeping generalities, the excessive claims, and the violent lapses of logic were peculiarly his own, but they were charged with a resonant poetry. He did not in those early days speak of the dictatorship of the proletariat but only of its supremacy, its power. He expected it to become the ruling class as the result of revolution, and then, according to *The Communist Manifesto,* it would sweep away "the conditions of the existence of class antagonisms, and of classes generally, and will therefore have abolished its own supremacy as a class." The supreme proletariat, he was saying, would then dissolve into a classless society.

It is precisely at this point that Marx's romantic vision becomes

170 The Dialogue with Corruption

cloudy and unconvincing. He resembles the romantic poets who place the beloved beyond reach, infinitely desirable and infinitely far away, and when by magic the knight appears in her presence, he sees not the real object but a visionary presence; and the vision fades. The classless society, the age of freedom, was not so easily acquired, nor was it likely that the supreme proletariat, once it had seized power, would abolish itself. Joachim of Floris in the twelfth century had announced the coming of the Age of the Holy Spirit after a transitional period following the Age of the Father, and he too had spoken of that mysterious dissolution as one age follows another:

JOACHIM OF FLORIS	KARL MARX
1. Age of the Father, obedience to the letter of the law.	1. Age of Capitalism, obedience to its laws.
2. Age of the Son, of the Eternal Gospel. Transitional period between the letter and the spirit.	2. Age of dictatorship of the proletariat. Transitional period between capitalism and Communism.
3. Age of the Holy Spirit. The church will be purified, the hierarchy will wither away, and man will enter into a period of worship, brotherly love, and freedom.	3. Age of true Communism. Society will be purified, the state will wither away, and humanity will enter a new era of complete freedom.

But these were dreams, not to be changed into reality without a miracle. Marx, himself an *isolato,* alienated from the world around him, thought of that classless society as his rightful home and luxuriated in it, even though it had no existence and was not likely to have any existence. Nevertheless, he lit a fuse that continued to burn long after his death. He had hoped to free men from their chains by offering them a vision, and instead he bound them more firmly in their chains. He thought he was speaking outside the established tradition, but instead he was speaking within a long established tradition and with the accents of romanticism. The dream turned into nightmare and corruption.

We are still living in a romantic age, and the *isolato* is still firmly embedded in our culture. We dream our terrifying nightmares and wake to find they are reality. In 1914—the date is important—André Gide published *Les Caves du Vatican (Lafcadio's Adventures),* which he had been contemplating for twenty years. The central incident of this novel is an absolutely motiveless crime committed by the brilliant and elegant Lafcadio Wluiki, the illegitimate son of Count de Baraglioul. On a railway journey Lafcadio finds himself in the same compartment as Amédée Fleurissoire, a meek little man who is coming to Rome because he has heard that the pope has been arrested and imprisoned in the Vatican cellars. Lafcadio knows nothing about him, but in a moment of boredom, reminding himself that he has saved two children from a fire and that therefore in some curious way he is entitled to take a life, he throws the man out of the compartment, killing him. It is a gratuitous and disinterested act. Lafcadio is mildly annoyed because in the brief struggle he has lost his hat.

Les Caves du Vatican is an important work because it describes an attitude of mind that was becoming commonplace. With its publication, the motiveless act entered literature. With the same careless indifference and irresponsibility the kaiser and the Austrian emperor would launch a meaningless war in which uncounted millions would be killed. The dissolution of classes was taking place, but in a form that had not been expected by visionary prophets; they were being dissolved in the mud of Flanders and Silesia. The military machine became more and more inexorable and arbitrary; it was bureaucratic, inefficient, self-serving; it assumed all power to itself and was so engrossed in killing that it was indifferent to the proclaimed purposes for which the war was being fought. The long stalemate on the Western Front served the military machine very well, for the machine was not concerned with the numbers of soldiers killed or the yards of territory gained; it was concerned to perpetuate itself. The railroad carriage was all of Europe, and an armed Lafcadio was throwing everyone out. A constant stream of orders was being issued on all fronts; the orders said, "Kill"; but which was responsible, the automatic machine that issued the orders or the poor devil in the trenches who did the killing? In all the belligerent countries the military bureaucracy seized the entire life of the country and squeezed it dry. If the populations of France and Germany were reduced to thirty men each, the military machine would have continued issuing senseless orders. Outwardly Europe appeared to be fighting a civil war; in fact, it had surrendered to the military, who were marvelously equipped to issue orders even if no one was left to obey them.

During the war years there lived in Munich a man who was busily attempting to place all of human history in an intelligible framework and who, by studying the past, hoped to prophesy the future. He was desperately poor, lived in a slum, took his meals in cheap working-class restaurants, haunted the libraries, dressed in secondhand clothes, and wrote by candlelight because he could not afford electricity. His name was Oswald Spengler, and the work he was writing so diligently was *The Decline of the West*, which was published in 1918. On a vast wall chart he had listed all the great civilizations and their achievements, discovering unsuspected correspondences between them. Each had its spring, summer, autumn, and winter. Sometimes he found it necessary to bend history a little, so that the correspondences would appear in the right season. The age of Sesostris III (ca. 1850 B.C.) was equated with Periclean Athens, the Umayyad dynasty, and eighteenth-century Europe, the Europe of Haydn, Mozart, Watteau, and the French Revolution, all characterized by a presentiment of their coming end. Winter was setting in, and soon Europe would be in full decline, its art forms exhausted, its will to survive so weak that it could no longer sustain a living civilization. And what then? Spengler had, one suspects, come to his conclusion even before his long, patient, crotchety examination of the morphology of civilizations. His final conclusion was that Western civilization would dissolve and that a world civilization would emerge under the rule of a new Caesar "who approaches with quiet, firm steps."

Marx and Spengler agreed on dissolution; they disagreed about how the process would be carried out. Neither accepted the possibility that the survivors would object strongly to their dissolution. Both composed threnodies on civilizations that were not yet dead, though they appeared to be dying.

While Spengler was writing his morphology of civilizations from outside, as though standing on a star, Marcel Proust was describing from inside the decay of French society. Writing his *Remembrance of Things Past,* Proust resembled a chemist who places an object in a solution and watches it decompose, scrupulously recording the subtle stages of its dissolution. French feudal society, which had survived emperors and kings, no longer had any reason for existence. It possessed some residual wealth and imposing titles. "You are only a baron," Monsieur Verdurin remarks to Baron de Charlus. "You forget," Charlus replies, "that I am also Duc de Brabant, Damoiseau de Montargis, Prince d'Oloron, de Carency, de Viareggio and des Dunes." He is in an excellent mood and smiles indulgently until Madame Verdurin asks him whether he knows some ruined old nobleman who would like to work as a porter. "Why, yes, but I wouldn't advise it," he says. "I would be afraid for your sake that your smart visitors would call at the lodge and go no further."

Charlus is feudalism in full decay, smelling to high heaven. Wrapped up in his own importance, contemptuous of everyone except the pope and some reigning monarchs whom he regards as legitimate representatives of royalty, he wanders through the novels like a running sore. He is a defeatist, perhaps a spy, a pervert who likes to lie chained on a bed while a boy beats him with a whip studded with nails. By thinking so fondly of men, he has become almost a woman. He powders his nose, paints his lips, his belly protrudes, his behind sticks out, he rarely smiles because he is half-ashamed of his gold teeth. With his tight smile and enormous eyes, his pallor, his jerky walk, and his overwhelming sense of his own importance, he is almost a personification of death. Proust poured all his great gifts into the portrait of Baron de Charlus, who is far from being a caricature. He is the breath of corruption transformed into flesh, larger than life, almost as large as death.

Gustav von Aschenbach, the hero of Thomas Mann's novella *Death in Venice,* is the Germanic counterpart of Baron de Charlus. He speaks harshly to his inferiors and takes enormous pleasure in the title of nobility granted to him on his fiftieth birthday for his great contributions to literature. Nevertheless he is a kindly man, generous, ascetic, stoic, superbly intelligent. In Venice he falls helplessly in love with a young Polish boy, Tadzio, remarkable for his honey-colored ringlets and pale, cameolike profile. They never speak to one another, but Aschenbach suffers the agonies of the damned in pursuing his unrequited love affair. "But what is self-possession? What is reason, moral sense, what is art itself compared to the rewards of chaos?" Cholera has descended on Venice, people are leaving the city in haste, but Tadzio remains, hovering like a mirage over the sand, his perfect beauty filling the aging author with the wildest fantasies. One suspects that Marx and Spengler with their dreams of the coming dissolution were also seeking for the rewards of chaos, projecting their personal mythologies upon the world. Aschenbach is luckier, for he dies in his deck chair while gazing at Tadzio, who is standing knee-deep in the waves, his hand on his hip, smiling invitingly.

"We know now that our civilization is mortal," wrote Paul Valéry at the end of World War I. Yet Europe, in its agony and corruption, survived a second war even more terrible than the first. Riddled with a hundred diseases, waging interminable civil wars, it was taking a long time to die.

Lord Acton, Nietzsche, and Dostoyevsky

When Lord Acton delivered himself of the famous apothegm "Power tends to corrupt and absolute power corrupts absolutely," he was not intending to be clever. He was speaking passionately about a subject he had examined with great care and fascinated horror over many years of intense scholarship. He had known many powerful men and was on terms of intimacy with Gladstone, the British prime minister, whom he regarded as one of the most honest and least corrupt of men. At a time when kings still wielded power he was able to study them at close quarters in half the courts of Europe. Like Ibn Khaldun, he was an aristocrat who based his study of history on direct observation of complex historical events. Ironically he was no stranger to corruption. He stood for Parliament, won the election, and resigned a few months later when it was learned that his agent had been accused of bribery and corruption for stuffing the ballot boxes.

John Emerich Edward Dalberg-Acton was born in Naples in 1834. His paternal grandfather, Sir John Acton, had been the lover of the queen of Naples, and although an Englishman he became prime minister of the kingdom of Naples. He was a totally ruthless man and superintended the reign of terror at Palermo after revolutionaries failed in their revolt against the kingdom. John Dalberg-Acton's maternal grandfather was Emerich Joseph, duke of Dalberg, whose family line could be traced without any difficulty to the twelfth century. By the fifteenth century the family had acquired such distinction that whenever the Holy Roman Emperor was crowned, the cry "Is any Dalberg present?" became part of the ceremony. A Dalberg was always present. They were dukes and grand dukes, archchancellors, chamberlains, ambassadors, bishops, and archbishops. Archbishop-Elector Karl Theodor von Dalberg threw in his lot with Napoleon and became Prince-Primate of the Confederation of the Rhine, only to lose the title when Napoleon was overthrown. He was a friend of Goethe and cultivated the friendship of other poets and scholars. The Dalbergs were courtiers and scholars, deeply religious. They took quite seriously a family legend that they were descended from the family of Jesus of Nazareth and were not averse to reminding lesser mortals of their exalted ancestry.

There was no priggishness in John Dalberg-Acton. He was the devoted scholar, more Dalberg than Acton, humble and proud by turns, holding fast to the faith that knowledge and faith were in an eternal partnership and that freedom was as sacred as the church. Hence, although a devout Catholic, he sometimes found himself at odds with the papacy. He had a vast knowledge of church history; there were many popes for whom he had no respect at all; sometimes in his essays he would point accusingly at their errors, their falsehoods, their cynicism and consummate brutality. This did not endear him to the Consistory. In 1870 there was held in Rome the first ecumenical council since the Council of Trent three centuries earlier, and many doctrinal matters, including the infallibility of the pope, were discussed. Acton was appalled by the doctrine of papal infallibility; he was also appalled by the increasingly rigid dogmatism of the church. A new despotism was emerging. The church, having lost its territorial power to the Risorgimento, was determined to build up an iron edifice of dogma as the basis of its spiritual empire, more reactionary in the closing years of the nineteenth century than it had been in the Middle Ages. Heartsick, Acton rebelled. Among the fruits of his rebellion was the determination to write an immense *History of Liberty*. He never wrote it—the subject was too vast even for his comprehensive scholarship—and he spent the rest of his life accumulating books, manuscripts, and notebooks, the source material for the many-volumed history. When he died, his card catalogue with millions of entries was found, but there was not a single written page. He had delayed too long, the details were too absorbing, he was too talkative, too busy, too undisciplined, even to make a beginning.

Rich, gregarious, constantly traveling among his various estates in England, Italy, Bavaria, and on the Riviera, he was an aristocratic amateur, but unlike most aristocrats he possessed a lifelong devotion to the idea of liberty. He detested censorship, intimidation of every kind, all attempts at suppression, all denials of intellectual freedom, regarding them as morally wrong and humanly intolerable. To the end of his life he was troubled by the fact that the church, the fountain of all the revealed knowledge of God, could have instituted something so murderous as the Inquisition.

Earlier historians had shown little interest in morality. Morality, it appeared, was divorced from history. In Acton's mind morality lay at the heart of the historical mystery and could not be wished away. Power, which historians regarded as one of the facts of life, to be treated with indulgence and occasional suspicion, Acton regarded as tainted with evil. "History is not a web woven with innocent hands," he wrote in one of his notebooks. "Among all the causes which degrade and demoralize men, power is the most constant and the most active." All popes, kings, governments were in his view engaged in a miserable game of expediency, beholden to no one, in love with power for power's sake, continually designing laws that tended to degrade and demoralize the people they ruled.

But if power is essentially evil, it is nevertheless necessary, for how otherwise can governments exist? Acton was prepared to face this problem pragmatically, saying in effect that the only permissible power is that which extends and prospers individual liberty. There is no class of people who can be entrusted with power. "The danger is not that a particular class is unfit to govern," he wrote. "Every class is unfit to govern."

There could therefore be no simple solution to the problem. All classes, all political groups, all religious groups, are suspect. Once a class, a political party, or a church has obtained power, it becomes intolerant of the claims of other classes, other political parties, other beliefs. Intolerance waits in the wings and can be kept off the stage only by the diffusion of power among the largest number for the equal security of all. In ancient Athens, under Pericles, such a society had come into existence for the first time. All problems were discussed in open debate; the rich were made safe against envy and the poor against oppression; no one class, no political party, no church predominated. But with the death of Pericles the hopes of a free society were destroyed, tyrants ruled, debate ended, the arbitrary whims of the rulers took the place of the desires of the people, the classes were at each other's throats, and the aristocracy perished in the Peloponnesian War. Was society so weak that it could not sustain the effort to be free? Reluctantly Acton came to see that most of history was merely a record of tyrannies.

The temper of his mind was profoundly pessimistic, but he held fast to the belief that liberty is not a means to a higher political end —it is itself the highest political end. Without it, a man was simply a slave or a tyrant. Both were ignoble and intolerable; both were offensive to human dignity; both were absurdities. There was an overwhelming human need to construct a society where slavery was unthinkable and tyranny impossible. Human justice demanded nothing less than that the slaves should be lifted up and the tyrants cast down.

Such were the beliefs he had held for the greater part of his life. He expressed them in many short essays, regarding them as almost too obvious to argue about. He expressed them trenchantly, without fire, like someone who has grown a little weary of them. Then quite suddenly in the late spring of 1887, in a letter addressed to the historian Mandell Creighton, who was writing a five-volume *History of the Papacy During the Period of the Reformation,* Acton struck out. The third and fourth volumes of the history had fallen into his hands, he had written a review attacking it strongly, and Creighton wrote heatedly asking for an explanation. Acton replied with his famous letter demanding that historians judge the morality of the actions they describe, all the more when it is a question of a pope condemning thousands of innocent people to their deaths. What particularly offended Acton was Creighton's seeming detachment amounting to indifference before all the horrors of the Inquisition:

A man is hanged not because he can or cannot prove his claim to virtues, but because it can be proved that he has committed a particular crime. That one action overshadows the rest of his career. It is useless to argue that he is a good husband or a good poet. The one crime swells out of proportion to the rest. We all agree that Calvin was one of the greatest writers, many think him the best religious teacher, in the world. But that one affair of Servetus outweighs the nine folios, and settles, by itself, the reputation he deserves. So with the mediaeval

Inquisition and the Popes that founded it and worked it. That is the breaking point, the article of their system by which they stand or fall. . . .

What amazes and disables me is that you speak of the Papacy not as exercising a just severity, but as not exercising any severity. You do not say, these misbelievers deserved to fall into the hands of these torturers and Fire-the-faggots; but you ignore, you even deny, at least implicitly, the existence of the torture-chamber and the stake. . . .

You say that people in authority are not to be snubbed or sneezed at from our pinnacle of conscious rectitude. I really don't know whether you exempt them because of their rank, or of their success and power, or of their date. The chronological plea may have some little value in a limited sphere of instances. It does not allow of our saying that such a man did not know right from wrong, unless we are able to say that he lived before Columbus, before Copernicus, and could not know right from wrong. It can scarcely apply to the centre of Christendom, 1500 years after the birth of our Lord. . . .

I cannot accept your canon that we are to judge Pope and King unlike other men, with a favourable presumption that they did no wrong. If there is any presumption it is the other way against holders of power, increasing as the power increases. Historic responsibility has to make up for the want of legal responsibility. Power tends to corrupt and absolute power corrupts absolutely. . . .

Acton's argument had been gradually progressing to this point, which was so final and inescapable. A devout Catholic, he was thinking first about the corrupting power of the papacy, and the image constantly present before his eyes was that of the torture chambers and the fires of the Inquisition, morally so inexcusable that heaven cries out for vengeance. The prose is controlled, but we are aware of a sudden flaring up of consciousness as though only now at last had he come to grips with the central problem of history. The bleak words are his judgment on Catholic history.

But Acton had not yet finished with his concept of power, which seemed to surprise him a little. He had begun the argument by proclaiming that Mandell Creighton was a bad historian because he glossed over the vices of the popes, and ended by discovering that the popes in their use of their absolute power were criminals. So were many other people whom historians regard affectionately. His letter continues:

Great men are almost always bad men, even when they exercise influence and not authority: still more when you superadd the tendency or the certainty of corruption by authority. There is no worse heresy than that the office sanctifies the holder of it. That is the point at which the negation of Catholicism and the negation of Liberalism meet and keep high festival, and the end learns to justify the means. You would hang a man of no position, like Ravaillac; but if what one hears is true, then Elizabeth asked the gaoler to murder Mary, and William III ordered his Scots minister to extirpate a clan. Here are the greater names coupled with the greater crimes. You would spare these criminals, for some mysterious reason. I would hang them, higher than Haman, for reasons of quite obvious justice; still more, still higher, for the sake of historical science.

Acton objected to the two standards of morality—one applied to great historical figures and the other to lesser mortals who were judged according to higher standards. All is forgiven to kings and popes. History grants them immunity, even a full pardon, even when they admit their crimes and glory in them. But history is written by historians who, when they grant immunity and pardon to great criminals, become accessories to their crimes. Elsewhere in his letter to Creighton, Acton reinforces the argument by an appeal to ordinary common sense. "What I said is not in any way mysterious or esoteric," he wrote. "It appeals to no hidden code. It aims at no secret moral. It supposes nothing and implies nothing but what is universally current and familiar. It is the common, even the vulgar code, I appeal to."

The case against historians who gloss over the crimes of kings and popes—or, as they do more frequently, praise them for committing acts for which common men would be damned—is put with force and conviction, but it is not completely proved. Acton assumes that there is only one morality, but he points out that kings and popes have always insisted that morality does not apply to them, that they are above the law, that they have the power to grant pardons and therefore may be assumed to have the power to pardon themselves. Custom and tradition have exalted them above ordinary mortals. Why, then, should they be judged like ordinary mortals?

Acton answers in effect that there is no way out. If there are two standards of judgment, then history is a game played according to two sets of rules, which are not complementary but at odds with one another. The historian, too, becomes corrupted by power, not that he wields any power, but that he becomes the slave of the powerful, an ignominious panderer, a man of straw. And just as previously Acton had stated his ultimate conclusions on the nature of power, so he stated his ultimate conclusion on the nature of history:

The inflexible integrity of the moral code is, to me, the secret of the authority, the dignity, the utility of history. If we may debase the currency for the sake of genius, or success, or rank, or reputation, we may debase it for the sake of a man's influence, of his religion, of his party, of the good cause which prospers by his credit and suffers by his disgrace. Then history ceases to be a science, an arbiter of controversy, a guide of the wanderer, the upholder of that moral standard which the powers of earth, and religion itself, tend constantly to depress. It serves where it ought to reign; and serves the worst cause better than the purest.

Acton was speaking violently about a violent subject—murder, which he considered a mortal sin. He was also speaking about the corruption of historians who excuse sinners of high rank, and this too he regarded as a sin, perhaps a mortal one. The distortions and lies practiced by scholars, whether consciously or unconsciously, made him heartsick. He could think of no conceivable reason why murder in the form of the Inquisition should have been permitted and encouraged by the church, which had taken as its motto *Ecclesia abhorret a sanguine* (The church abhors bloodletting). The fact that the Inquisitors did not themselves set fire to the faggots but instead surrendered their victims to civil magistrates with a sanctimonious formula—"We abandon thee to the secular arm, beseeching it affectionately, as Canon Law requires, that the sentence of the civil judges may spare you death or mutilation," only aroused him to further indignation. The "affectionate" address to the civil magistrates, if taken literally, could mean only that the victim was not to be put to death; the civil magistrates understood the words in a contrary sense. Everything attending a sentence of death is full of ambiguities, but this was the ultimate ambiguity: HE MUST NOT BE PUT TO DEATH = KILL HIM.

From such ambiguities comes the corruption of all moral values and of the intelligence. The Inquisitors were not only murderers; they were also liars, hypocrites, bearers of false witness. They were committing crimes far more heinous than those committed by their victims. The responsibility lay with the church. In a letter to Mary Gladstone, Acton drew up a balance sheet. The church had helped the poor, protected marriage, abolished slavery and human sacrifice, and prevented war. All this was to the profit and advantage of the people. But against this must be set the crimes committed by the church toward unbelievers and heretics. "Here her responsibility is more undivided; her initiative and achievement more complete." The church was guilty of abominable crimes.

In Acton's view the church was guilty of deliberately concealing its crimes and employing its most masterful propagandists to obliterate traces of the crimes or to drown them in holy water. He cites as an example Saint Charles Borromeo:

> He occupied the highest stations, with success and honour; he is held in high, in enthusiastic reverence by the most intelligent Catholics, by converts, by men who, in their time, have drunk in the convictions, haply the prejudices, of Protestant England; the Church that holds him up as a mirror of sanctity stands and falls with his good name; thousands of devout men and women would be wounded and pained if you call him an infamous assassin.

Yet Acton had no difficulty proving that Charles Borromeo *was* an assassin, for the church had never denied the authenticity of a letter written by him urging the assassination of Protestants and adding that he hoped the murderers would be remunerated. Many similar letters were written from the papal chancery. What was surprising was to discover the signature of a man who was later canonized and offered the most extraordinary marks of respect and devotion:

> The writer of that letter lies in the most splendid mausoleum that exists on earth; he has been canonized by the lawful, the grateful, the congenial authority of Rome; his statue, in the attitude of blessing, looks down from the Alps on the plain of Lombardy; his likeness is in our churches; his name is upon our altars; his works are in our schools.

Confronted by the immorality of the church, Acton confessed himself a devout Catholic who detested every immoral act committed by the church, and therefore a Catholic with reservations. It was an untenable position, but he held to it. In an anguish of tortured idealism he wrote in one of his notebooks: "They sent forth murderers. They doomed to hell as they believed by the power of the keys all who interfered with the murder. They canonized the assassins. All this on a larger scale, longer and more effectively than the old man of the mountain."

Inevitably Acton suffered a crisis of conscience. He felt completely isolated and useless. What was the use of writing history when the powerful had already subverted history to their own ends? They made their own history, elaborated their own excuses, exonerated their own criminals, and artificially created their own reputations. They bent historians to their own wills and thought nothing of it. These were not small matters, and he raged against them with unconcealed horror. To the long letter to Mandell Creighton in which he outlined his views on the corruptions of power and the historian's duty to report corruption when he sees it, Acton added thirty-five brief apothegms intended as a corrective, or a medicine, to the historian who finds himself swayed by the powerful. His apothegms are still valuable today, particularly these:

A Historian has to fight against temptations special to his mode of life, temptations from Country, Class, Church, College, Party, authority of talents, solicitation of friends.

The most respectable of these influences is the most dangerous.

The historian who neglects to root them out is exactly like a juror who votes according to his personal likes or dislikes.

In judging men and things, Ethics go before Dogma, Politics or Nationality.

Put Conscience above both System and Success.

History provides neither compensation for suffering nor penalties for wrong.

The Reign of Sin is more universal, the influence of unconscious error is less, than historians tell us. Good and evil lie close together. Seek no artistic unity in character.

A good cause proves less in a man's favour than a bad cause against him.

The final judgment depends on the worst action.

Character is tested by true sentiments more than by conduct. A man is seldom better than his word.

History is better written from letters than from histories: let a man criminate himself.

No public character has ever stood the revelation of private utterance and correspondence.

In public life, the domain of History, vice is less than crime.

Active, transitive sins count for more than others.

The greatest crime is Homicide.

The accomplice is no better than the assassin; the theorist is worse.

Faith must be sincere. When defended by sin it is not sincere; theologically, it is not Faith. God's grace does not operate by sin.

Transpose the nominative and the accusative and see how things look.

Crimes by constituted authorities are worse than crimes by Madame Tussaud's private malefactors. Murder may be done by legal means, by plausible and profitable war, by calumny, as well as by dose or dagger.

Acton's letter to Mandell Creighton remains the *locus classicus* for the nineteenth-century study of corruption. He isolated the virus, identified it, and discovered that it was much more dangerous, more prevalent, and more infectious than anyone had suspected. If "Power tends to corrupt and absolute power corrupts absolutely" represents his central discovery, he also made many minor discoveries and hammered out in the thirty-five apothegms a credo worthy of the historian's art. Never again did he write with so much penetration and power.

When Acton began writing his famous letter, in the late spring of 1887, he was on holiday in the south of France, at Cannes. By strange chance there was living nearby a man who was to have a far greater influence on European history than Acton and whose ideas were directly contrary to his: Friedrich Wilhelm Nietzsche. Acton celebrated freedom; Nietzsche celebrated tyranny; and neither could conceivably have understood the other. At this time Nietzsche was writing the scattered notes that, when collected, would bear the title *The Will to Power*. He was a sick man, poor, dispirited, little known outside a small circle of friends. He was living on a small pension granted to him by the University of Basel, and he was already showing signs of the madness that would soon take complete possession of him. He sang the praises of the Superman, hard, murderous, totally immoral, his sharpened senses capable of exulting in his triumph over the mob, riding roughshod over two thousand years of Christian prejudice, and hammering into shape a new world of conquerors and slaves. *The Will to Power* is an astonishingly vengeful book. Nietzsche's hatreds spill over, and most of all he hated the bourgeois Christian liberalism of his time. Acton wrote, "The accomplice is no better than the assassin; the theorist is worse." Nietzsche offered himself as the theorist for the new assassins who would take over the world.

Against Acton's apothegms can be set the opposing apothegms of Nietzsche in praise of all the things Acton detested:

> The corrupt ruling classes have ruined the image of the ruler. The "state" as a court of law is a piece of cowardice, because the great human being is lacking to provide a standard of measurement. Finally, the sense of insecurity grows so great that men cower in the dust before *any* forceful will that commands. N.B. *Scorn* for the kings who have only the virtues of petty virtuous people.
>
> We resist the idea that all great human beings have been criminals (only in the grand and not in the miserable manner), that crime belongs to greatness (—for that is the experience of those who have at-

tempted to command and of all those who have *descended* deepest into great souls).

The democratization of Europe is at the same time an involuntary preparation for the rearing of tyrants—taking the word in all its meanings, even in its most spiritual sense.

One has no right to existence or to work, to say nothing of a right to "happiness." The individual human being is in precisely the same case as the lowest worm.

We must think of the masses as unsentimentally as we think of nature: they preserve the species.

To look upon the distress of the masses with an ironic melancholy: they want something we are capable of—ah!

Workers should learn to feel like soldiers. An honorarium, an income, but no pay!

Absolute commands; terrible means of compulsion; thus tearing the workers away from an easy life. The others must *obey,* and their vanity demands that they appear to be dependent, not on great men, but on "principles."

So Nietzsche goes on to describe the new world composed of "sovereign individuals who resemble only themselves" and "the others," who are bonded into perpetual slavery. The vision was prophetic, for both the Communists and the National Socialists created political systems where "the others" were enslaved and the Supermen strode high above the categorical imperatives of morality. These heartless apothegms, thrown off like machine-gun bullets, have no philosophical basis; they are incitements to action, and they had a profound effect on Hitler, who saw himself as the destined Superman who would preside over all lesser mortals. This was a position Nietzsche had previously selected for himself, for there was found among his manuscripts a piece of paper with the words "Since the old God has been abolished, I am prepared to rule the world." More prophetically he wrote in *Ecce Homo:* "I know my fate. One day my name will be associated with something tremendous—a crisis without equal on earth, the most profound collision of conscience, a decision that was conjured up *against* everything that had been believed, demanded, hallowed so far. I am no man. I am dynamite."

What is obvious is that Nietzsche had little understanding of the human condition and no respect for humankind. If Man = Worm, then tyranny is no doubt a useful method of government. But if Man = Worm is a total falsehood, then the elaborate systems of tyranny have no meaning, the argument on behalf of the Superman collapses, and "the sovereign individual who resembles only himself" becomes a myth.

But even though he spoke like a raving paranoid, Nietzsche sometimes helps us to see how the errors of fascism and bolshevism came about. He lived in a decadent age and had some singularly apposite things to say about the corruption of his time. He wrote in the early pages of *The Will to Power* a kind of critique of European corruption:

> Skepticism is a consequence of decadence.
>
> The corruption of morals is a consequence of decadence (weakness of the will, need for strong stimuli).
>
> Attempted cures, psychological and moral, do not change the course of decadence, do not arrest it, are physiologically *zero*.
>
> Nihilism is not the cause but merely the logical result of decadence.
>
> In the belief that we are choosing a remedy, we choose something that hastens exhaustion. Christianity is an example (to name the greatest example of such an aberration of the instincts), and "progress" is another.
>
> The supposed causes of decadence are its consequences.
>
> *The state of corruption.* To understand how all forms of corruption belong together without forgetting Christian corruption (Pascal, for example) as well as socialist-communist corruption (which derives from the Christian—from the point of view of the natural sciences, the socialists' conception of the highest society is the lowest in order of rank). Also the corruption "that lies beyond," as if outside the real world, the world of becoming, there was another world of being.

With the corruption "that lies beyond" Nietzsche announced one of his most staggering inventions, for he was hinting at the existence of corruption in the absolute and ideal world of being. The idea occupied him for only a moment and then he abandoned it forever, for other and more important ideas attracted him. He enjoyed turning everything upside down. Starting with the assumption that Christianity is evil, progress deplorable, and nihilism inevitable, he turned the tables on the modern age by insisting that the perfection of politics is represented by Machiavellianism, which is not completely attainable. He wrote in *The Will to Power*, "Machiavellianism *pur, sans mélange, cru, vert, dans toute sa force, dans toute son âpreté,* is superhuman, divine, transcendental, it will never be achieved by man, at most approximated." Then at last he offered some consolation to the poor slaves who were destined to live under the jackboots of the Supermen.

Acton was deeply concerned with morality; Nietzsche threw morality out of the window. "Moralists," Nietzsche declared, "should display the gestures of virtue, but never submit to virtue. A great moralist should be a great actor." That, according to Acton, was the trouble with the rulers of this world. They acted out the appearance of virtue and went on killing.

Nietzsche's accomplishment is that he permits us to see corruption *from the inside*. Wholly corrupt, he accused all other philosophers of corruption. Even Socrates was condemned because he suffered from the disease of moralizing, and Pascal because he corrupted reason. Nietzsche condemned pitilessly, exulting in his cruelties. After reading his works one has the curious impression of having wandered through a tropical forest where the air is stagnant, where the jungle weed is choking the roots of the trees and heavy creepers weigh down the branches, while here and there in the gathering darkness strange, brilliantly colored orchids are gleaming. Yet this madman sometimes possessed a penetrating insight, and he possessed a terrifying gift of prophecy.

Dostoyevsky, too, possessed the gift of prophecy. Like Nietzsche he saw the coming of the Caesars. "We shall triumph and shall be Caesars, and then we shall plan the universal happiness of man," says the aged Grand Inquisitor to Christ in the story told by Ivan Karamazov in *The Brothers Karamazov*. The story, told with consummate power, shows Christ, robed in the utmost purity, confronting the Grand Inquisitor, who is corruption incarnate.

The Legend of the Grand Inquisitor is an allegory set in Seville in the sixteenth century at the height of the Inquisition. Day after day the people come to witness the heretics being burned in the presence of the Cardinal-Inquisitor, the king, the court, the knights, the most charming ladies of the court, and the entire population of Seville. Then Christ appears, moving silently among the crowds, and on the steps of Seville cathedral he raises a dead girl lying in a small white open coffin. Immediately there is confusion, the people sobbing and crying, and at that moment the Cardinal-Inquisitor arrives on the scene, tall and gaunt, with a withered face and sunken eyes, wearing the coarse cassock of a monk rather than the scarlet robes of a cardinal. The Cardinal-Inquisitor orders the arrest of Christ, who is led away to one of the dungeons of the Inquisition. That night Christ is confronted by his accuser in a dark prison cell.

There follows a long exchange between Christ and the accuser which is one of the most extraordinary dialogues ever written, all the more extraordinary because Christ says nothing at all. Yet, as Dostoyevsky describes the scene, Christ's silence accuses the accuser at every turn. His unspoken words possess great force, not so much denying the claims of the Cardinal-Inquisitor as denying any real existence to him and the powers he represents. Meanwhile the Cardinal-Inquisitor threatens to have Christ burned at the stake and puts forward a massive argument in favor of tyranny against the freedom Christ promised to the world. It is not freedom that men want. They want bread, protection, hope in their earthly future, for they are all weak and pitiable creatures. The Cardinal-Inquisitor presents himself as the provider of all their needs, guarding and superintending their lives in the name of Christ, well aware that he is using Christ's name falsely. He says:

We alone shall feed them in Thy name, declaring falsely that it is in Thy name. Oh, never, never, can they feed themselves without us! No science will give them bread so long as they remain free. In the end they will lay their freedom at our feet, and say to us, "Make us your slaves, but feed us!" They will understand themselves, at last, that freedom and bread enough for all are inconceivable together, for never, never will they be able to share between them! They will be convinced, too, that they can never be free, for they are weak, vicious, worthless and rebellious. Thou didst promise them the bread of Heaven, but, I repeat again, can it compare with earthly bread in the eyes of the weak, ever sinful and ignoble race of man?

And if for the sake of heavenly bread thousands and tens of thousands follow Thee, what is to become of the millions and tens of thousands of millions of creatures who will not have the strength to forego the earthly bread for the sake of the heavenly? Or dost Thou care only for the tens of thousands of the great and strong, while the millions, numerous as the sands of the sea, who are weak but love Thee, must exist only for the sake of the great and strong? No, we care for the weak too. They are sinful and rebellious, but in the end they too will become obedient. They will marvel at us and look on us as gods, because we are ready to endure the freedom which they have found so dreadful and to rule over them—so awful it would seem to them to be free. But we shall tell them that we are Thy servants and rule over them in Thy name. We shall deceive them again, for we will let Thee come to us again. The deception will be our suffering, for we shall be forced to lie.

As the Cardinal-Inquisitor speaks, it becomes increasingly clear that he has not been forced to lie, that indeed his entire attitude toward the people is one of the utmost contempt and he has deliberately chosen the path he is following against all the other choices he could have made. When he says, "The deception will be our suffering," he is merely presenting a lawyer's brief for damages sustained in the course of duty. There is no suffering, only exultation and self-admiration. He has set out to win the world, to corrupt it, to ensure the willing obedience of multitudes of slaves by assuming the burdens that are rightfully theirs. The anxiety and agony of making their own free choices are removed from them. They are free to be happy, and "only we, we who guard the mystery, shall be unhappy." But the Cardinal-Inquisitor bears the burden of his unhappiness lightly. The dictator has emerged in the darkness of the prison cell.

Christ rejects the dictator's claim, but he rejects it silently, for there are no words which have power to convince the dictator that he is wrong, that he is embarking on a course that is fatal both to him and to the people who accept his authority or are tricked into accepting it. Christ answers by being Christ. The Cardinal-Inquisitor yearns desperately for an answer, however bitter, however terrible. Instead Christ silently approaches him and kisses him on his bloodless, aged lips, and the old man goes to the prison door and says: "Go, and come no more. Come not at all, never, never!" And then Christ walks away through the dark alleyways of Seville, having spoken not a single word, made no promises, offered no rebukes. The silence is deafening. Christ, wandering away into the darkness, is all the more present, all the more the figure who consoles men in their sorrows and answers their prayers.

The Cardinal-Inquisitor, presenting himself as a kind of angel of pity who willingly assumes the terrible burdens imposed on mankind, is not an altogether convincing advocate. He is too self-regarding, too proud, too satanic, as he acts out the role he has given himself. Dostoyevsky gives him the best lines, but they are best only because Christ is silent. He is Nietzsche's Superman robed with the authority of the church.

In his *Notes from Underground,* which should more accurately be called *Notes from Under the Floorboards,* Dostoyevsky depicts the man "who could not even become an insect," full of spite and self-loathing, living in a single miserable room which in his eyes is no better and no worse than a moldy corner under the floorboards where mice and insects live. He rages against the world, but without passion. He rages out of boredom and ill temper. It annoys him that $2 + 2 = 4$. He is acutely conscious that he has nothing to live for, and concludes quite logically that he can at least derive some enjoyment from his own degradation. Even if something better were offered, even if the whole world turned into an exciting pleasure garden, he would be too bored to make the effort to wander into it. He is one more, and perhaps the nastiest, of those "superfluous men" who were minutely studied by the Russian novelists of the nineteenth century. He is not so much corrupt or corrupted as a focus of corruption, a sore that has been repeatedly scratched, a wound that will never heal, surrounded by maggots. "We are oppressed at being men," he complains. "We are stillborn, and for generations have not been begotten." This is not quite true, for in his desultory fashion he runs after prostitutes and delivers moral lectures about the higher life that awaits them when they have abandoned prostitution. He rages at the materialism represented by the Crystal Palace, which he has recently seen in London: science will ennoble our lives, all things will be arranged scientifically, methodically, according to the latest inventions; and he believes none of it. The Crystal Palace is merely an anthill that someone will one day stamp out with his boots. Just as he repudiates science, socialism, and the hideous boredom of industrial society, so he repudiates the whole world. "The whole world can perish," he announces, "as long as I can have my cup of tea."

But there remains a lingering hope that all these boring horrors, all this corruption of life, will give way at last to a new, fresh, innocent life of faith. While writing the book Dostoyevsky wrote in his diary:

> The teaching of materialism—universal corruption and mechanical science mean death.
> The teaching of history and philosophy—the annihilation of corruption leads to God and eternal life.

Again and again Dostoyevsky returned to the theme of the boredom and corruption of the present age and the pure, unsullied life that seems to be so near and so far away. In a story called "The Dream of a Ridiculous Man," written toward the end of his life, he describes a man very much like the hero of *Notes from Underground* who is so bored with life that he buys a revolver in the hope that he will have the courage to blow his brains out. One night, when returning home, he is accosted by an eight-year-old girl who is dreadfully frightened and needs help. He rejects her and she runs madly across the street in search of someone else who will help her. But when he reaches his lodging, he is filled with a sense of guilt, places the revolver on the table and once more thinks of shooting himself. Instead he falls asleep and has a strange dream.

He dreams that he has shot himself and been buried and is somehow wafted out of his coffin and led across the infinite spaces of a dark night to another earth, in appearance exactly like the one he has just left but inhabited by people living in a Golden Age. The scene reminds him of an island in the Greek archipelago. The people are calm and gentle, know no sin, possess no creed or church, hold their children in common, cherish wisdom rather than knowledge, and feel very close to flowers, animals, and the stars. They like singing songs about one another and praise each other like children. They have no fear of death, for all live to an old age and their deaths are like falling asleep. They believe in the immortality of the soul and are sure that after death they will live in a greater communion with the universe. They never weep, for they know no sorrow.

These happy, laughing creatures welcome the stranger in their midst, sing songs for him, caress him, teach him their wisdom, allow him to move freely among them. The time comes when he begins to corrupt them, for he is still a nihilist. "Like a vile trichina, like a germ of a plague infecting whole kingdoms, I contaminated all this earth, so happy and sinless before my coming." The people learn to lie and become addicted to cruel sensuality and jealousy, which leads to the first murder. They form political parties, become criminals, invent justice, introduce social programs, and set up a guillotine. They remember the Golden Age only as a dream, as something that happened to them in a legendary past, and they make an idol of it, set up temples and worship it, and fight over it. Saints who come to warn them against the false and evil things they are doing are pelted with stones. Slavery emerges; the weak submit to the strong, on condition that the strong help them subdue those who are weaker still. There arises a group of men who believe that even now it might be possible to bring about peace in this bitterly quarrelsome community. Wars break out, and both sides contend that they are aiming toward a harmonious and rational society. To hasten things, "the wise" exterminate those who are "unwise." Proud men, who demand all or nothing, bring about intolerable suffering, and strange cults emerge, calling on men to destroy themselves "for the sake of the everlasting peace of annihilation."

Meanwhile, the man who has brought about these evils characteristically finds himself both exultant and contrite, exultant because the sight of suffering gives him pleasure and contrite because he is aware that he is responsible for their suffering, because he has brought corruption, pollution, and falsehood among them. "I, I alone, have done this!" he exclaims, exulting in the earth men have polluted more than in the paradise they had once lived in. To atone for his sins, he begs them to raise a cross and crucify him on it, but they only laugh at him for his folly and threaten to put him in a madhouse if he persists in making a nuisance of himself. They tell him he has committed no crimes; he is not responsible; everything is happening as they wanted it to happen. He thinks of killing himself but lacks the strength. He wants them to lay violent hands on him, but they treat him with indifference. He rages against them for being his willing victims, for having left their paradise to build an absolutely corrupt society. And at this point he wakes up.

"The Dream of a Ridiculous Man" is perhaps an allegory but it is also a prophecy. The dream was to come true much sooner than anyone expected. At first in Russia, then in Germany, there came into existence societies more corrupt than any that had existed in the world before. In the Communist and Nazi labor camps absolute corruption appeared for the first time, demonstrating that there is no limit to men's power to degrade, humiliate, and murder their fellow men. Less than forty years after Dostoyevsky's death the age of the great corrupters began.

The Coming of
the Dark Ages

Absolute Corruption, Phase I: Soviet Labor Camps

I n the Lenin Library in Moscow there are some letters written by Lenin to his mother addressed to "Her Excellency Maria Ulyanova." She was the widow of an aristocrat who had been the director of schools in an entire province and had been raised by order of the tsar into the lower orders of the nobility. Lenin was well aware that he had inherited this lesser patent of nobility, and when it was proposed at a meeting of the Central Committee after the revolution that all aristocrats should be liquidated, he turned to the other members of the committee and said: "Hm, hm, we really can't do that. Kamenev, too, has some kind of rank in the orders of nobility. We'll have to change that a little." The Central Committee thereupon issued an order that all aristocrats, except those performing important services to the state, should be liquidated.

To the end of his life Lenin acted like an aristocrat. He had an aristocratic temper, an aristocrat's disdain for lesser mortals, their lives and property. He even talked like an aristocrat, slurring his *r*'s and lisping a little. He was aware of his intellectual superiority to everyone else. Small, stocky, red-bearded, with a mind as pene-trating as a recoilless rifle, he dominated everyone he encountered with ruthless efficiency. He had a ferocious temper, which he kept in check, and his large brown eyes sometimes appeared to give off electric sparks. Trotsky, who was very close to him, spoke of the melting look in his eyes when he was deeply moved or when he was with someone he genuinely liked; at such times his eyes shone with a love light. He was a profoundly complex man, as one might expect from his mixed ancestry. He was part Russian, part German, part Swedish, and part Chuvash, a race of Turkic tribesmen living on the banks of the Volga. It was an inflammable mixture, and he set Russia on fire.

In the early fall of 1917, when Lenin was hiding in the Finnish marshes after the failure of his first attempt to take power, he wrote a short book called *State and Revolution,* which he intended as a blueprint for the destruction of the tsarist state and the birth of the new communist state. It is a book that one reads today with incom-prehension and bewilderment, for it reduces all problems to their ultimate simplicities. Lenin believed he possessed a great gift for ex-pressing the heart of a problem, and he certainly possessed the gift of trenchant statement. In a letter to Gorky he wrote: "Any religious idea, any flirtation with a deity is an inexpressible abomination. Any deity is stupidity." In this way he resolved all theological problems.

In *State and Revolution* he solves political problems with the same ease. The existing state will be utterly overthrown, and there will follow "a state that is democratic *in a new way* (for the prole-tariat and the poor in general) and dictatorial *in a new way* (against the bourgeoisie)." Lenin does not work out any consistent program. The only light he throws on the form the new revolutionary govern-ment will take is given in a passage where he speaks of control and accounting:

> In order to abolish the state, it is necessary to convert the functions of the public service into such simple operations of control and ac-counting which are well within the capacity and ability of the vast majority of the population, and ultimately of every single individual.

The Chinese philosopher Lao-tzu believed that government should become "as simple as cooking little fishes." Lenin appears to have believed that it would become as simple as running a post office. He was one of those "great simplifiers" whose existence in the twentieth century had been prophesied by the nineteenth-century historian Jacob Burckhardt.

"Control and accounting" inevitably involve bureaucracy, and bureaucracy is never a simple operation. Lenin himself detested bureaucracy. He told Klara Zetkin, "I hate bureaucracy heartily; it paralyzes and corrupts from above and from below." Nevertheless, he came to accept the existence of a totalitarian bureaucracy that would control the lives of the Russian people in a manner more far-reaching, more corrupt, and more deadly than in any other country on earth. In *State and Revolution* he spoke, too, of the excesses that might perhaps be committed during the revolution, excesses some people might want to suppress. Lenin saw no need for suppressing these excesses, because the armed people themselves would put an end to them "as simply and readily as any crowd of civilized people, even in modern society, interferes to put a stop to a street fight or to prevent a woman from being outraged." For Lenin there were no problems. Everything would be done "simply and readily."

When Lenin came to power, he learned that nothing was simple. To survive in power he had to build up a bureaucracy, a secret police, and an army loyal to him. Instead of the dictatorship of the proletariat there was the dictatorship of one man, Lenin, who ruled as though the people were the enemy to be suppressed, rooted out, executed. The excesses were not put down by a crowd of civilized people but were encouraged by Lenin himself. In an article called "How to Organize the Opposition," written in the first week of January 1918, he proclaimed his unyielding purpose: "to purge the Russian land of all kinds of insects." By *insects* he did not mean the royal family, the aristocrats, the rich landowners, the army officers fighting against him. He meant all those who did not jump immediately to his orders, malingerers in the print shops, Bolsheviks who made errors of judgment, farmers who did not bring in supplies quickly enough, anyone he suspected, rightly or wrongly, of not being in complete sympathy with him. Lenin was determined to crush the enemy, and the enemy was everywhere.

In *State and Revolution,* his blueprint for the coming upheaval, Lenin twice cites with approval the dictum of Engels: "The proletariat needs the state, not in the interests of freedom, but in the interests of the repression of its opponents, and when it becomes possible to speak of freedom, the state as such ceases to exist." In his eyes "the state" and "freedom" were a contradiction in terms. The ultimate state, the state in which "it becomes possible to speak of freedom," had no existence. Thus in all the foreseeable future the state was to remain an instrument of repression against whatever enemies the proletarian government sought to destroy. A few days after the October Revolution Lenin called on the workers to "take all the affairs of state into your own hands." It was a strange speech, for never for a moment did he relax his hold on all the affairs of state.

Lenin became just one more of the many dictators who have come to power with the determination to exploit their power to the uttermost, wherever it leads them. Maxim Gorky, who knew him well, was appalled by the prospects confronting Russia, and in the liberal newspaper *Novaya Zhizn* he openly attacked Lenin for his destructive fanaticism. Without mentioning Lenin by name he portrayed a revolutionary leader who could be no one else:

> He thinks he is completely emancipated, but inside he is chained by the heavy conservatism of zoological instincts, fathered by a thick mesh of petty grudges, which he has no power to rise above. The habits of his thought drive him to seek in life and in man above all the negative phenomena; in the depths of his soul he is full of contempt for man, on whose behalf he suffered once or a hundred times, but who has himself suffered too much to notice or appreciate the torment of another. . . . He has toward people the attitude that an untalented scientist has toward the dogs and frogs picked for cruel scientific experiments, with the difference that the untalented scientist, though uselessly tormenting the animals, does it in the interests of man, while the revolutionary during this time is not consistently sincere in his experiments on people. People for him are simply objects, the more suitable the less exalted they are. . . . He is a cold fanatic, an ascetic; he emasculates the creative force of the revolutionary idea.

It is a cruel portrait, but a truthful one; and though Gorky subsequently made his peace with Lenin he never completely came to terms with the Bolshevik Revolution. What alarmed him was precisely the Bolshevik attitude toward freedom. In the same newspaper shortly after the revolution he wrote fearlessly, "Lenin, Trotsky, and their collaborators have already been fouled with the rotten poison of power, as is witnessed by their shameful attitude toward freedom of expression and freedom from arrest and toward the whole sum of those rights for the triumph of which democrats have fought."

Lenin was a profoundly complex person, but in his innermost heart there was an ice-cold core. "The bitter lesson: to regard all persons without sentiment, to keep a stone in one's sling," he wrote after an early defeat. Thereafter he continued to regard all persons without sentiment, as though they were merely figures in a ledger.

When he arrived in Petrograd in 1917, having traveled from Switzerland in a sealed train provided by Kaiser Wilhelm II, and possessing ample funds provided by the German government, Lenin proposed to launch a communist revolution that he hoped would quickly engulf the whole world. He envisaged a very sudden revolution: the capture of the government, which in those days ruled from Petrograd. He did not pause to ask whether the long-suffering Russian public wanted to be ruled by him. He proposed to act suddenly, ruthlessly, at the moment when the existing revolutionary government was weakest. The tsarist regime had been overthrown long before Lenin arrived from Switzerland; he envisaged a second revolution—short, sharp, and brutal, sweeping away all the members of the government who were not Bolshevik or Bolshevik sympathizers. His revolution would therefore be the second revolution to confront a war-weary people exhausted by food shortages and all the inevitable dislocations following the February Revolution. This time he promised himself there would be a real revolution, final and absolute.

Karl Radek, who was one of Lenin's closest associates, tells the story of how he was walking along the Nevsky Prospekt, the main street in Petrograd, shortly before the October Revolution, and found himself looking at the magnificent shops, the banks, the insurance companies, the palaces of the nobility, and it occurred to him that in a few days they would no longer serve their original purposes, for the Bolsheviks would simply expropriate them. All the old familiar ways of life would vanish. It seemed to Radek, as he watched the people hurrying along the street, that there was something dreamlike in the scene, a strange sense of the evanescence of all things overcame him, and for a long time he reflected on the vanity of human hopes. How absurd that they should be going about their affairs as though nothing would ever happen to them! Soon the huge black hammer would descend on them, and they would be running about helplessly like ants when an anthill is overturned, not knowing where to go or what to do or whether their lives still possessed a meaning.

There is no record that Lenin ever had any qualms about seizing power. He did not concern himself with the fact that the revolution must by its very nature destroy whole classes of people and must inevitably bring about large-scale famine and civil war. He saw himself as a man who would take command of the ledger, rearrange the double-entry bookkeeping, cancel many figures, and arrive at a suitable sum total. "The simple operations of control and accounting which are well within the capacity and ability of the vast majority of the population" would of themselves bring about the socialist state. When he declared, "We shall now proceed to construct the socialist order," he was placing himself in the position of Dostoyevsky's Grand Inquisitor, who said, "We shall triumph and shall be Caesars, and then we shall plan the universal happiness of man." He had already triumphed and he was already Caesar.

At this time the Bolshevik Party consisted of about 25,000 members, largely recruited from the industrial district of Vyborg: sailors, railroadmen, and a small nucleus of intellectuals of whom the most powerful and influential after Lenin were the now forgotten Alexey Rykov, who was immediately appointed People's Commissar for Internal Affairs, and Lev Bronstein (Trotsky), who had recently returned to Russia from a long exile in the United States. The real strength of the party lay with the army, which was disaffected and demoralized by the defeats of the late summer. Lenin had seized the Winter Palace, arrested most of the members of the government, and established his own government. To consolidate his position, he ordered an election, and out of nearly 40 million votes cast, the Bolsheviks received 9,562,358 and the Social Revolutionary Party received 17,490,837. The Bolsheviks were decisively defeated in the only free election held in Russian history. Lenin remained in power. The votes of the electors were a matter of indifference to him.

On November 23, 1917, two days before the elections, Gorky wrote in *Novaya Zhizn* an appeal to the working class not to vote for the Bolsheviks. This time he mentioned Lenin by name, calling him "a Russian aristocrat who has many of the moral traits of that decayed class" and charging that he was about to impose on the Russian people "a cruel experiment which is doomed to failure from the beginning." Gorky's verdict was a bitter and brutal one: Lenin was totally incompetent and risked dragging Russia into the depths. Nothing was to be gained by entrusting the state to his hands.

From the moment when he lost the election Lenin decided upon a ruthless policy of oppression. The Cheka, the Extraordinary Commission for the Suppression of the Counterrevolution, was instituted with Felix Dzerzhinsky, a Polish revolutionary of aristocratic origin, at the head. At the beginning most of the agents of the Cheka were Latvians who had no hesitation in arresting, torturing, and killing Russians. Lenin made it clear that he was determined to wipe out all classes except the peasants and workers. The monarchists and the aristocracy were rounded up; the professional classes were left in a kind of limbo, some to be killed, others to be kept alive because they would be useful to the revolution; the rich merchants and the bourgeoisie were to be eliminated; and members of other political parties were arrested as counterrevolutionaries. Dzerzhinsky operated on the principle that his task was to inspire mortal fear everywhere, and there was no better instrument for inspiring fear than mass arrests and executions. When Gorky attempted to intercede for the intellectuals on the grounds that the country needed their brains, Lenin answered, "In actual fact, they are not the nation's brains, but shit!" It was on this level of rage and vindictiveness that Lenin made his judgments about who should or should not be arrested and put to death.

Although Lenin had no clear understanding of the kind of state he proposed to inflict on Russia and spent comparatively little time thinking about the nature of the state once he was in power, he had a very clear understanding about his enemies—who they were, and what should be done to them. They included the entire body of the Social Revolutionaries, the largest revolutionary party in Russia, and everyone who was remotely connected with the revolutionary provisional government that was in power between February and October 1917. Dzerzhinsky's chief assistant was Yakov Peters, a Latvian, who was impatient with investigations and trials and who enjoyed shooting his victims in the nape of the neck. Already, within the first two months of the revolution, the Cheka had become a state within a state, lawless, imperious, inventing its own rules which were constantly changing, and enjoying the continuous benediction of Lenin. Thus there began the long reign of the Bolshevik terror which has continued without interruption to the present day.

Lenin's fame as the founder of the first Communist state has obscured his responsibility for the continuing terror. He founded it, ordered it, justified it, saw that it was properly financed, and defended Dzerzhinsky from all attacks, for there were some Bolsheviks who thought the Cheka was transforming the revolution into a mercilessly efficient punitive organization that might soon start devouring Bolsheviks. Under Lenin, the largest of the Solovetsky Islands, famous for their ancient monasteries, was transformed into a concentration camp. The island lies in the far north beyond the Arctic Circle, and in the first winter half the prisoners froze to death. Yakov Peters organized execution squads that roamed the country. The war fought by the Soviet government against the Russian people had begun.

On August 30, 1918, Moisey Uritsky, head of the Petrograd Cheka, was assassinated by a young student, and on the same day Fanya Kaplan made an unsuccessful attempt to assassinate Lenin but succeeded only in severely wounding him at close range with a Browning pistol. Fanya Kaplan was a member of the Social Revolutionary Party and in her statement immediately after the shooting she said, "I shot him because he has betrayed the revolution." She had bad eyesight, which affected her aim. Previously she had attempted unsuccessfully to kill a tsarist official in Kiev and had been sentenced to eleven years' forced labor. While Lenin hovered between life and death, Yakov Sverdlov, who was president of the new Communist state, issued an order to "All Soviets of Workers, Peasants and Red Armymen's Deputies, All Armies, All, All," urging them to mount a merciless mass terror against the enemies of the revolution. In Petrograd, 512 prisoners were immediately shot, and 300 more were shot during the following month, while all over Russia the Cheka shot prisoners at random. About 15,000 prisoners were shot in revenge for the wounding of Lenin and the killing of Uritsky. The Red Terror was largely directed against the Social Revolutionaries. Lenin quickly recovered and was soon back at his desk ordering more executions.

He was a revolutionary, not a statesman. He knew how to destroy a state but not how to build a society. A studied ruthlessness and a smiling serenity were characteristics vividly remembered, but he also possessed to an alarming degree the quality the Russians call *proizvol,* which signifies a wild, pervasive arbitrariness of authority. He was one of those who give terrible orders lightly. Early in 1918 he settled down to work in a large office in the Kremlin in Moscow, with a battery of telephones in the corridor outside. It was his command post, his private generator of power, his study, his library and maproom. On his desk was a statue of a monkey gazing at a skull; the statue was intended as a commentary on Darwin, but it could just as easily be taken as a commentary on the destructive rule of a personal dictatorship. The dictatorship of the proletariat was a myth; the dictatorship of Lenin was a reality.

Lenin owed much to Karl Marx, whose theories he distorted, but he owed more to Sergey Nechayev, the extraordinary revolutionary who died in the Alexis Ravelin, the most carefully guarded corner of the Peter-Paul Fortress in St. Petersburg, in 1882, when Lenin was twelve years old.

Nechayev was a phenomenon of quite exceptional importance because he was the first to hammer out a theory of the conspiratorial overthrow of the state based on the premise that only a small handful of determined men, fanatically loyal to the revolution, was needed. He was not in the least interested in what happened to the state once its destruction was accomplished; it was enough that the state would no longer exist. Lenin delighted in the simplicity of Nechayev's revolutionary techniques. He said:

> People completely forget that Nechayev possessed unique organizational talent, an ability to establish the special technique of conspiratorial work everywhere, an ability to give thoughts such startling formulations that they were forever in one's memory. It is sufficient to recall his words in one of his leaflets, where he replies to the question, "Which member of the reigning house must be destroyed?" He gives the succinct answer, "The whole responsory."* The formula is so simple and so clear that it could be understood by everyone living in Russia at a time when the Orthodox Church held full sway; when the vast majority of the people, in one way or another, for one reason or another, attended church, and everyone knew that every member of the Romanov house was mentioned at the great responsory. The most unsophisticated reader, asking himself, "But which of them is to be destroyed?" would see the obvious, inevitable answer at a glance. "Why, the entire Romanov house." But this is simple to the point of genius.

When Lenin came to power, the same ruthlessness was employed to the same chaotic ends, and he very quietly ordered the destruction of "the whole responsory," invented slogans he had no intention of acting on, and set all opposing parties at one another's throats, while waging a war of complete extermination against them. Like Nechayev, he was dedicated to the destruction of the state without having any clear ideas about the new state he would bring into existence, and in fact the new state was just as domineering as the old, used many of the same forms, and differed chiefly in the number of prisoners it held in its jails and labor camps. Like Nechayev, Lenin practiced deceit as a fine art. He climbed to power on the slogan "All power to the Soviets," and then disbanded the Soviets. Almost his first act in power was to sign a decree returning the land to the peasants, but he had not the slightest intention of letting them keep the land. He followed Nechayev in all particulars except one. Nechayev's program had included the defiant statement "We deny free will and the assumed right of society to punish." Lenin denied free will, but he exercised the right to punish to the utmost.

* The prayer for the royal house recited in the Orthodox Church.

With Nechayev we see the future coming into focus. His *Revolutionary Catechism* was his supreme achievement as a founder of revolutionary doctrine. In twenty-six paragraphs he outlined four fundamental themes: the character of the true revolutionary and his relationship to other revolutionaries, to society, and to the people. Karl Marx once wrote that the *Revolutionary Catechism* was a hodge-podge of Schiller's *The Robbers* and Dumas's *The Count of Monte Cristo,* which is no more sensible than saying that Marx's *Communist Manifesto* is a hodge-podge of Heine's *Germany, A Winter Journey* and the novels of Eugène Sue and Georges Sand, from which the manifesto quotes extensively. The *Revolutionary Catechism* is a harsh and compelling document that exists in its own right, although its sources are to be found in Tieck, Jean-Paul Richter, and many early writers of the romantic period. The character of the true revolutionary is described brilliantly. He is a doomed and dedicated man, totally amoral, totally tyrannical, completely devoid of human sympathy. "Night and day he must have only one thought, one aim—merciless destruction. Striving cold-bloodedly toward this end, and always indefatigable, he must be prepared to destroy himself and to destroy with his own hands everything that stands in the path of the revolution." Nechayev paints the portrait of an ascetic, passionless and austere, dedicated to "terrible, total, universal and merciless destruction."

The revolutionary's methods are clearly stated: murder, blackmail, and corruption. In six categories Nechayev outlines the proper conduct to be shown toward each social class. The tsar, his entourage, his ministers, the military leaders must be killed; a few high officials who can be relied upon to act with formidable repressive measures will be spared but only because their repressive measures will powerfully assist the course of the revolution. Other high officials will be blackmailed and used on behalf of the revolution: "Their dirty secrets will be ferreted out, and they must be transformed into slaves. Their power, influence, and connections, their wealth and their energy will form an inexhaustible treasure and a precious help in all our undertakings." The fourth category consists of liberals and lesser officials who will believe that the revolutionaries are blindly following them when in fact they are being compromised and used for revolutionary purposes. The fifth category consists of demagogues who believe they are directing the revolution but can be easily directed; a few of them will become genuine revolutionaries, while the rest can be compromised and destroyed. The sixth category consists of women. Nechayev believed that women would play an important role in the revolutionary struggle, for they were expected to subvert and seduce men in authority, purloin compromising documents, and create the greatest possible degree of havoc.

Nechayev's *Revolutionary Catechism* implies a harsh verdict on humanity. One of the characters of Dostoyevsky's novel *The Possessed* says, "To level the hills is a good idea." Nechayev shows succinctly, clearly, and almost without emotion how the leveling process can be carried out. Lenin carried it out.

Again and again Nechayev insists that the revolutionary struggle must be carried out mercilessly. It does not matter how many people are killed; the only thing that matters is that the state should be completely uprooted and all the existing state institutions, traditions, and classes utterly destroyed. Nechayev revels in the turmoil and bloodshed, and is wholly corrupted by the vision of himself as the archconspirator presiding over the destruction of a civilization. Like Lenin, who pronounced in 1894 that Marxists must be "bloodyhanded" (*sangviniki*), Nechayev seems determined to drown Russia in blood as a punishment for her past sins. Whether anyone would escape alive was a matter of profound indifference to him.

Lenin never saw an execution and had not the remotest conception of what it was like to be tortured. Under the tsarist regime political prisoners were generally dealt with leniently. There were exceptions, of course, and Dostoyevsky's account of penal servitude in Omsk, as described in *Notes from the House of the Dead,* does not reflect any credit on the penal system under the tsars. Terrible punishments were inflicted on prisoners, men were sometimes flogged to death, sadistic guards amused themselves by humiliating the inmates, and the prison at Omsk was nearly as murderous as Auschwitz. But there was one significant difference between the prison camps of nineteenth-century Russia and those of twentieth-century Russia. According to the *Great Soviet Encyclopedia* the number of prisoners working at hard labor in tsarist Russia during the nineteenth century ranged from five thousand to ten thousand. In the thirties of this century the number of prisoners in Soviet prison camps ranged from ten million to twenty million.

Lenin was arrested for revolutionary activity in 1895 and a year later he was exiled to Shushenskoye in Siberia. The punishment was not severe. He was given a house, he received as many books as he wanted, his wife was permitted to live with him, and he was allowed to keep his hunting rifles. He was not permitted to carry on revolutionary activity while in exile, but he had very little difficulty smuggling out letters couched in violent revolutionary terms. No one under Lenin's dictatorship was treated so leniently.

Lenin's Cheka was an instrument of total coercion, and Lenin inspired it with his own fanatical devotion to mass executions. The heads of the Cheka lived dangerously. Felix Dzerzhinsky died peacefully in his bed in 1926, but most of his successors died from bullets fired into the backs of their heads. Dzerzhinsky was succeeded by Vyacheslav Menzhinsky, a man of some culture, learned in many languages. He was poisoned in 1934. Genrikh Yagoda, who succeeded him, was dismissed in 1936 and shot two years later. Nikolay Yezhov ruled for two years so terrible that they came to be known as the Yezhovshchina, "the age of Yezhov." In 1938 he was removed from office and given the minor post of Commissar for River Transport; he was liquidated the following year. Lavrenty Beria, a Georgian and the author of a famous and wholly inaccurate history of the Communist Party in Georgia, which celebrated Stalin as the sole genius of the Russian Revolution, ruled over the Cheka for fifteen years. He was moon-faced, unsmiling, businesslike; he could have been taken for a clerk in a railroad office. Like Heinrich Himmler, whom he resembled to a surprising degree, he was one of those morose and frustrated men who find an intense satisfaction in being the instrument of massacre. He was liquidated by Stalin's heirs in 1953.

All the leaders of the Cheka, which later came to be called the OGPU, the NKVD, the NKGB, the MVD, the KGB—the different names describe the same bureaucratic murder machine—were corrupt men who rejoiced in the exercise of their power to terrorize all of Russia. They had the power to destroy and maim, to torture and drive to madness, to reduce men to abject, quivering servitude. They discovered that it was very easy to destroy, and they lost count of the innocent people killed in the cellars of the Lubyanka Prison in Moscow. Yezhov, a thin-faced dwarf—he was only five feet tall— was responsible during his two-year reign for the deaths of three million people. His reign coincided with the great purge trials that led to the execution of the Bolshevik Old Guard, but most of the three million received no trial. Instructions were sent out on ticker tape from the Moscow headquarters: "Execute five hundred at Omsk." No names, no explanations, no instructions on the method of execution. The machinery was well oiled and ran smoothly. The Cheka was a state within a state, which gradually acquired absolute rule over vast areas of Russia. It was an independent satrapy that obeyed its own rules. Once arrested, a man was worth nothing, for he lived at the mercy of sadistic guards trained to be totally merciless.

The Russian prison camps, spread out from the far north to the far east, were among the greatest horrors of our time. Here absolute corruption held sway. Here life was totally devoid of meaning, for the camps were totally senseless. The only purpose they served was to satisfy the power lust of the dictator and his appointed deputies, who were able to remind themselves that millions of people lived or died at their pleasure. "How important I am! I have ten thousand laborers working for me, and if some of them die, I can always arrest more. They are always dying! Probably this is because I charge a 50 per cent commission on their allotment for food. I am sorry I have to starve them, but it is all in a good cause, and it is more interesting when there is a large turnover." The commandant of the prison camp smiles into his shaving mirror and silently applauds himself for having landed a good job with a fine house and excellent prospects. With luck he will become the commandant of a camp with a hundred thousand prisoners, or even of a camp with a million prisoners.

Trotsky was of the opinion that under a properly organized Communist state the entire population could and should be placed under military rule and converted into a permanent work force. The idea, from the point of view of Communist rule, had everything to commend it. It was efficient, centralized, final. The Communist rulers could get on with the business of governing without fear of contradiction, for the work force was under martial law and anyone who criticized the government was immediately executed. The population was maneuverable: the inhabitants of a city could be moved to another city without excessive dislocation. Somewhere in Moscow there would be a vast map with colored counters, each representing a hundred thousand people, and these could be moved about at will. In this way canals could be dug, rivers could be made to change course, the deserts could be planted with wheat. In theory the Communist government rejected the idea; in fact the idea was carried out in the prison camps, which constitute Trotsky's permanent memorial.

The Soviet government had not the slightest difficulty filling the prison camps. Just as telegrams would be sent under Yezhov's signature ordering executions for no reason whatsoever, so it was possible to send telegrams ordering the arrest of five thousand people from Nizhni-Novgorod and their immediate transportation to the Soviet far east. The telegram had the force of an imperial decree, and no one could dispute it. The five thousand were selected at random or chosen from existing lists of comrades whose absolute loyalty to the state had not been proved to the entire satisfaction of the local police. Other lists were compiled by the Cheka and submitted to Stalin, who glanced over them and wrote his initials on each page, signifying his approval. Similarly with the death lists. In a speech describing the insane lengths to which Stalin would go to cultivate the myth of his own great personality, Nikita Khrushchev revealed that the original death lists compiled by Yezhov and submitted to Stalin had been discovered. The lists were all lengthy, sometimes containing a thousand names. Three or four times a week, sometimes every day, a new folder of lists would appear on Stalin's table for his approval. Stalin read the folders, sometimes removed or added a name, and dutifully wrote his signature on the last page. Molotov also read the folders and added his signature. During the Yezhovshchina, which lasted less than two years, 383 death lists were submitted to Stalin and Molotov and approved by them.

The covering letters were also discovered. There were slight variations, depending upon the nature and character of the victims. Usually the letter took the following form:

Comrade Stalin,
I am sending for your approval four lists of people to be tried by the Military Collegium:

List No. 1	(General)
List No. 2	(Former military personnel)
List No. 3	(Former personnel of the NKVD)
List No. 4	(Wives of enemies of the people)

I request sanction to convict all in the first degree.

YEZHOV

The letter belongs to the category of things that can be listed under the heading of murderous hypocrisy, not in the first but in the ultimate degree. Nothing in the letter meant what it said. The Military Collegium had no existence as a trial court and simply rubber-stamped the decisions already made by Stalin, whose signature on the last page of the folder was a death sentence from which there was no appeal. "I request sanction to convict all in the first degree" was bureaucratese for "I have obeyed your orders and made up a list of prisoners condemned to death." Stalin, like Lenin, had a high regard for bureaucratic formulas. There must be a proper application to the appropriate authority; there must be the semblance of a trial; the final verdict must be approved by the appropriate authority, and the sentences must be carried out in the appropriate manner. All this was expressed in a letter that placed Stalin in the role of judge and prosecutor while permitting Yezhov to play the role of executioner. The letter was a tribute to Stalin's sense of his own bureaucratic efficiency.

Since the average number of names on each list was eight hundred and about four lists were seen each week, Stalin cursorily examined some three thousand names every week over a period of two years. He cannot conceivably have known even by reputation more than a tiny fraction of the people he condemned to death, and the reading of the names was therefore an exercise in self-glorification, a solemn recital of his own absolute powers. Such lists were presented to him from the time he achieved supreme power in 1926 until he died in 1953. His exercise in self-glorification was thus an extensive one. Although his death sentences were perhaps most numerous during the Yezhovshchina, there were other periods, particularly at the end of World War II and in the last years of his life, when they approached the same figures. Death was something Stalin dispensed quietly and casually, without any emotion whatsoever. His corruption took the form of an endless traffic with all the death-dealing forces available to him. Even more than Nechayev and Lenin he was dedicated to "terrible, total, universal and merciless destruction."

The dead were sometimes luckier than the men and women thrown into the labor camps. The camps were designed to punish prisoners by a long process of degradation. Sentences were usually for ten or twenty years, and all those days and nights were spent in total misery. Each food bowl was shared by four or five half-starved prisoners; latrines were inadequate; and the bunks were too few and too crowded to permit restful sleep. As in the German prison camps, common criminals, thieves and murderers were given positions of authority. Reports on the behavior of "political" prisoners, by which was meant prisoners arbitrarily arrested in those mass roundups which were the particular amusement of the Cheka, were written by common criminals now transformed into bureaucrats. Sometimes fights broke out between the criminals and the "politicals," but since the criminals were better fed and possessed the authority that derives from "fulfilling a bureaucratic function," they were usually able to beat the "politicals" to a bloody pulp. According to the accepted class structure of the Communist state, a thief or even a murderer was regarded as infinitely superior to a "political," who became from the moment of his arrest an "antistate person." His crime was so heinous that he was regarded as belonging to the bottom stratum of the state.

Although the existence of the prison camps in Russia was widely known in the West from the accounts of former prisoners who escaped, and although everyone in Russia was aware of their existence and there was scarcely anyone who had not seen the Black Marias in the streets and prisoners roped together in the charge of blue-capped Chekists, a conspiracy of silence prevailed in both Russia and the West. It was as though the camps had become so familiar a part of the mental scenery that they passed unobserved. They existed in vast numbers; a map marked with their locations would have shown the country pockmarked with disease spots. Perhaps the very immensity of the camp population prevented men from thinking about the prisoners in human terms. While millions of people were being degraded and massacred, the Soviet Union continued to advertise itself as a workers' paradise.

In Russia the camps were an open secret; they were talked about privately and discreetly; nearly everyone had a relative in a prison camp. Nevertheless the prisoners had no official existence and the prison camps were never mentioned in the newspapers. Not until Alexander Solzhenitsyn published *One Day in the Life of Ivan Denisovich* with the permission of Nikita Khrushchev was the existence of the camps publicly acknowledged. Solzhenitsyn did not recount the horrors, though he hinted at them. Instead he described the slow draining of physical strength, the hard labor, the rations that were barely sufficient to keep a man alive, the endless misery. He described a world of perpetual degradation and hopeless misery. Men could live, but life was senseless, for there was nothing to live for. The sap was sucked out of the body, and the prisoner was reduced to a living husk.

Why did the camps come into existence? Partly, of course, because Lenin had willed them into existence in his desire to inflict punishment on all those he regarded as his enemies. In his essay "How to Organize the Competition," written in January 1918, he proclaimed the necessity of "purging the Russian land of all kinds of harmful vermin"—drunkards, hooligans, prostitutes, malingerers, counterrevolutionaries. They were to be submitted to execution or, failing that, to "punishment at forced labor of the hardest kind." The vermin must be purged, rendered harmless, cleansed. The *chistka,* the "cleansing process," was established and by degrees imperceptibly acquired the meaning of *likvidatsiya,* or "liquidation." Henceforth Russia was at the mercy of men who cleansed and liquidated implacably without being able to invent a single consistent explanation for all the suffering they inflicted on the people. A totalitarian dictatorship cannot explain; it can only suppress.

Something very similar to the Communist *chistka* occurred in the sixteenth century when Ivan the Terrible divided his subjects into two estates, the *zemshchina* and the *oprichnina.* He ruled over both, but the *oprichnina,* "the separated estate," was designed as the instrument for punishing the *zemshchina,* "the earthly estate." Among the *oprichnina* were the nobles who were fanatically loyal to Ivan and whose chief interest was to loot and despoil the *zemshchina.* Raiding parties were sent out, hundreds of thousands of people were murdered or tortured into revealing where they had hidden their treasures, and on one occasion Ivan led an army of *oprichniki* to the great city of Novgorod, murdered half the population, and drove off with all their valuables. The *oprichniki* wore black cloaks, rode on black horses, carried brooms to signify that they were cleansing the world of vermin, and tied dogs' heads to their saddlecloths as badges. The *zemshchina* lived in fear and trembling of the *oprichniki,* hoping against hope that Ivan would abandon this insane division of the country between the looters and the looted, the murderers and the murdered. After seven years Ivan turned against the *oprichniki* and murdered them in their turn because they proved to be totally incompetent in a war against the Tatars.

The historian confronted with the phenomenon of the *oprichnina* finds himself at a loss to explain why an autocratic tsar found it necessary to divide his country into two estates and set one against the other. He can surmise only that Ivan, who possessed a genuinely criminal nature, created an autonomous criminal state to satisfy his own criminality. Karl Marx, who made a special study of Russian history, had a less charitable explanation for the strange savagery of the tsars. He thought it derived from the many years when the Russians lived under the Tatar yoke and the grand prince of Muscovy, acting as a kind of viceroy of the Tatar khan, fought the other Russian princes on the khan's behalf. A slave himself, he fought to enslave his fellow Russians. Here Marx describes the character of Grand Prince Ivan Kalita:

Forced to dissemble before his masters the strength he really gathered, he had to dazzle his fellow serfs with a power he did not own. To solve his problem he had to elaborate all the *ruses* of the most abject slavery into a system, and to execute that system with the patient labour of a slave. Open force itself could enter as an intrigue only into a system of intrigues, corruption, and underground usurpation. He could not strike before he had poisoned. Singleness of purpose became with him duplicity of action. To encroach by the fraudulent use of a hostile power, to weaken that power by the very act of using it, and to overthrow it at last by the effects produced by its own instrumentality—this policy was inspired to Ivan Kalita by the peculiar character both of the ruling and the serving race.

Marx was writing in English, a language he had not yet mastered, but there is no doubting the sense of his argument. Ivan Kalita needed to corrupt the Russians in order to keep them under the heel of the Tatars, and thus there grew up throughout Russian history the concept of the two Russias, one enslaving and the other enslaved.

Certainly the Russian serfs never suffered so much as the prisoners in the labor camps. Serfdom, abolished in 1861, arose again in 1918. Lenin never understood the normal human desire for freedom, and even if he had understood it, he would have discarded it because it did not fit into his grand design. "So long as the state exists, there is no freedom," he wrote in *State and Revolution*. "When there is freedom, there will be no state." In the same essay he wrote, "Our ultimate aim is the destruction of the state—i.e., of all organizational and systematic violence, all violence committed on human beings in general." But the state continued to exist, more unyielding than ever because he was in charge of it.

Perhaps never in history has so much violence been committed on human beings on so vast a scale as in the Soviet Union. To this day the horrors of the prison camps continue; the Cheka is entrenched as a permanent separate estate, and it will continue forever and ever, *in saecula saeculorum,* unless in the fullness of time the Russians arise and burn down the camps, saying: "This is corrupt, inhuman, and degrading. There is only one thing to be done—to throw it into the trash can of history!"

We have to ask ourselves what purpose is served by sending millions of people into concentration camps. By uprooting them, by reducing them to slavery, by treating them with inhuman barbarity, an appalling weight of suffering is imposed on them—to what end? We have to ask ourselves whether there is a rationale for the Russian concentration camps. When we probe deeply into the origins and history of the camps, we discover no reason for them at all. Totally irrational, they serve no purpose except to satisfy the obscure psychological needs of a handful of frightened men who have seized power and are determined to maintain it at all costs, even the cost of ruining the nation.

Only on the most minimal basis can it be said that the concentration camps serve the economy of the country. The cost of transporting the prisoners and administering the camps far exceeds the gains brought about by their labors. Except in the Kolyma goldfields and in the building of the White Sea Canal, the labor of the prisoners has been very largely unproductive. The economy of the entire country has been disrupted in order to feed a constant flow of prisoners into useless occupations. The human economy as measured in the lives of these millions of prisoners has also been disrupted. Mountains of ledgers record the names, occupations, and former addresses of the prisoners, the work tasks entrusted to them, their behavior toward the guards, whether they carried out their norms, whether they made disrespectful remarks, and any other information that might be useful to the bureaucracy in administrative charge of the prisons. Bureaucracy thrives; countless pages are filled with reports made in quadruplicate; the ledgers are carefully preserved because it is in the nature of bureaucracy to preserve ledgers.

But in fact all this labor on the part of the prison clerks is just as useless as the labor of the prisoners. No one, least of all Stalin, cared what happened to the prisoners. They were expendable, because all Russians were expendable. "What is one generation?" Stalin asked when talking to Churchill about the terrible upheavals of the thirties, those upheavals which he had ordered and for which he alone was responsible. It was perfectly possible to destroy an entire generation and in the history books it would appear merely as a hiatus or as an asterisk. But in Stalin's mind all generations were equally expendable. There was no limit to the number of people he would have killed if he had thought it would be to his advantage to kill them.

The concentration camps are spread over vast regions of European and Asiatic Russia; hundreds of thousands of guards, prison officers, interrogators, and judicial officials are employed to ensure that some twenty million prisoners are suitably punished by being reduced to mindless servitude. All this is a total waste of human resources. Over the heads of all Russians there dangled during the reign of Stalin, like the sword of Damocles, the prospect of a ten- or twenty-five-year sentence of imprisonment and hard labor, not for having committed a crime against the state, but because it amused the rulers from time to time to punish them for no reason at all. People were punished because they existed or because it was felt necessary that sacrifices should be made to some unknown god or perhaps—and this was most likely—because Caesar felt an obscure need for sacrificial victims. After Stalin the number of prisoners grew less, but the bureaucratic system remained unchanged.

The real rulers of Russia were not the delegates elected from a single party to the Supreme Soviet but Stalin and the secret police. In effect it was a military dictatorship with the blue-uniformed officers of the Cheka in command. That they were corrupt and merciless was less important than that they were corrupt and merciless in the bureaucratic manner, which is to say wholly corrupt and wholly merciless. They obeyed orders to the letter, lacked any sense of humanity and human dignity, and felt themselves, like the *oprichniki* before them, to be surrounded by enemies who must be stamped out at all costs. That the enemies were their own brothers and sisters seems never to have occurred to them.

What is most terrible about the Soviet system is the absence of choice. There is a norm of work, a norm of behavior, a norm of obedience, and woe betide anyone who does not perform according to the appropriate norm. There are no places of refuge; there is no way to escape from the all-seeing eye of the secret police. One can imagine a military dictatorship that at least presents men and women with the right to choose the manner of their deaths and to offer their views on the military dictatorship. One can imagine a dictatorship that issues a questionnaire asking for a few personal preferences within a limited field of enquiry. It would be neither long nor exhaustive but would contain essential information. But military dictatorships are not interested in obtaining information from the subject peoples; they are deaf and blind, and they believe that to punish is to govern. When the condemned prisoner asks, "Why am I being punished?" there is no answer.

The tragedy is that the Russian Revolution began so hopefully. The young students of the *narodniki* movement in the 1880s and 1890s fanned out over Russia to educate the peasants in the hope of bringing about a revolution that would bring liberty, brotherhood, and equality to all. No more idealistic students have ever lived. But the revolution, when it came, was a grotesque caricature of a revolution led by "a shepherd with an iron staff." "Starting out from unlimited freedom," says Shigalyov in *The Possessed*, "I end with unlimited despotism." It was a strange development, and Shigalyov

QUESTIONNAIRE ADDRESSED TO THE SUBJECT PEOPLE

To be completed in triplicate and returned immediately to your local command post. Extreme penalties will be incurred in the event of delay.

Circle one

1. Do you want to be ruled by a military dictator?   Yes   No

2. In your view, should the military dictator rule
   for five years, for ten years, or for life?   _____

3. Do you object to torture?   Yes   No
   If you object, please state whether you object
   a little, very much, wholeheartedly.   _____

4. Do you approve of abortion   Yes   No
                   parricide   Yes   No
                   assassination   Yes   No
                   mass suicide   Yes   No

5. Do you want to be killed?   Yes   No

6. Would you prefer to be killed by
                   garroting   Yes   No
                   shooting   Yes   No
                   clubbing   Yes   No
                   poison   Yes   No
                   being thrown into a furnace   Yes   No

7. Have you any preferences concerning your appointed executioner? Would you prefer him to
   be   bearded   Yes   No
                   blue-eyed   Yes   No
                   Christian   Yes   No
                   other   _____

8. Will you adore at all times the person and public image of your military dictator?   Yes   No

(Signature) _____ *(Date)* _____

was surprised by his findings. We, who are less surprised because we have seen unlimited despotisms at work, are confronted with the task of holding on to our remaining freedoms with all our strength, for to do less is to see all freedoms vanishing and to become mindless pawns in a world given over to absolute corruption.

Absolute Corruption, Phase II: German Extermination Camps

When the Allied troops, advancing through Bavaria, drove down the winding road which branches to the left from the main highway between Augsburg and Munich, they found near the village of Dachau a high-walled camp inhabited largely by dead and dying prisoners. They learned that within those walls three hundred thousand prisoners had been put to death. For the first time the reports that had been coming out of Central Europe began to seem credible; there had been vast murder factories in the German Reich —how vast we shall never know.

Dachau, however, was a comparatively small camp. At Auschwitz more than three million people had been murdered over a period of three years. Most of them were gassed to death and then thrown into the crematoriums; the men who shoveled the corpses into the furnaces were themselves prisoners and knew that in the course of time they would meet the same fate. Nothing comparable to this mass extermination had ever happened before; even the great Mayan sacrifices—at which, according to Torquemada, seventy-five thousand prisoners were once killed over a period of four days—were small in comparison with this terrible holocaust. Why did it happen? This, too, we may never know for certain. All we can do is examine the history and the workings of the extermination camps and try to discover how they came about.

These camps were usually situated in marshy areas, in the neighborhood of obscure villages, near forests and quarries, and not far from a railroad. Their sites were carefully chosen, and it was hoped that their remoteness would prevent news of their existence from becoming known. The barracks of the prisoners were long, low buildings covered with green tar paper and arranged to form an enormous grid of streets. The barbed-wire perimeter was interrupted every thirty or forty yards by high watchtowers often manned by two soldiers armed with machine guns, one directed upon the camp, the other directed upon the roads leading to it. From high pillars along the perimeter of the camp and down the main avenues hung floodlights, and at night the entire area was usually floodlit. The light was very hard, a "white, purplish blue" according to the survivors. At night the camp took on a look of harsh unreality, and a man walking along the paths between the buildings threw many shadows. Only the guards walked about at night.

By day the camp was a hive of activity. Work gangs were moving about, sadistic punishments were being administered, slave laborers were working in factories, SS officers were making tours of inspection, and trains were continually arriving to deposit the latest load of prisoners. The newcomers were immediately divided into two groups, those who were provisionally allowed to live and to work as slave laborers and those, including the very young, the sick, and the elderly, who were consigned directly to the gas chamber. A doctor standing in the railroad siding glanced at each prisoner for a moment and made an instant judgment, pointing to the left if the person was about to die and to the right if he was to be given a temporary lease on life. The doctor wore the uniform of an SS officer, and there was no appeal from his quick judgments.

As in the Soviet labor camps, the well-oiled machinery of death ran smoothly: condemned prisoners were marched from the train to the gas chambers and were dead within thirty minutes of their arrival. Many of them must have known the fate reserved for them. They were marched in the direction of two-story buildings surmounted by enormous, red-brick chimneys, tapering toward the top, from which arose great tongues of flame and clouds of thick, black smoke bearing the unmistakable odor of burning flesh and scorched hair.

Those who were condemned to live were not necessarily luckier than those who were condemned to die. Their lives were usually harsh, brutish, and brief. The camps were machines for manufacturing martyrs, for the guards knew exactly how to prolong an agony and had invented hitherto unknown ways of killing. Each prisoner trained himself to obey instantly and to be as inconspicuous as possible. This was not always easy, for all prisoners were classified and each was required to wear a badge identifying his class. Criminals wore a green triangle, political prisoners wore a red one, Jehovah's Witnesses a purple one, homosexuals a pink one, gypsies a black one, and Jews wore a yellow star of David.

The general plan of the camp helps to suggest its purpose. Seen from above, it resembled a walled medieval city dominated by a cathedral, which in this case was the crematorium. The feudal nobility occupied a well-guarded corner of the city and lived in considerable luxury, served by the disenfranchised workers who lived in barracks. All the familiar appurtenances of a well-organized city were present: shops, brothels, hospitals, a stadium, a cinema, factories, police posts. There were, however, very few shops, no hotels, and the prisoners were rarely permitted to use the post office. The city administration was in the hands of a small elite, which received its instructions from Berlin. The camp commandant was rarely seen, for he was busy signing documents, writing reports, and supervising the extensive bureaucracy. In a place apart was the chief doctor; on him rested the selection of the prisoners who were to die. In medieval terms he represented the inquisitor, whose priestly function was to choose the sacrificial victims for the fire. The rituals of the camp were complex and changeable, but the ultimate act of worship was always the same: the offering of the blood.

Just as the feudal city gradually gave place to a city dominated by the bourgeoisie, so the camps gradually found themselves halfway between feudalism and rule by the bourgeoisie. There were not enough guards and officers to run the camp efficiently, so prisoners gradually assumed positions of power and responsibility. The *Kapos* in charge of the barracks, the *Sonderkommandos* who worked at the crematorium, and others who worked in the kitchens and hospitals and fulfilled administrative functions enjoyed special privileges and thus resembled an emerging bourgeoisie. At Buchenwald this emerging power fell to the Communists, who protected their own and saw to it that Catholics and Socialists were given the heaviest tasks; they had no hesitation in killing anyone who threatened their power.

The term *Kapo* comes from *Kamaradschafte Polizei,* "comradely police," but there was not much real comradeship. Many of the *Kapos* were professional criminals, murderers who rejoiced in the opportunity to continue their profession inside the camp. It was a comparatively simple matter for a *Kapo* to lure a prisoner he detested near a hospital and then quietly put him to death with an injection of strychnine, morphine, or evipan, or simply by injecting air into his veins or by injecting chloroform into his heart, which killed him in about forty seconds.

The commandants of the extermination camps were no psychologists. They knew very little about human behavior under stress, but they were pragmatists who learned very quickly. They wanted to kill, and they were indifferent about who did the killing. So it came about that a large number of prisoners in the extermination camps were killed by prisoners, who were themselves killed later. Once the extermination camps had been built, supplied with an adequate number of prisoners and equipped with death-dealing instruments, there was in theory no reason to staff it with armed guards and skilled murderers: the prisoners could be made to exterminate each other like gladiators in the arena.

The extermination camps institutionalized sadism. There was nothing new in this, for common criminals in the Soviet labor camps, given positions of power and authority, had long been accustomed to torment and murder their charges. This was officially approved and became part of the ceremony. But in Russia as in Germany there was always the danger that if common criminals were appointed to high positions in the camp there would come about a complete breakdown in the machinery of camp government. This rarely happened. The common criminals found an outlet for their criminality in riding roughshod over the prisoners; they rejoiced in their authority. Since the government was itself criminal and all the officers in charge of the camps were criminals, and since the laws regulating the camps were drawn up by criminals for criminal purposes, it was not surprising that murderers, perverts, and sadists acquired high positions. In an age of criminality the innocent were driven to the wall, and the criminals survived.

The practice of the extermination camps under the Nazis was the result of a long process of development. The original murder camps were small cellars in the workers' quarters of Munich. Here the first storm troopers tortured and murdered their enemies, who were nearly always but not invariably Communists. The bodies were thrown into the river or left on the streets to strike fear into the hearts of peaceful citizens. This was gang warfare, for the Communists were doing the same thing to the Nazis. On both sides men were engaged in open, advertised murder, taking full credit for their acts. By 1931, when the war between the Nazis and the Communists in Munich was at its height, disused warehouses were being transformed into concentration camps. These were primitive affairs, tentative and exploratory. No one quite knew what to do with the prisoners, and Hitler was not yet ready to assume the responsibility of butchering all the prisoners who fell into his hands. National Socialism was still wearing the mask of legality, and Hitler hoped to receive financial help from the bourgeoisie. Nor were the Communists eager to precipitate mass murder. Thus there came about one of the strangest events in the early history of the war between the Communists and the Nazis—a quiet exchange of prisoners.

With Hitler's seizure of power in 1933 the situation changed abruptly. All over Germany concentration camps were opened to take care of the thousands of Socialists and Communists who were under arrest. They were brutalized, starved, and beaten, but the formulas of degradation had not yet been worked out in detail. Hitler was too busy creating a totalitarian state to pay much attention to his prisoners. Just over fourteen months later came the Night of the Long Knives, when he struck blindly at all his imagined enemies and in a single day killed at least a thousand people (though he admitted to killing only seventy-four), declaring that he had been compelled by the circumstances of the time to assume the role of judge and executioner.

The Night of the Long Knives is a brilliantly inventive misnomer for a peculiarly terrible experience—the dictator giving way to a frenzied blood lust. The events did not take place at night and long knives were notably absent. Many of the men shot to death were Hitler's loyal followers, who died shouting, "Heil Hitler!" This day was the turning point. Thereafter Hitler gave himself up to private vengeance and the corruption of Germany for his own ends.

After that day the Brown Shirts, known as the SA (*Sturmabteilung*), the ill-disciplined army that had brought Hitler to power, lost their privileged position. Thereafter Hitler relied on two incomparably more powerful weapons—the German army and the highly disciplined SS (*Shutzstaffel*), commanded by the former chicken-farmer Heinrich Himmler.

Two weeks after the Night of the Long Knives, on July 13, 1934,

Hitler delivered a speech at the Kroll Opera House in Berlin in which he attempted to explain and justify his actions. In this extraordinary speech he spoke about the four kinds of destructive agents who had been let loose upon the world, using words that echo Nechayev's *Revolutionary Catechism*. He described first the "international disintegrators," who fight on the barricades and resort to mass terror. Then he described the discontented politicians, those who have been removed from office and are therefore all the more determined to employ deceit and trickery in order to regain office. The third group of destructive agents consisted of those who were uprooted by World War I and had lost all sympathy for an ordered human society. Members of this group were filled with hatred against authority, finding satisfaction only in "some conspiratorial activity of the mind perpetually plotting the disintegration of whatever at any moment exists."

In Hitler's description of the third group of destructive agents, the reader soon recognizes that he is unconsciously drawing a self-portrait. He is the archcorrupter perpetually plotting the disintegration of society.

Hitler's fourth group consisted of people who carried out their destructive activities "even against their own will," nihilists by instinct, by habit, and by avocation. "They are," Hitler explains, "men whose own nothingness allows them to look upon the world as nothingness." They have no roots, they have nothing in common with the millions of people who form the mass of the nation, and they perform their terrible acts in order to bring some excitement to their otherwise completely purposeless lives. These people are especially dangerous because they carry within them the malignant bacteria of doubt, uncertainty, and unrest; lies and suspicions fester in them; fear breeds from them; and soon the whole nation is reduced to a state of hysteria by the uncontrollable advance of the fatal disease.

Hitler's speech on July 13, 1934, provides one of the few occasions when an archcorrupter has described the phenomenon of corruption. He seems to have been perfectly aware that he was describing himself and the members of his own conspiratorial organization. Like those psychopaths who sometimes announce their crimes publicly, knowing that no one will believe them or thinking that their crimes have been so well hidden that no one will ever discover the evidence, he seemed to be daring the audience to accept the only possible conclusion—that he was describing himself.

Throughout his public life Hitler practiced the arts of corruption with a steady and unflinching purpose. Like Nechayev, who believed it was possible for a man or a small group of men to bring about the destruction of a whole state, Hitler believed that it was within his power to destroy whole nations and to conquer the world. He could do this only by the slaughter of millions and millions of people, a prospect that did not in the least disturb him, for he was one of those who "look upon the world as nothingness." It mattered nothing to him that hundreds of thousands of Russian prisoners were allowed to starve to death or that the German army at Stalingrad perished as a result of his own miscalculations. But it was in the extermination camps that his genius for corruption reached its greatest extent.

In the spring of 1940, after the corpse of Poland was divided between Russia and Germany and while the Wehrmacht was poised to attack France, Heinrich Himmler received Hitler's approval to build a new concentration camp at Oswiecim, a small town lying close to a railroad on the main line from Vienna to Cracow. It was a town of about twelve thousand inhabitants, mostly farmers. Once it enjoyed a modest prosperity. There were an abandoned tobacco factory and an abandoned military post, of which all that remained was an army barracks consisting of six large buildings. There were birch groves and pine woods, and the low, marshy ground bred millions of mosquitoes in summer. In autumn and winter heavy mists rose from numerous stagnant pools. Cracow lay to the east, about an hour's drive by automobile and four or five hours by farm cart.

The site was selected because of the very obscurity of the place. The chief advantage was the proximity of the railroad; the seven abandoned buildings served as the core of the camp. Many camps were beginning to arise in various parts of Poland, and no special importance was attached to the new one. Meanwhile, the boundaries of Poland were changed, and all the region around Oswiecim was incorporated in the German Reich. The town itself was now officially known by its German name, Auschwitz.

From May 1, 1940, when the camp was opened, to January 17, 1945, when the guardians of the camp fled before the advancing Russian armies, Auschwitz was the site of a stupendous experiment in mass murder. From a miserable, sleeping town set down in the clayey marshlands it became an industrial city where essential war products were produced by slave labor and where those who were too old, too young, or too ill to labor were herded into gas chambers and incinerators. It would be a mistake to assume that mass murder was the chief industry of Auschwitz. Mass murder was a by-product of the huge industrial complex of arms workshops, chemical factories, synthetic gasoline and rubber factories, railway repair yards, quarries, forestry and farm enterprises all conducted by slave labor. Siemens and Krupp between them managed most of these enterprises. They bear the heaviest responsibility for the existence of the camp, for they rejoiced in the unending supply of free labor continually pouring into their factories from nearly every country of Europe. Heavy industry and mass murder went hand in hand.

On May 1, 1940, SS Hauptsturmführer Rudolf Höss arrived in Auschwitz to take up his duties as commandant. He had sharp, foxy features, dull eyes, a thin mouth, a way of ingratiating himself with his superiors. He had been adjutant to the commandant at the prison camp at Sachsenhausen since 1938 and he was known as a man who could be relied upon to act mercilessly at all times. He had served in World War I and afterward worked as a farmhand in Silesia and Schleswig-Holstein. In 1923 he committed a murder and was sentenced to ten years' imprisonment but was pardoned five years later and released from prison. In 1932, the year before Hitler came to power, Rudolf Höss joined the Nazi Party. In the following year, by the purest chance, he caught the eye of Heinrich Himmler while in command of a team of SS horsemen on a farm in Pomerania. Himmler admired men who kept a good seat on a horse. In 1934 Höss was given an administrative appointment at Dachau, and four years later he was sent to Sachsenhausen.

When Höss arrived in Auschwitz with a small staff, it never occurred to him that he would soon be in charge of the world's largest extermination camp. He had been promised a position where his abilities would be given full rein, but very little was being done to help him. Some Poles were being housed in the army barracks; they had been arrested for continuing the fight for a free Poland, and were soon liquidated. The camp was only a camp in embryo. Early in 1941 Himmler came to Auschwitz on a tour of inspection and gave orders that new buildings were to be put up and the marshlands drained. Later in the year, after the German attack on Russia, Himmler ordered Höss to prepare for the arrival of a hundred thousand Russian prisoners. Höss was empowered to take over the neighboring town of Birkenau (meaning "birch grove") and construct a large camp there. Auschwitz-Birkenau, straddling the railroad line, was still only an embryo. IG-Farben began building a synthetic rubber factory in the spring of 1941, but it was not in operation until the autumn. By that time the situation had changed drastically. The Germans were carving deep into Russia, and Hitler was prophesying that both Moscow and Leningrad would fall before the end of the year.

At some time during the summer of 1941 Rudolf Höss learned for the first time that Auschwitz was destined to become a vast extermination center. When writing his autobiographical notes he could not remember the exact date, but it was probably in the early days of August. He met Himmler in Berlin and was told that Hitler had decided upon the Final Solution of the Jewish Problem. The existing camps were far too small for the massive operation he intended, and Auschwitz was to be given all the facilities needed for an unprecedented expansion. Höss later recalled that the meeting with Himmler took place in the greatest secrecy, and Himmler's adjutant, who was nearly always present at such meetings, was ordered from the room. Höss was told that Auschwitz had been chosen because of its easy access by rail and because the entire area could be sealed off. He was also told that Sturmbannführer Adolf Eichmann would shortly visit him at Auschwitz to discuss details.

In fact, very little was done. Many months passed before Eichmann came to Auschwitz, and even after the Wannsee Conference held on January 20, 1942, when the representatives of all the ministries involved met to decide upon the exact measures to be taken against the Jews, nothing was decided. Hitler had ordered that all the Jews living in Europe were to be liquidated, but he had come to no conclusion about the time, the place, or the method. He seems to have hesitated not because he was uncertain of his aims but because he wanted the destruction of the Jews to come about in a single fiery holocaust. After conquering Russia he proposed to hurl the Wehrmacht against England, Ireland, and Turkey; and there are ominous indications that the Jews of these countries would also have been included in the holocaust.

But for the moment there was a long pause, while the Wehrmacht argued bitterly that it needed skilled Jews for the war effort and Himmler argued just as bitterly that he had a mandate from Hitler to destroy Jews wherever they could be found, sparing only the irreducible minimum needed for the war effort, and these would be taken under the wing of the SS. (Many of the surviving documents of this period are written in veiled language. There are repeated mentions of "removal" and "resettlement"; both meant "death.") But there were no clear-cut lines of responsibility, and there seemed to be a general disposition to wait until the final conquest of Russia. Meanwhile the paperwork mounted up, and Auschwitz continued to grow slowly and not very effectively.

In the spring of 1942 Höss visited the concentration camp at Treblinka to enquire into the best methods of mass extermination.

He found that victims were being herded into sealed rooms and asphyxiated by exhaust gases from internal-combustion engines. The process was slow, undependable, and unwieldy. Höss was of the opinion that some better method could be found and began experimenting on Russian prisoners with the vapor from prussic-acid crystals, which brought death within five or ten minutes, depending on the temperature and humidity of the air. These amethyst-colored crystals, in containers labeled Zyklon B, were provided by IG-Farben. When Eichmann arrived at Auschwitz, he seems to have thought that mass executions by monoxide poisoning on the Treblinka model would solve the most pressing problem. Höss gave him a demonstration of the effectiveness of prussic-acid crystals, and it was agreed that henceforth this method would be used exclusively.

Now at last the part of the Auschwitz-Birkenau concentration camp that was devoted to mass extermination went into full gear. Eichmann promised an ever-increasing supply of boxcars filled with Jews from all over Europe. The design and construction of the huge gas chambers and crematoriums were speeded up as the first big convoys began to arrive. Mass executions of Jews began in July 1942. Since the gas chambers had not yet been erected, executions took place in two large farm buildings in a remote area of Birkenau. The buildings were made air-tight, heavy wooden doors were provided, and concealed peepholes were installed to allow the SS men to look in. Condemned Jews were marched to these barns, made to undress behind a screen of hurdles, and then ordered to go inside. Large notices on the doors read *Disinfection Room,* and the victims were led to believe that the barns served as disinfection chambers. Many held back, for there was something distinctly ominous about these buildings hemmed in by birch forests. Those who held back too long were struck with riding whips or rubber truncheons, or shot.

Compared with what came later these mass executions were still primitive affairs. About 250 people could be killed at a time. The bodies were then hosed down, gold rings and gold fillings were removed, and they were then taken to a cremation pit and burned. After about six hours, the bones were removed and pulverized with heavy wooden hammers. In this way, day after day, and every day, about 1,000 people were reduced to sufficient powder to fill a small truck. The powder was sold as fertilizer or thrown into the Vistula River, which flowed nearby.

Before the end of the year the process had been speeded up with the installation of the first officially designed gas chamber and crematorium. This time the gas chamber could hold three thousand people at a time and they could all be killed in five minutes. Jews were marched from the train to a vast whitewashed entrance hall where there were notices in German, French, Greek, and Hungarian reading *Bath and Disinfection*. This entrance hall, about six hundred feet long, was brilliantly lit, with benches around the walls. Above the benches were numbered coat racks, and in the middle of the hall were white columns with more benches below them. The Jews were ordered to undress, to hang their clothes and shoes on numbered coat racks, and on no account to forget the number. Everything about the room was intended to deceive: the gay posters, the numbered racks, the benches, the brisk and kindly behavior of the guards, all were designed to lull any mounting suspicions. The victims were allowed about fifteen minutes to undress and then they were instructed to walk to a second room, which was equally large, equally well lit, with a central row of white columns like the first room, but without benches. When they were all inside, a hoarse command rang out: "SS and *Sonderkommandos* leave the room!" Then the doors swung shut, the lights were turned off, and the prisoners were left in darkness.

Those who were near the center of the room may have guessed where death came from. It came from the white columns, which did not support the roof at all, and were made of light sheet metal amply perforated to permit lethal gases to escape and within a few seconds to fill the entire room. A moment after the doors swung shut, the first of four green canisters of Zyklon B was opened by a man wearing a gas mask and the contents were poured down one of the columns. The contents of the remaining canisters were quickly poured down three other columns. Experiments had shown that this was the optimum amount of poison needed to kill two or three thousand people.

The man wearing the gas mask was a *Sanitätsdienstgefreiter,* "deputy health service officer." He arrived at the gas chamber in an automobile furnished by the International Red Cross, with the red cross on a white background clearly marked. He had picked up the canisters from their place of concealment—the projection booth of the local cinema.

About ten minutes later, after the screaming had died down, the lights came on again, and soon powerful ventilators were sucking the gas from the room. Dr. Miklos Niyszli, a Hungarian Jew pressed into service as a specialist in forensic medicine by Dr. Josef Mengele, the camp's chief medical officer, has described the scene:

228 The Coming of the Dark Ages

The bodies were not lying here and there throughout the room, but piled in a mass to the ceiling. The reason for this was that the gas first inundated the lower layers of air and rose but slowly towards the ceiling. This forced the victims to trample one another in a frantic effort to escape the gas. Yet a few feet higher up the gas reached them. What a struggle for life there must have been! Nevertheless it was merely a matter of two or three minutes' respite. If they had been able to think about what they were doing, they would have realized they were trampling their own children, their wives, their relatives. But they couldn't think. Their gestures were no more than the reflexes of the instinct of self-preservation. I noticed that the bodies of the women, the children, and the aged were at the bottom of the pile; at the top, the strongest. Their bodies, which were covered with scratches and bruises from the struggle which had set them against each other, were often interlaced. Blood oozed from their noses and mouths; their faces, bloated and blue, were so deformed as to be almost unrecognizable. . . .

The Sonderkommando squad, outfitted with large rubber boots, lined up around the mountain of bodies and flooded it with powerful jets of water. This was necessary because the final act of those who die by drowning or by gas is an involuntary defecation. Each body was befouled, and had to be washed. Once the "bathing" of the dead was finished, the separation of the welter of bodies began. It was a difficult job. They knotted thongs round the wrists, which were clenched in a viselike grip, and with these thongs they dragged the slippery bodies to the elevators in the next room. Four good-sized elevators were functioning. They loaded twenty to twenty-five corpses to an elevator. The ring of a bell was the signal that the load was ready to ascend.

The process was so smooth, so mechanical, and so automatic that mistakes were rarely made, and the gas chambers and the crematorium achieved their daily quotas without difficulty. Himmler could congratulate himself on his success. By April 1944 there were 20 full-scale concentration camps and 165 satellite labor camps. "How our business has grown!" he remarked contentedly, little knowing that most of the camps would be abandoned later in the year.

The extermination camps introduced a strange new language. To be killed in the gas chamber was called "going to the movies," because the movie theater housed the Zyklon cylinders. It was also the storehouse for the whipping block and the gallows. *Kanada* was the name given to the warehouse full of hair, gold teeth, clothes, shoes, jewelry, and toys removed from the prisoners. Prisoners who had sunk into a state of apathy were called *Mussulmenschen;* they were greatly feared, for their apathy was contagious. What was surprising was that people were able to survive at all in those camps, which were lighted at night by the flames of the crematorium.

The terror of the camps was so great that there was very little resistance from the prisoners. At Auschwitz there was only one known attempt at revolt. This was organized by the future Polish minister-president Josef Cirankiewicz. Some automatic pistols and grenades, manufactured by women working in the Krupp fuse factory, were smuggled into No. 3 Crematorium, which was blown up early in October 1944. But the revolt failed, and most of those who took part in it were shot.

In outward appearance the German and Russian concentration camps looked very much alike. There were the same merciless and arbitrary punishments, the same coarse guards recruited from the criminal class, the same rows of desolate wooden barracks laid down as meticulously as a Roman camp, the same watchtowers and search-lights and barbed-wire entanglements. A heartless, mechanical bureaucracy ruled. Filth and misery and torture reduced the prisoners to mockeries of themselves, and only the bravest and luckiest survived. The camps were places where men were stripped of the last vestiges of their human dignity, and this was done deliberately, according to plan, in the manner approved in the appropriate regulations, without any feeling of guilt, for a bureaucracy does not feel guilt. It was done by both the Germans and the Russians on a scale so breathtaking that it staggers the imagination. Two powerful dictatorships were engaged in a kind of race as to which of them could murder and reduce to shambling caricatures of humanity the largest number of its own people.

If one could have flown over a German concentration camp and then a Russian concentration camp, one would have seen remarkable similarities of design. It could hardly be otherwise, for essentially they served the same purpose—the planned degradation and destruction of the prisoners. Since the prisoners were expendable, their ultimate fate was of no concern to the government. If, as sometimes happened, a Russian prisoner was released from a camp and allowed to go home and resume his career, the explanation was not to be found in any leniency on the part of the prison authorities; it was simply that the prisoner had slipped through the bureaucratic mesh, as fish will sometimes slip through a net. If one in a hundred prisoners somehow manages to live out his term and is eventually released from prison, it does not prove that the prison is inefficient. It simply proves that when a man is sentenced to twenty-five years' imprisonment, he sometimes outlives his prison term. There was no appeals court; there were no pardons; there were no commutations of sentences. Both the Germans and the Russians upheld the rigor of the law. That the laws were insane was not a matter that ever troubled the vast bureaucracies, which administered the laws to their own advantage.

The Germans and the Russians were alike in setting up their concentration camps in frontier regions so that in the normal course of events very little would ever become known about the management of the camps. The administrators and the guards were sworn to secrecy. The guards were rarely given holidays; they, too, were prisoners. In theory they were not permitted to strike or punish a prisoner except under extreme provocation or after all due legal processes had been first explored. In fact they did as they pleased in the full knowledge that they would not be punished for their acts. There exists an extraordinary document signed on December 2, 1942, by Heinrich Himmler, ordering the guards in the concentration camps never to use physical violence "except as a last resort when hard labor, close arrest, and the withholding of food have proved to be ineffective." Himmler also threatened condign punishment to guards who stole money from the prisoners. He observed correctly that corruption should have no place in a corrective facility. Nevertheless, guards frequently beat prisoners and continually subjected them to extortion. Himmler of course knew very well what was happening in the camps; his orders were merely face-saving devices. Significantly, the order against physical violence in the camps was issued at the time of the Battle of Stalingrad, when the first wave of fear concerning the eventual fate of Germany shocked the leaders of the SS into an agonizing reappraisal of their methods. By this time the extermination camps were operating at full capacity. It was too late to reverse the trend, and the order of December 2, 1942, had no significance whatsoever.

The camps were governed by a system of complex, methodical regulations issued from headquarters, but these regulations were subject to the personal interpretations of the guards. There were thus two systems of laws. Both were insane, and both elevated lawlessness to a fine art. In Germany and Russia the methods were roughly the same, although there were important differences of principle. The two gigantic murder machines were activated by different fuels, the compression chambers were of different shapes, and the axles were greased with different lubricants. Although they resembled each other, they had different purposes:

RUSSIAN PRISON CAMPS	GERMAN PRISON CAMPS
The desire to punish.	The desire to kill.
Crushing of the will.	Crushing of the body.
Forced confessions.	Assumption of guilt.
A continuous process.	To be terminated within a fixed time span.
Aim: to impose conformity.	Aim: to eliminate nonconformity.
Method of punishment: hard labor, starvation rations, brutality, slow death from exhaustion.	Method of punishment: hard labor, starvation rations, brutality, sudden death from gas chamber or bullet.
Show trials.	Trials held rarely.
The prisoner knows what to expect.	The prisoner is deliberately misled about his fate.
The prison system is autonomous and self-generating, a permanent state within a state.	The prison system appears to be autonomous and self-generating but is in fact impermanent, a temporary state within a state.
The chiefs are liquidated one by one.	The same chiefs hold office throughout.
Terror applied with more or less constant pressure.	Terror applied with constantly mounting pressure.
Reflects the psychotic personalities of Lenin and Stalin.	Reflects the psychotic personality of Hitler.

Both the Russian and the German prison camps belong to the category of appalling errors which are justified and perpetuated because they serve the purposes of a few powerful, corrupt officials—men who are too lazy and incompetent to devise different and better methods to deal with their real and imagined enemies, men who derive satisfaction from inflicting suffering and death. The camps served the personal purposes of their creators. They did nothing whatsoever for the general good and were immensely wasteful of the most valuable of all resources: human skills and intelligence. They were vast, festering wounds that inevitably weakened the body politic. They provided massive evidence that the national government was corrupt, incompetent, and absurd, and therefore needed to be replaced. The existence of prison camps on such a massive scale testified to the weakness and insecurity of the dictator, not to his strength. They provided accurate barometers measuring the extent of the dictator's fear.

A useful fiction frequently repeated during the Nuremberg trials is that Hitler knew very little about the extermination camps and was not especially interested in them. The fiction relies on the fact that there are almost no surviving documents linking him to the camps. But the absence of documents shows only that Hitler took care that no documents should survive, not that the documents never existed. He was fully informed about the camps, received a constant stream of emissaries from the SS, and at least twice a day received reports from Himmler, and these reports came to him even when he was living for months on end in his concealed command post in East Prussia. He knew at all stages exactly what was going on and gave his directives by telephone and in secret conversations with Himmler, which took place *unter vier Augen*, "between four eyes." A whole department in his Chancellery was devoted to the planning and administration of the camps, with Philip Bouhler acting as his personal representative.

Bouhler was soft-faced and youthful-looking, resembling nothing so much as a lecturer in philosophy, which is what he had been until he was caught up in administrative duties in the Chancellery. Completely corrupt, he became chief censor of German school books; wrote a flattering life of Hitler, which was full of inaccuracies; and went on to write a book called *Napoleon, the Comet-Path of Genius,* which Hitler read avidly, finding, as Bouhler had hoped he would find, strange similarities between the genius of Napoleon and the genius of Hitler. Bouhler had been placed in charge of the euthanasia campaign, and for him it was merely a short step from euthanasia to mass murder. He was only forty-five when the war ended. The obscure, quiet-spoken Bouhler with the thick, horn-rimmed spectacles, a cautious and somewhat scholarly man, was one of the chief architects of mass murder. He vanished after the war, and no trace of him was ever found.

Stalin, too, took a deep personal interest in the camps. He studied them minutely, planned the sites, appointed the chief administrators, and read the lengthy reports issued by the Cheka for limited circulation among top officials. He knew exactly what was happening in the camps. Stalin and Hitler had far more in common than either of them suspected, and they understood each other well. Both were absolutely corrupt, dedicated killers, totally immoral. They placed no value on the lives of people, even those who helped them and perhaps especially those who helped them. Man = Zero. But if man is a worthless cipher, no harm is caused if he is killed and, indeed, it may be preferable to kill him. The only purpose he serves is to be used or to be killed.

According to the general belief, the mass murders in Hitler's concentration camps were incomparably more terrifying and more deadly than the mass murders in Stalin's labor camps. The facts are otherwise. Hitler's extermination camps went into high gear in the summer of 1942 and operated with increasing momentum for a period of thirty months. By November 1944 they had ceased to operate with any efficiency, and during the last six months of the war the machine broke down. Prisoners continued to die of malnutrition, typhus, random killing by the guards, and the exhaustion that came from forced marches in advance of the Russian armies. About six million men, women, and children died in the German camps. The Soviet prison camps have existed for nearly sixty years and about twenty-five million people have died in them or been killed by the execution squads of the Cheka. The staggering figures show that the Russian terror has been far more destructive than the German terror.

There are enough similarities between the German and the Russian camps to suggest that they sprang ultimately from the same cause. They sprang from the attitude of mind that regards Man = Zero as a formula to be applied wherever it is expedient, wherever it offers some advantage. If a problem is difficult, destroy the problem. If men are in the way, shoot them. In August 1918, Lenin sent an urgent telegram to the Novgorod Soviet: "Apply mass terror immediately, execute and exterminate hundreds of prostitutes, drunken soldiers, former officers, etc." The telegram was a nihilist's scream of despair. It said, "Massacre etc." There was no need in Lenin's mind to define "etc." On May 17, 1922, a week before he suffered his first stroke, he wrote urgently to the Commissar of Justice recommending a new criminal code that would openly proclaim the necessity, justification, and legitimacy of terror, forgetting that terror by its very nature is not susceptible to law. In this way, shortly before he passed from the scene, he announced the discovery of his final formula: Legality = Illegality.

Such men bear down with an intolerable weight on the human race. Their purpose is to destroy, not to build. The appalling vacuity and deadliness of their ideas have the quality of an obsession. Their small-spirited, mean, and violent minds are obsessed with human frailty; they will reshape man in their own image, and those who refuse to be reshaped will be stamped out, like vermin. Lenin repeatedly called his enemies or imagined enemies vermin, and so did Hitler. In the German concentration camps the inmates were called *Ungeziefer,* "vermin," on official documents. But the real vermin were those who succeeded by trickery in placing themselves in positions of power, thought of themselves as "great men," corrupted everything they touched, and trafficked with death.

Death was always their accomplice, always working to their advantage. He was so easy to summon, and he worked with such efficiency. He wore unfamiliar faces: sometimes he was a jar of blue crystals labeled Zyklon B, sometimes he was a telegram signed by Lenin, sometimes he was an open grave. Whatever disguise he wore, death was the master, not the slave.

One of the most resourceful of dictators, the last survivor of the triumvirate that once included Hitler and Mussolini, is Generalissimo Francisco Franco, who plunged Spain into a bloodbath and emerged as the undisputed ruler of a country drained of blood. Small, pompous, and absurd, he was all the more terrible for his absurdity. Like Hitler and Mussolini he designed huge monuments in his own honor. The greatest of these monuments is a cross of concrete nearly 500 feet high and weighing 200,000 tons, with an immense crypt intended to hold all the dead of the Spanish Civil War. Franco's own tomb will dominate all the others. It is called Santa Cruz del Valle de los Caidos, the Holy Cross of the Valley of the Fallen. All over Spain the dead were disinterred, Nationalists and Republicans alike, and reburied in the vast mausoleum where eventually the dead Franco will keep a watchful eye on them through all eternity.

The mysterious compulsions that rule in the recesses of the minds of dictators are manifest in that enormous cross and still more enormous cavern where death is sovereign and the generalissimo in all his panoply becomes death's earthly vice-regent. He said once, "To me alone God has granted the destiny of Spain," and he might have added, "The dead, too, have been entrusted into my care." At the heart of the mystery of corruption there is always this trafficking with death.

Franco's cross towers over the valley, a monument to his pride, his corruption, and his ferocity. It tells us nothing about the immensity of the human tragedy brought about by his decision to conquer Spain even if it meant that half the Spaniards would have to be killed. Nor is it likely that he will long remain in the marble tomb he has built for himself amid the fallen.

Perhaps it is the very immensity of the tragedy that blinds us to its causes. We can see the men who brought the tragedy about— Lenin, Stalin, Hitler, Franco—and we half accept the idea that they are the product of historical and social forces, and the world might be in the same plight if they had never lived. But the more we examine them the more we recognize that they were very similar in their character and in their methods. Above all they possessed the desire to dominate at all costs, even if there was no one left to dominate except the dead.

Sometimes but very rarely we can grasp the extent of the human tragedies they imposed on the world. The classic text is provided by a German engineer, Hermann Gräbe, who described the SS rounding up the Jews and slaughtering them in a mass grave in an abandoned airfield in Volhynia:

Without screaming or weeping these people undressed, stood around in family groups, kissed each other, said farewells, and waited for the sign from the SS man who stood beside the pit with a whip in his hand. During the 15 minutes I stood near, I heard no complaint or plea for mercy. I watched a family of about eight persons, a man and a woman both about fifty, with their children of about twenty to twenty-four, and two grown-up daughters about twenty-eight or twenty-nine. An old woman with snow-white hair was holding a one-year-old child in her arms and singing to it, tickling it. The child was cooing with delight. The couple were looking on with tears in their eyes. The father was holding the hand of a boy about ten years old and speaking to him softly; the boy was fighting his tears. The father pointed to the sky, stroked his head and seemed to explain something to him.

At that moment the SS man at the pit shouted something to his comrade. The latter counted off about twenty persons and instructed them to go behind the earthmound. Among them was the family I have just mentioned. I well remember a girl, slim and with black hair, who, as she passed me, pointed to herself and said, "Twenty-three." I walked around the mound and stood in front of a tremendous grave. People were closely wedged together and lying on top of each other so that only their heads were visible. Nearly all had blood running over their shoulders from their heads. Some of the people shot were still moving. Some were lifting their arms and turning their heads to show that they were still alive. The pit was already two-thirds full. I estimated that it already contained about a thousand people. I looked for the man who did the shooting. He was an SS man who sat at the narrow end of the pit, his feet dangling into it. He had a tommy gun on his knees and was smoking a cigarette. The people, completely naked, went down some steps which were cut in the clay wall of the pit and clambered over the heads of the people lying there, in the place to which the SS man directed them. Some caressed those who were still alive and spoke to them in low voices.

The scene, described so quietly, seems to be taking place in a nightmare. We hear only the voice of a young woman pointing to herself and saying, "Twenty-three" and the cooing of a baby. We do not even hear the gun shots. There is the sense of something happening beyond all understanding, as in a vision, or as though it happened in the long-distant past. We tell ourselves that this is not the real world and such things cannot happen now, and then we realize that somewhere in the world it is still happening and we are powerless to prevent it.

The Corruptions
of Our Time

In the chapter called "Walpurgis Night" in Thomas Mann's *The Magic Mountain* there is a curious description of patients in a tuberculosis sanatorium amusing themselves with a new game. They sit at a table with their eyes closed and try to draw a pig. Some succeed better than others. One man is able to draw a quite recognizable pig, with the eyes and pointed ears in the right place, the tiny legs properly situated under the rounded little belly, and the curving line of the pig's back ending appropriately in a little ringlet of a tail. He has accomplished the portrait of a pig with unfaltering accuracy. But when others play the same game, they unfailingly produce abortions lacking all coherence. The eyes are outside the head, the legs inside the paunch, the tail curls far away from the rear end, and the lines intended to portray the body of the pig do not meet. Sometimes there is something faintly resembling a pig, but generally these portraits have not the slightest resemblance to a pig or to anything on earth.

What has happened? Quite clearly a man drawing from memory

with his eyes closed is at a disadvantage. Unless he has a practiced skill, he draws in unrelated fragments, hoping they will relate to one another when the drawing is completed. He knows perfectly well the general shape of the pig—nothing could be more familiar—but in the darkness he is totally unable except in rare instances to re-create the familiar form. If he had been asked to draw a horse, he would fail even more calamitously.

Thomas Mann tells the story to illustrate the strange fragmentation of the minds of the patients in the sanatorium; he is telling a parable; the patients are themselves fragments. In them the forces of death are stronger than the forces of life, and they lack the organic tension that permits men to enjoy life. Dying, they give themselves up to small intrigues, wild fantasies, sudden rages. They are all touched by corruption, separated and fragmented.

One can imagine a civilization that reaches a critical state, explodes, and leaves nothing behind except a few unrelated fragments —a dishwasher, some coils of telephone wire, a marble statue of blindfolded Justice, and a Declaration of Independence. It would be difficult to make a plausible reconstruction from these disparate objects. We meet the same kind of difficulty when we attempt to reconstruct the lives of Neolithic men from a few surviving artifacts. Perhaps if we could hear them speaking, everything would be made clear and we would understand their lives perfectly. What is missing above all is the sound of their voices. We see them in fragments, but they were not themselves fragmentary.

Fragmentation occurs when a civilization is in decline. "Only connect," wrote E. M. Forster, seeing in the act of connection the essential element of civilization. But when the civilization is breaking down, the connections can no longer be made. The voices are confused. The ceremonies are being performed, but no one knows what god is worshiped or whether indeed there is any god behind the altar. All that was previously orderly, comprehensible, and conditional becomes disorderly, incomprehensible, and unconditional. Life may go on, but all that makes life worth living has been fragmented. This is the phenomenon described by the poet W. B. Yeats:

> *Things fall apart; the centre cannot hold;*
> *Mere anarchy is loosed upon the world,*
> *The blood-dimmed tide is loosed, and everywhere*
> *The ceremony of innocence is drowned;*
> *The best lack all conviction, while the worst*
> *Are full of passionate intensity.*

Yeats was speaking prophetically, for all this was to come about in Europe during World War II. But it is not, of course, necessary that a state of anarchy should come about as the result of a war. It can happen in peacetime. The postal service goes on strike; telegrams are deliberately delivered to the wrong address; food supplies are held up; the dictator has died, leaving behind a long tape-recorded speech which is played interminably on the radio; in the speech he urges the people to crush the enemy, but the name of the enemy is never mentioned. It is even easier in a highly industrialized state to bring about a state of anarchy. All that is necessary is to pull a few switches and take command of the telephone exchange and radio station. The modern city and especially the modern metropolis is amazingly vulnerable.

A modern city, unless ruled and organized by very wise and efficient men, consists of a series of interlocking fragments with little communication among them. In this jigsaw puzzle some of the pieces do not fit properly; there is a good deal of overlapping; authority is divided; and there is almost no sense of a common purpose. *Asabiyya* is notably lacking. When a shock wave passes through the city, the jigsaw tends to disintegrate. What appeared to be strong proves to be abysmally weak precisely because there is no coherence between the fragments. What appeared to be an iron bar proves to be compacted iron filings which, when the shock is delivered, become nothing more than a black powder that blows away with the first gust of wind. "Only connect." But there can be no connection between atoms of powder blowing away in the wind.

In an industrial civilization *asabiyya* is one of the first casualties. There is little sense of belonging or of purpose; religion no longer provides a substantial faith; a man lives for his family and for survival. Because survival is so difficult, because he is confronted with a soaring inflation and danger in the streets, he becomes more and more aware of the small, helpless creature he is, and he fights to survive, thinking only of himself and his immediate dependents. He has no sense of community with his neighbors, even with his next-door neighbor. He may know by sight a few people in the street where he lives, but he has no particular feeling for them. He is a stranger living in a world of strangers.

The phenomenon of alienation in industrial societies is as old as the Industrial Revolution, when for the first time men were reduced to statistics. The very nature of industrial society has worked toward the annihilation of man as a being existing in his own right and made in the image of God; instead, he discovers that he possesses few rights and can no longer believe that he possesses any sacred function. He is driven back into himself, in loneliness and despair, conscious of his vulnerability, his terrible inadequacy. He has an obscure feeling that society has been put together haphazardly like the pig in Thomas Mann's story. He is an atom, and there exists no magnet to draw all the atoms together.

Hence there arises what may be called the Genovese syndrome. In March 1964, in the Kew Gardens district of New York, a twenty-eight-year-old woman, Kitty Genovese, parked her car at 3:30 A.M. near the Kew Gardens railroad station and began to walk the short distance to her apartment. A man followed her and stabbed her. She screamed, lights went on in the neighboring apartment houses, people saw what was happening—and did nothing. The man walked away from the young woman, then returned, and stabbed her again. Miss Genovese staggered to her feet and attempted to reach her own apartment house. A city bus passed; it did not stop. Voices could be heard from the open windows. Someone shouted to the man, who was clearly visible, to leave the young woman alone; and these voices, instead of keeping him away, made him all the more determined to carry out his plan of murdering her. He went away, returned, and struck her for the third time as she lay slumped at the foot of the stairs in her own apartment house. Her screaming died down, the lights went out, and the man got in his car and drove away.

About a quarter of an hour passed before anyone telephoned the police. A neighbor of Miss Genovese who had witnessed the crime telephoned a friend in Nassau County for advice, and then, very reluctantly, he made his way over the roof of the apartment house and reached the apartment of an elderly woman. He did not make the call to the police himself. Somehow he succeeded in persuading the elderly woman to assume this responsibility. Asked why he took so much time to report to the police, he answered, "I did not want to get involved."

None of the thirty-seven people interviewed by the police felt he had acted disgracefully. All were indifferent, or they were afraid to become involved, or they quietly accepted the fact that such things happened and it was not their responsibility to prevent them. One man, asked why he had done nothing, replied, "I was tired, and went back to bed." Each of the thirty-seven people who saw the murder was within reach of a telephone, and none would have been in the least danger if he had called the police. The *New York Times* in an editorial written two weeks later asked: "Does residence in a great city destroy all sense of personal responsibility for one's neighbors? Who can explain such shocking indifference on the part of a cross section of our fellow New Yorkers? We regretfully admit that we do not know the answers."

Nevertheless, the answers are not hard to find; they lie in the fragmented nature of New York society. Street crime has become commonplace. In 1973 there were 1,680 reported murders in New York, which has a population of 8 million. Tokyo with a population of 11.6 million had 196 murders in the same period. The New York Police Department offers no hope that the number of murders will grow less. Murder has become endemic as a result of permanent local conditions, those conditions being widespread poverty, hopelessness, lack of faith, lack of real authority, lack of cohesion. The fragmentation continues, and New York is fast approaching the situation prophesied by H. G. Wells in an interview in 1933. The New York *American* carried headlines over the interview: H. G. WELLS VISIONS THE ENTIRE WORLD IN THE CLUTCHES OF ORGANIZED CRIME: SEES ERA OF DESERTED ROADS, FORTIFIED BANKS, BARRICADED HOMES.

The people who refused to go to the aid of Kitty Genovese even though the necessary aid consisted of nothing more than going to a telephone and calling the police were corrupted by fear and by apathy. Some feared for their lives, some feared the police, some were so frightened that they were no longer capable of reasoning and of taking conscious action, and some, perhaps the majority, were indifferent because it was happening to someone else somewhere else. It was not their affair, and they were not their sister's keepers. There was no law saying they must report the crime. It was too terrible to think about it, and so they stopped thinking about it and slept peacefully.

The sin against God is to regard people as things; Kitty Genovese became a thing, a statistic, a short paragraph in the evening newspaper. But she was not forgotten. In that strange episode where nothing happened except that a knife struck three times men saw the shape of the future.

The difficulty is to reconcile oneself to a future so bleak and so dangerous. Every year the number of murders rises and the police are powerless to prevent them. There are forty million handguns circulating in the United States; two and a half million are sold each year. Considerably more than 50 per cent of the guns are bought by people who are desperately frightened of being murdered. Next year more guns will be sold, and still more in the following year.

The relentless march of these figures implies an ever more dehuman-ized society.

In 1914 the poet Rainer Maria Rilke wrote, "The world is no longer in the hands of God; it is in the hands of men." Shocked into a state of stupor by the war, the poet quickly recovered and wrote poems in praise of the German army, which he later regretted. The poet T. S. Eliot speaks of God departing from the city in *Choruses from "The Rock":*

> *When the Stranger says: "What is the meaning of this city?*
> *Do you huddle close together because you love each other?"*
> *What will you answer? "We all dwell together*
> *To make money from each other"? or "This is a community"?*
> *And the Stranger will depart and return to the desert.*

The question is left open whether the Stranger will ever return to the city, and under what conditions. If life in the city consists merely of making money from each other, we are left with the impression that he will never return. The sense of the God who is absent, *Deus absconditus,* is inescapable in the slums of a city.

"If there is no God, then everything is permissible," says one of the characters of Dostoyevsky, using words that must serve as a chorus to any study of corruption. What Dostoyevsky meant by "everything" is far from being everything. He meant "every kind of evil, every outrage, every rape, every murder." If there is no God, then crime, even those crimes that shriek to heaven, is justified in human terms, because no other terms exist. If there is no God, mor-ality vanishes, the Ten Commandments are held in abeyance, the laws of the land are of no consequence, and the important thing is not to be found out. But if everything is permissible, it is permissi-ble to everyone, and only the law of the jungle prevails. If there is no God, then all things are in a state of corruption and the world is a charnel house. If there is no God, then a decent human society is no more justifiable than a murderous military dictatorship; for de-cency involves morality, and morality involves God. If there is no God, mass murderers are justified in their acts. If there is no God, there is no law.

Such are the implications of Dostoyevsky's words, and they are not easy to live with. Translated into another idiom, they read: "Since there is no God, I may be as corrupt and murderous as I please, and only those who are more corrupt and more murderous will be able to stop me. The world is nothing more than loot."

On the morning of March 16, 1968, there occurred in Vietnam, in the small hamlet of Mylai in Quang Ngai Province, a few miles inland from the South China Sea, an incident that may be remembered hundreds of years from now, for the people of Asia have long memories. It was not an isolated incident; other very similar incidents had occurred countless times, though rarely on such a large scale; but there was about this particular event a peculiar fatality, as though it represented the end of a long historical process, the moment of dissolution, the final obscene product of what was once, before corruption set in, intelligent, noble, and life-giving. At Mylai the American army suffered one of its most terrible defeats.

At 8:30 A.M. the first American assault troops arrived by helicopter just outside the hamlet. They were under the command of Captain Ernest Medina, a thirty-three-year-old former enlisted man who on the previous evening had given his men a pep talk in which he said their mission was to destroy the hamlet and everything in it including the animals, the houses, and the stores of grain. He declared later that he did not at any time order his men to kill women and children. This is probably true, but since he did say, "Destroy everything living; don't take any prisoners; everything in the village is the enemy," the question whether he specifically ordered the killing of completely defenseless persons is immaterial. The hamlet was to be wiped out.

Exactly why it had been chosen for destruction was not clear, although it was known that the 48th Viet Cong Battalion had recently been in the vicinity of the hamlet and was no doubt using it as a supply base, as it used all the other hamlets in Quang Ngai Province. The entire province had been declared a "free-fire zone," indicating that the Vietnamese peasants were suspected of being sympathetic to the Viet Cong, and at various times most of the hamlets had been attacked by assault troops or bombed from the air. But the troops who entered Mylai clearly did not expect to find any substantial number of Viet Cong in the hamlet; otherwise the helicopters would not have landed less than two hundred yards away, within rifle range of the enemy. They were on a "search-and-destroy" mission. "Search" was less important than "destroy."

Although the operation was a very simple one, headquarters was determined that it should be successful. A very senior officer, Major General Samuel Koster, circled the hamlet in a helicopter to observe the "search-and-destroy" mission. Helicopter gunships with overwhelming firepower also circled the hamlet and shot at everything that looked suspicious. Captain Medina set up his command post in a rice field outside Mylai and kept in close touch with his troops. Tape machines recorded conversations between the helicopters and the command post with the result that we know from minute to minute what was happening at Mylai.

What happened was exactly what the officers intended to happen. There were no Viet Cong in the hamlet, but a few were hiding nearby, and some of them actually witnessed the massacre that followed. It was an indiscriminate massacre. Women, children, and old men were systematically clubbed to death, bayoneted, blown to pieces with hand grenades, marched off in columns and mowed down with machine-gun fire, or thrown into a wide irrigation ditch and shot in much the same manner as the Nazis killed the Jews in the Ukraine. No youths or grown men were seen. There was blood everywhere. American soldiers were running around and shooting women and children in the doorways of their huts. Those trying to flee were thrown into the bunkers built for protection against air raids, and when there were enough people in the bunker, a hand grenade was thrown in. "Charlie" Company, under Lieutenant William Calley, an undersized former bellhop and dishwasher from Miami, was attempting to organize the massacre. He was completely successful. He ordered the peasants to be herded into the irrigation ditch, and then he shot at them with automatic fire until they were nothing more than a blood-red jelly. The women instinctively attempted to cover their children with their bodies, but most of the children died. When the shooting was over, one little boy crept from beneath his mother and went running back to the village. Lieutenant Calley hurried after the boy, carried him back to the ditch and shot him. Of the five hundred inhabitants of the hamlet, there were no more than about fifteen survivors. Nine of these, two old men, two women, and five children, were rescued by two Americans and flown by helicopter to safety.

At the orders of Captain Medina the entire hamlet was burned to the ground, the grain stores were destroyed, and the livestock was killed. He had set up his command post in the village and took part in the shooting. He appeared to be very calm and evidently knew what he was doing. Lieutenant Calley was in a state of frenzied excitement, shouting hoarsely, enjoying his newfound power to murder the enemy and insisting, whenever his orders were queried, that he was the boss. According to the official version of the engagement published on the following day in the *New York Times,* there had been a battle resulting in the killing of 128 enemy soldiers; 2 Americans had died and 12 had been wounded. These figures were completely imaginary. A few days later General William Westmoreland, the commander of the U.S. forces in Vietnam, sent a telegram congratulating "Charlie" Company for outstanding action on the battlefield and for having delivered a heavy blow to the enemy.

General Westmoreland either knew nothing about the massacre, in which case he was grotesquely ignorant about matters under his command, or he did know about it, in which case the telegram was part of the official cover-up. General Koster, flying in a helicopter above the hamlet, certainly knew about it.

The army covered up the massacre at Mylai so successfully that more than a year passed before any serious enquiry was undertaken. This happened because a former GI, Ronald Ridenhour, who had taken no part in the massacre but had once flown over the dead hamlet after the massacre took place, was haunted by all the stories he heard about it and decided to write to the president and to a number of senators and congressmen to ask for an official enquiry in the name of "the principles of justice and the equality of every man." He sent altogether thirty letters, received eight acknowledgments, but only two congressmen took a personal interest in the letter. They were Morris Udall of Arizona and Mendel Rivers of South Carolina, who was chairman of the Armed Services Committee. The letter was written well and had the ring of truth in it. The army quickly decided to embark on a cautious investigation, but many months passed before Captain Medina and Lieutenant Calley were arrested and placed on trial.

The massacre at Mylai was only one of many massacres committed by the American forces in Vietnam. Massacre was an essential element in the overall strategy of inspiring terror in the enemy. Whole villages were bombed until nothing remained but rubble, or they were engulfed in napalm, with men, women, and children burned to cinders. At the close of each day's business the American army produced the required statistics: the body count. We know now that body counts were fraudulent and represented little more than elaborate guesswork and wish fulfillment; they were not entirely imaginary because they represented the hopes and despairs of the American army.

The body counts in Vietnam, announced every day as regularly as clockwork, quoted in all the newspapers and recited by the Secretary of Defense with an air of total authority, represent one aspect of corruption that has the gravest importance, for it is precisely when men become statistics that they are in the greatest danger of being used by corrupt and incompetent men. Statistics of the imaginary dead in Vietnam served many purposes. They satisfied the army, which could then construct projections on the course of the war. They satisfied some Americans at home who felt that the body counts demonstrated the inevitability of victory, since the North Vietnamese and the Viet Cong dead were reported in the hundreds of thousands while the Americans and the South Vietnamese dead were reported only in the hundreds. The monotonous repetition of the figures day after day gave them a certain validity; and all the time they were quietly producing the poison of corruption. They were manipulated lies.

Very early in America's involvement in Vietnam things went terribly wrong. President Kennedy believed the South Vietnamese could win the war against the North Vietnamese only so long as it was *their* war. At the same time he believed in sending armaments, officers, and enlisted men to aid the hard-pressed South Vietnamese. The officers and enlisted men, who were called advisers, numbered more than thirty thousand. *Their* war and *our* war became subtly confused. When President Johnson succeeded President Kennedy, there was no longer any confusion: *their* war became *our* war. The president's chief assistants were well-meaning and well-educated men, administrators and professors, who might have been expected to understand that the situation in Indochina was infinitely complex and not to be solved by simple methods. Robert McNamara, McGeorge Bundy, Walt Rostow, and Dean Rusk were intelligently alert when it came to dealing with American problems; they had not the faintest idea what was happening in the minds of the Indochinese, and they did not care. They were imaginatively sterile and in love with their own power. They found it easy to lie, and they lied grotesquely, miserably and interminably. They bear the responsibility for the fantastic growth of the American forces in Indochina until the time came when there were half a million American troops in the country, fighting a war they could not possibly win. The youth and treasure of the United States poured into Saigon. After 1964, when the American involvement acquired massive dimensions, the wasting of American resources went on unimpeded; and South Vietnam, ruled by a succession of military dictators, became a sewer of corruption.

The solution had been found: total American involvement in the war, the use of overwhelming force, the destruction if necessary of entire cities, entire towns, entire districts. The interests of the Vietnamese were not considered. They were statistics, "gooks," subhuman, poverty-stricken, therefore zero. The American army believed that most of the peasants—and the population consists almost entirely of peasants—favored the Viet Cong. Therefore there was no need to preserve them or safeguard their lives in any way. All were expendable.

The American government made no effort to explore the minds of the Vietnamese people. In the fifteen years of military involvement not a single book was translated from Vietnamese into English. No effort was made to understand the history and culture of Vietnam and the long-established habits and customs of the Vietnamese. Crude force was the only instrument. Antipersonnel bombs were used, in contravention of the Geneva Convention; defoliation poisons were spewed from airplanes to kill all growing plants; the uses of napalm were perfected; the most powerful industrial country in the world was pitted against the secret armies of the Viet Cong, who took cover in darkness and moved silently in the undergrowth. It was an uneven battle, for the Viet Cong had all the advantages: the human understanding, the knowledge of their own people and of their land, the certainty that they were fighting against an invader. Few wars are won by weapons alone. The Americans had forgotten the human element. We had lost the war before it began. Most Americans thought of it in terms of body counts, numbers of hamlets destroyed, numbers of sorties by infantrymen, numbers of strikes by bombing planes, numbers of areas defoliated. In terms of numbers we won the war daily. But the war, despite the evidence of American successes, continued unabated. The Vietnamese were dying in hundreds of thousands, and few of the survivors felt they owed any debt to the Americans.

The Vietnam War was a strange war, fought outside the rules of war. In Washington and Hanoi experienced generals sat over their maps, moved strips of colored plastic, gave orders on the telephone, and sat back to await the results of their deliberations. The Communist generals were as coldly inhuman and detached as their American counterparts. The Americans finally withdrew from Vietnam. We had gained nothing, lost fifty thousand men, wasted our treasure, and brought about massive social dislocations both in Vietnam and in the United States.

The United States had the resources to win the war in Vietnam, but not by fighting. If we had established a peace army; if we had genuinely helped the poor, the weak, and the oppressed with food and medical care; if we had attempted to bring education and advanced agricultural methods to the Vietnamese peasants and learned their language and customs and helped them to form a representative government, we would have found willing allies wherever we went. Instead the task of winning the war was given over to the American military machine, which by the nature of things was incompetent to win men's minds. Americans had the choice: to bring life or to bring death. Because the men in charge of the war were corrupt and indifferent to the human suffering of the peasants, we lost the war. After a particularly ferocious bombing of a South Vietnamese town, an American major said, "We had to destroy it so that it would remain free." All this destruction played into the hands of the enemy. Like an insane and ignorant child America was meddling with an age-old culture of Southeast Asia and destroying it piecemeal.

Naked power has its limitations, since power is a generator of corruption and corruption in its turn tends to dilute the effectiveness of power. The Vietnamese were perfectly aware of the dilution of American power. They saw the fighting machines, the bombers, the gunships, the heavy artillery, all the gleaming, death-dealing instruments, which in theory should have won the war within a month, and they saw that the war was not won and that the machines were more vulnerable than anyone had thought possible. The fighting machines inflicted appalling damage, but the war went on. Every American victory was a defeat, for every dead enemy became a martyr, and every martyr produced ten living soldiers. The war was not being fought with machines; it was being fought with invisible weapons. The *asabiyya* of the Vietnamese peasants, the consciousness that the white races no longer had any effective role to play in Asia, the knowledge that the Asians possessed an endurance denied to the West—all these played their part. The peasant held fast to his humanity and demanded that it should be respected. It was not respected by the Americans, and the peasant drew the logical conclusions.

American involvement in Vietnam was a disaster of the first magnitude. The falsified body counts, the "fragging" of American officers with grenades thrown by their own men, the underground "tiger cages" where Viet Cong prisoners were held, the murder of civilians, the defoliation of the landscape, the appalling financial corruption in the docks at Saigon, the succession of military dictatorships with each new dictator being chosen by the American authorities—these were the signs of an unhealthy and corrupt government in Washington which seemed, as the war continued, to be beyond hope of redemption. Under President Lyndon Johnson and then under President Nixon the administration of the war in Vietnam took on the colors of parody. Each president repeatedly addressed the nation and wearily repeated a succession of barefaced lies concerning the prospects of imminent victory. They did not believe their lies; their television images betrayed them; they spoke haltingly, as criminals speak when confronted with their crimes; and they continued in every way possible to conduct the war with secret maneuvers designed to keep the American public in ignorance of what was actually happening.

The American people had no control of these events. Power had been seized by a small group of secretive men who successfully resisted enquiry about their activities. The American public was not permitted to know that Cambodia was being bombed or that defoliation was being practiced on a massive scale or that appalling massacres were taking place. The checks and balances had broken down, the democratic processes were discarded, the lies continued. Someone invented the term "credibility gap," to be applied to presidents and senior members of the government. It was an awkward term, but it enabled American correspondents to talk to the presidents and remind them of their "credibility gaps." It would have been more difficult and perhaps more dangerous to tell them to their faces that they were barefaced liars.

Corrupt men are always liars. Lies are their instruments, their pleasure, their solace. In time they come to believe their lies, or rather to half-believe them. They test out their skill in lying in the Area of Confusion, where they serve their apprenticeship in corruption, and when they have passed through the gate into Toward Absolute Corruption, they lie more adroitly, certain at last that they have acquired the keys of power. But, strangely, both President Johnson and President Nixon were inept liars. They lied so obviously, so heavily, that they lacked conviction even in their smallest lies.

Foreign governments were well aware of President Nixon's reputation for lying. The tragedy was not that the president lied; the tragedy was that American honor was involved.

Corrupt men choose other corrupt men for their allies. The men around President Nixon were by common consent such a gang of poltroons as has rarely decorated the White House. They were criminals who rejoiced in their criminality, predatory, vicious, and self-serving. It is not remarkable that President Nixon had chosen them, for he attracted into his service men who were most like himself.

What is remarkable is that they advertised their criminality and were so convinced that they were unassailable that they failed to take the most elementary precautions. They comprised a mafia that was different from the traditional Mafia in that the CIA, the FBI, and the Justice Department protected and assisted them. It rarely occurred to them that reporters had long ago detected their criminality and were lying in wait for them. They talked like mafiosi, acted like mafiosi, quarreled among themselves like mafiosi. Unlike mafiosi, they had no code of honor, and when their misdeeds were discovered, they bitterly accused one another. They resembled the Pazzi conspirators in Florence who were hanged by the legs upside down and in their dying agonies bit one another.

In foreign affairs, too, President Nixon had a predilection for corrupt men. He was especially close to General Yahya Khan, the military dictator of Pakistan. Fat, ungainly, and theatrical, Yahya Khan claimed to be a descendant of Nadir Shah, a former slave who rose to become shah of Persia and successfully waged war against the Afghans, the Turks, and the armies of the Mughal emperor, and whose most memorable feat was the sack of Delhi. Nadir Shah was one of those emperors who took special delight in massacres, and even to this day his name is spoken with bated breath in North India. Yahya Khan's belief in his imperial ancestry became more fervent when he was drunk. In fact his father was a small farmer from the obscure village of Chakwal some sixty-five miles southwest of Rawalpindi.

Pakistan, which came to birth after the partition of India in 1947, consisted of two large areas separated by the entire width of India. West Pakistan was inhabited by Punjabis, Pathans, Sindhis, and Baluchis, mostly tall, fair-complexioned, and thick-boned. East Pakistan was inhabited by the small, dark, thin-boned Bengalis. In West Pakistan most people spoke Urdu and Punjabi; in East Pakistan they spoke Bengali. What these two separate countries had in common was their religion, Islam, and a government that exercised power from Islamabad in West Pakistan. The people of East Pakistan, who regarded themselves as a colony of West Pakistan, were determined to achieve a measure of independence. They intensely disliked the military government ruling from Islamabad, which was arbitrary and clearly favored the Punjabis at the expense of all the other inhabitants of Pakistan. The generals and the officers ruled, and there were very few positions open to Bengalis. The military government had attempted to ban the use of the Bengali language in

East Pakistan, but without success. In the early spring of 1971 tempers were at flash-point. The Bengalis had voted solidly for the Awami League led by Sheikh Mujibur Rahman, who insisted on permitting the Bengalis to manage their own affairs short of complete independence, and the military dictatorship was faced with a dilemma. Either it could continue to act in spite of the Awami League or it could destroy the Awami League. It chose to destroy the league.

On the night of March 25, 1971, American-built M-24 tanks advanced from the military cantonment just outside Dacca, the capital of East Pakistan, into the center of the city. Behind the tanks came the West Pakistani infantry. The orders given by General Yahya Khan, who flew off to Karachi early in the evening, were succinct: "Sort them out!" This meant, "Massacre everyone on the side of the Awami League and spare only those who approve of the military dictatorship." The tanks advanced on the dormitories of the University of Dacca; there was a general massacre of professors and students. The police barracks was attacked and set on fire, and there was a massacre of the Bengali-speaking police. The East Pakistan Rifles' barracks was also attacked, and there was another general massacre. The military believed that the students, the police, and the East Pakistan Rifles would offer the most serious resistance, and some of the events that happened that night may be considered as a preemptive strike. At the same time detachments of troops set fire to the thatched huts in the poorer parts of the city, posted machine guns outside and killed everyone who tried to escape. The pattern of terror and repression, which continued for nine months, was established that night.

General Yahya Khan was determined to destroy the Awami League at all costs, even if it meant killing two or three million people; and since the league was spread widely in East Pakistan and maintained an office and a political organization in every village, it was obvious that he would have to arrest or kill a very large number of people. Like Generalissimo Francisco Franco, who announced in 1936 that it might be necessary to kill half the population of Spain to prevent it from falling into the hands of the Socialists and the Communists, General Yahya Khan had no qualms about destroying his compatriots. Intellectuals, professional men, leaders of the Awami League, Bengali soldiers and officers, railroadmen, and students were rounded up, thrown into concentration camps, tortured, and killed. To all outward appearances the country was being run by the military, who soon discovered that they were incompetent administrators. Since most of the dockworkers and longshoremen at Chittagong, the chief port, had been killed or were in hiding, soldiers from West Pakistan were flown in to take their places; and since most of the railroadmen had also been killed or were in hiding, soldiers took their places as well.

Within three weeks East Pakistan was in a state of chaos. Large areas of Chittagong, Kushtia, Mymensingh, Rajshahi, and Jessore had been depopulated, and at night three million people were moving across the rice and jute fields, trying to escape to places of safety beyond the reach of the Pakistani army. Many of them went over the border to India, where some eight million refugees finally found shelter. Meanwhile the killing went on relentlessly. The Punjabi soldiers raped, tortured, and murdered at their pleasure. One of their minor amusements was to line up a group of helpless peasants so close to one another that it was possible to kill them all with a single high-velocity bullet. East Pakistan became a graveyard.

The news of the atrocities in East Pakistan reached the outside world. Anthony Mascarenas, a Pakistani journalist believed to be entirely reliable by the military authorities, was permitted to travel through the country and watch the military at work. His report, first published in an English newspaper, was an indictment of the anarchic and murderous rule of the military. From Calcutta came a stream of reports from daring Indian journalists who succeeded in entering East Pakistan. By June 1971 nearly every newspaper in the world was carrying accounts of the atrocities, which were denied by the government in Islamabad. There had been a few "unfortunate incidents," a few peasants had been killed, and most regrettably there had been a fire at Kushtia which had burned most of the city to the ground. General Yahya Khan maintained that his troops were merely keeping order.

President Nixon and Henry Kissinger were well aware that East Pakistan was living through a reign of terror. Accurate reports of the bloodbath were received regularly in Washington from the American consul-general in Dacca. But both Nixon and Kissinger owed a debt to General Yahya Khan, who for some months had been helping to prepare the groundwork for the *coup de théâtre* which Nixon had been secretly cherishing since the day he became president: the meeting between himself and Mao Tse-tung in Peking. In July Kissinger flew to India and then to West Pakistan. In India he had no word of sympathy for the Indians who were troubled by the vast invasion of refugees; in West Pakistan he promised General Yahya Khan a continual supply of armaments, knowing that they would be used to kill the people of East Pakistan. Then, in a much publicized secret journey, he flew to Peking to make the arrangements for Nixon's visit to Communist China.

The massacres in East Pakistan continued, but the military government of West Pakistan was becoming increasingly aware that the Bengalis were learning to fight back. The Mukti Bahini, the freedom army, armed with captured weapons and supplies from India, fought two pitched battles against the Pakistani army in September. Thereafter the fighting grew even more savage as the Pakistani government realized that it was confronted with a full-scale rebellion. A provisional government had been established by the Bengalis in April. Sheikh Mujibur Rahman was under arrest and believed to have been killed. The Bengalis spoke of a war that might last ten years, and they were prepared to go on fighting because the alternative was to live under a tyranny which was among the most terrible the world has ever seen.

The rivers of East Pakistan ran with blood; a thousand villages went up in flames; Bengali women were bayoneted to death after being raped by Punjabi soldiers; massacre became a way of solving all problems. Massacre satisfied the military, who duly reported the official body counts to Islamabad while minimizing their own losses. General Yahya Khan proclaimed that East Pakistan had been completely pacified at a time when the country was engaged in civil war. He appears to have known very little about the real situation in East Pakistan, and he did not care because he knew he could rely on the resources of a friendly China and an equally friendly United States. Like all the senior generals in the Pakistani army he was totally corrupt, and as always corruption blinded him to the true state of affairs. The destruction of East Pakistan was only the first step in his grandiose plan of conquest. The second step was the conquest of India, or at least of vast areas of northern India. On December 3, 1971, he ordered an invasion of India and a preemptive strike against Indian airfields. His plans were known to Nixon and Kissinger, who made no effort to stop him. They despised the Indians and would not have been in the least disturbed by an Indian defeat. The invasion of India was a fiasco; so too was the preemptive strike on the airfields. The Indians attacked East Pakistan and with the help of the Mukti Bahini destroyed the Pakistani army. On the racecourse at Dacca the commander-in-chief of the Pakistani forces signed the instrument of surrender on December 16.

Up to the last moment Nixon and Kissinger worked to avert the coming disaster to the Pakistani army. The U.S. Seventh Fleet, armed with nuclear warheads, was directed to sail into the Bay of Bengal, ostensibly to rescue American citizens in East Pakistan. Just as General Yahya Khan had acted in the stupor of corruption, scarcely knowing what he was doing, so Nixon and Kissinger also acted blindly and irresponsibly at a time when it was more than necessary to act calmly and intelligently. Happily the war was over before the nuclear fleet could bombard devastated East Pakistan.

On the night of the surrender General Yahya Khan addressed his people on the radio. He admitted that as a result of unfortunate circumstances the war in East Pakistan had been brought to a conclusion. He spoke in Urdu, slurring his words, for he was drunk and barely able to read from the paper in front of him. He praised himself and went on to praise the Pakistani army, which had just surrendered ignominiously, invoked Allah, and spoke as though all these terrible events had taken place spontaneously, as a result of the inevitable propensity of human beings to err. The war was lost —regrettable. East Pakistan no longer existed—regrettable. He did not mention the new nation, Bangladesh, that arose from the ruins of East Pakistan, martyred, streaming with blood, stupefied by the horrors it had seen. Like President Nixon when he resigned from office, Yahya Khan made no apologies; nor did he mention that there had been a surrender on the racecourse at Dacca.

Why were such things permitted to happen? Partly, of course, because the military elite of West Pakistan drew enormous financial profit from the bloody adventure. There were tariffs for men's lives. A Bengali industrialist or doctor in Dacca was permitted to live on condition that his entire bank balance was surrendered. Similarly, the village women were sometimes allowed to go free after surrendering their gold jewelry. The rape of the Bengalis' wealth was officially encouraged and protected by the military authorities. For all the West Pakistani soldiers, officers and soldiers alike, there was the emotional satisfaction of killing. The fact that they were killing their own people was a matter of indifference to them. The Bengalis in East Pakistan were nearly all Muslims, but the fair-skinned Punjabis had convinced themselves, or were convinced, that the Bengalis were Muslims of an inferior kind. Killing was an emotional relief from the stultifying life of the barracks.

General Yahya Khan had come to believe that the mantle of Nadir Shah had fallen on him and that he could do anything he pleased. He believed rightly that he was under the special protection of the president of the United States and the chairman of the People's Republic of China, both of whom provided him with armaments. The fact that India lay between East and West Pakistan was an added inducement to the general massacre, for it served as a warning to the Indians of what they might expect in the coming war with Pakistan. He was terrified by India, and his campaign against East Pakistan was conducted in the full knowledge that India would take cognizance of what he was doing. India, not East Pakistan, was the real enemy; and he hated the Bengalis of East Pakistan all the more because they resembled Indians and retained some elements of Indian culture. In as far as he could make rational decisions, his decision to strike at India on December 3, 1971, is completely understandable. What is not understandable is why he struck so feebly after publicly stating that he was about to order the attack and thus providing the Indians with ample warning. The man who ordered the greatest massacre of the post-World War II era proved to be an incompetent general so corrupted by power that he had lost the sense of reality. He was not iron; he was jelly.

General Yahya Khan provides a pitiable example of a man who came to supreme power without any of the necessary qualities for ruling. His corruption grew out of his weakness, not his strength. Like President Nixon, he was totally incompetent and therefore forced himself to wear the mask of a "great man" and to act on a grand scale: the worm imagined he was a dragon. Like Nixon he lacked any grace of mind, or kindness, or mercy. He blustered, consulted his "shadow cabinet," which consisted of his mistresses, exulted in his power to punish and to pardon, signed his decrees with enormous flourishes, and insisted like a medieval monarch that he should always be addressed by all his titles. He was the pure tyrant armed with the most sophisticated modern weapons.

Long ago John of Salisbury announced that "tyranny is a crime aimed against the body of Justice herself" and that "whoever does not seek to bring the tyrant to punishment offends against himself and the whole body of the earthly commonwealth." General Yahya Khan was not punished. A few days after his speech on the radio he was quietly eased out of office by Zulfikar Ali Bhutto, his perennial rival, who set about establishing his own dictatorship. General Yahya Khan was retired from the active list and given a house in Abbottabad, near the golf links. From time to time he complains bitterly to Zulfikar Ali Bhutto about his "servitude" and reminds his successor of the great services he has performed for his nation.

The tragic incompetence of rulers even when provided with well-trained and intelligent assistants was shown in September 1965 when Achmed Sukarno, who had proclaimed himself President for Life of the Republic of Indonesia—he had also granted himself the titles Supreme Helmsman, Great Leader of the Indonesian Revolution, Supreme Builder, Supreme Fisherman, Supreme Guardian of the Muhammadiyah, Supreme Educator, and First Pioneer of Freedom in Africa and Asia—suddenly decided that the time had come to install a Communist government in Indonesia with himself as Supreme Chairman. With the help of Colonel Utung, commander of the palace guard, and Dr. Subandrio, the prime minister, he instigated a revolt against the generals and the general staff. On September 30, 1965, six Indonesian generals were tortured and murdered. Their mutilated bodies were thrown into a well. General Abdul Haris Nasution, the minister of defense, was shot at but escaped unharmed; his five-year-old daughter was killed. The Indonesian Communist Party issued a call to arms and announced that a new government had been installed under Sukarno to transform Indonesia into a Communist state. The new government was short-lived. One of the surviving generals led the countercoup, and soon all over Indonesia Communists were being massacred in a popular uprising. Some three hundred thousand were killed during the holy war against the infidels that raged over the whole of Java and Bali and much of Sumatra. For a while the Communist guerrillas attempted to raise a civil war in Central Java; this failed; the survivors fled into the jungles and the limestone caves, where they were found cowering in the darkness. Plucked from the caves, they were immediately executed. It was the greatest disaster that had ever befallen a Communist party.

None of this would have happened if Sukarno had not been so corrupted by power that he was no longer able to come to terms with reality. He saw himself as all-powerful, a divinely appointed leader who was entitled to change the form of his government at will. Like General Yahya Khan, he lived among his mistresses and saw the world through the veils of his harem. Supreme in all things, he nevertheless found life empty and unrewarding, and he attempted to impose a Communist government on Indonesia merely because he was in search of excitement and a new title. To a remarkable and frightening degree he possessed what Emily Dickinson called "the zero at the bone," a corrosive emptiness that burned him out and left room only for the exercise of arbitrary power. He was a sick man, suffering from a disease of the kidneys, and he was being attended by Chinese doctors when he issued the call for a Communist dictatorship on the Chinese model. He was not punished, although he was directly responsible for the deaths of three hundred thousand men, women, and children. In theory he remained president for life. In fact he was president only in name, and General Suharto, one of the few surviving generals, succeeded in stripping him delicately of his powers until only the husks of power remained.

The scale of the massacres in Indonesia and East Pakistan was terrifying. In each case the massacre was brought about by the political incompetence of a corrupt and powerful man; and if these men had been strangled at birth the massacres would not have taken place. The damage that can be done by one corrupt man is breathtaking.

Long ago Nechayev showed how it was possible for one man or a very small group of men to overturn a state: all that was necessary was to find the Archimedian point and exert pressure. In theory a very small charge of dynamite in the proper place can bring a skyscraper crumbling down until it is nothing more than a heap of rubble; a single match can destroy a whole city; a bucket of poison in a reservoir can bring about the deaths of all the people whose drinking water is piped from it. All countries, all cities, are vulnerable.

One day in 1971 a policeman walked into the police property clerk's office in New York and quietly removed four hundred pounds of narcotics worth about $73 million at street prices. The police had accumulated this store of narcotics in countless raids on addicts and drug-traffickers, and now it was being sold back to the traffickers. New York was swimming in drugs, and the chief supply was coming from the police, who were being paid to suppress the drug traffic. No one could possibly count the number of murders and suicides and the increase in general misery brought about by this single theft.

It was an act comparable to a massacre, and significantly it happened during the presidency of Richard Nixon, who publicly extolled law and order, granted the police more powers than they had ever possessed, and abused his presidential authority to such an extent that a patient and long-suffering Congress finally succeeded in forcing him from office in disgrace.

The Corrupt
Presidency

R ichard Milhous Nixon, the former president of the United States, was born on January 9, 1913, in Yorba Linda, a farming village thirty miles inland from Los Angeles. His father, Frank Nixon, was black Irish, a man of towering rages, incapable of holding a job for long, and his mother, born Hannah Milhous, also Irish, was a quiet, strong-willed woman who kept her temper, was pleasant to everyone, and held firmly to her Quaker faith. Frank left school after only six years of education, but Hannah graduated from Whittier College and was well educated. She had five sons: Harold, Richard, Donald, Arthur, and Edward. Harold and Arthur died young, and at their deaths the family was shattered by grief. It was a very close-knit family, remarkable only because it survived the strains that come about when an educated woman marries a drifter.

At various times Frank Nixon was a conductor on the streetcars of Columbus, Ohio, he painted Pullman cars, drilled for oil, farmed, and kept a village store in a disused church. He had no settled aim in life, was constantly in debt, and fiercely resented his poverty. He instilled in his surviving sons the belief that the only sure way to live well was to acquire a good deal of money. Hannah was far less concerned with money than with her Quaker faith and with the necessity of doing good in the world. She genuinely liked to help people, even perfect strangers, and people in trouble would go to her.

Richard inherited many of his parents' characteristics: his father's rages, his mother's eagerness to do good works, her dogged persistence, her Quaker faith. From her, too, he derived his features, including the strange, lumpy nose that gave him something of the appearance of a comic actor and that was to become the delight of caricaturists.

Nothing in the boy's early life suggested that he was presidential timber. Its very ordinariness, close to the poverty level, gave it a kind of dignity. Because the freight cars of the Santa Fe Railroad passed close to the Nixons' house in Yorba Linda, young Richard dreamed of becoming a railroad engineer, and in later years he liked to remember the days when he watched the trains roaring past and vanishing into the distance. For a while Frank attempted to manage an orange and avocado farm at Yorba Linda, but he pulled up stakes when Richard was nine and settled in Whittier, closer to Los Angeles. Here he acquired a disused church and converted it into a general store, and Richard, always reclusive, used to hide in the abandoned belfry. He went to school in Whittier and later to college, where his grades were mediocre. He worked hard and learned to speak trenchantly, acquiring a reputation as a debater. Oratory fascinated him. He was fourteen when, during a summer spent in Prescott, Arizona, he earned his first fees as an orator. This was when he went to work as a barker in a concession at the Slippery Gulch Rodeo.

Whittier had originally been settled by Quakers and was named in honor of the gentle Quaker poet John Greenleaf Whittier. It was a small town with about twelve thousand inhabitants, a shipping point for walnuts, avocados, oranges, and lemons, and it was penetrated through and through with the philosophy of its founding fathers. Here at last Frank Nixon settled down with his general store, with his wife and his sons serving behind the counter. It was the only place where he acquired any roots. As he grew older, he became more embittered and he was constantly cursing politicians and lawyers, saying they were all corrupt. Richard announced that he would become a politician and a lawyer on the side of the people against the corrupters.

Such sentiments were not unusual among the dedicated Quakers of Whittier. They were on the side of the angels against the evil of the world. In his poem "The Tent on the Beach" Whittier speaks of how he left the haunt of the Muses to turn "the crank of an opinion mill" but continued to hear the voices of the Muses:

> *He heard the fitful music still*
> *Of winds that out of dream-land blew.*

Richard Nixon gave no sign that he heard the fitful music. He worked at his lessons, played football poorly, wore hand-me-downs, and excelled only in the hard-hitting oratory he had learned from his father. His affections were centered on his mother, who sometimes sat with him as he did his homework. Ironically, his first school debate was on the subject of whether it was better to own a house than to rent one. With his father's help he constructed his argument around the advantages of renting a house.

As he grew older, he developed a deep sense of property, dressed with care, walked purposefully, and made few friends. Shy and secretive, he was happiest in the belfry of the converted church. Later, when he became president, he liked to steal away from the Oval Office and work in a smaller office in a nearby building. He liked to hide, to be alone where no one could find him.

At Whittier College, which he entered on a partial scholarship provided in the will of his grandfather, Franklin Milhous, a prosperous fruit farmer, he was not regarded as an outstanding student although he worked so hard that he sometimes made himself ill. He had the competitive spirit but lacked the native intelligence to achieve distinction. It was the same in sports, in amateur theatricals, and in dating girls. He was not a failure but he was not a success, and this embittered him. He taught at Sunday School and played the organ, and his mother thought he might become a Quaker missionary in Central America. This was a career that never attracted him. He was more interested by the raucous fundamentalist evangelists who pounded their Bibles, rolled their eyes, and pronounced doom upon the world, and at a meeting held by one of these evangelists he made, as he wrote later, his "personal commitment to Christ and Christian service." He was not so much deeply religious as caught up by the drama and oratory of evangelism. Since oratory was the subject that interested him most, and since he had no intention of becoming a missionary, he began to think of becoming a lawyer. In 1934, on a full scholarship provided by the Duke Foundation, he was admitted to the Duke University Law School.

He was a hard worker, known for his "iron butt" and for his peculiarly solemn expression, as of a man who takes himself very seriously and is determined to live his own life, not popular, not unpopular, and terribly lonely. A classmate said he worked "almost fearfully." Such fearful work is not unusual among scholarship boys who receive very small allowances from home; he was deeply aware that he had nothing except his own hard work to fall back upon. He was graduated in June 1937, applied for a job in the FBI, was rejected, and then went the rounds of the great corporate law firms in New York, only to be rejected by all of them. Reluctantly he left the East Coast and took a train back to California. A law firm in Whittier accepted him, and by the end of his first year he was a partner. Wingert, Bewley & Nixon was the new name of the firm. An obscure lawyer in an obscure town, he seemed destined for obscurity and could expect to spend the rest of his life in Whittier. He married Pat Ryan, the daughter of a Nevada miner, who had worked her way through the University of Southern California, occasionally acted as an extra in Hollywood films, and was then teaching shorthand and typing at Whittier High School. She tended to dominate her husband, had none of Hannah Milhous's gentleness, and was fiercely ambitious.

The Japanese attack on Pearl Harbor in late 1941 changed their lives, as it changed the lives of all Americans. Almost at once Richard and Pat Nixon took the train for Washington. A well-paying job in the Office of Price Administration offered security, while Washington offered a close view of the way the country was being led under Roosevelt. But by the summer of 1942 Richard Nixon was bored with a job that was hopelessly bureaucratic and fundamentally distasteful to him. Although he was a Quaker and therefore under considerable pressure to avoid taking part in a war, he applied for and received a commission in the U.S. navy. In May 1943, after six months' training, he was assigned to the South Pacific Transport Command. He did no fighting. He was part of the complex machinery that brought soldiers and supplies to the staging areas, set up landing strips, arranged PX facilities, and helped to build latrines. It was not a particularly heroic period in his life, but it was crucial for his development, for he now concentrated on amassing as quickly as possible the largest possible amount of money. His chief contribution to the war effort consisted in entertaining other junior naval officers at poker, playing with such deadly seriousness that he became a master at the game and made a small fortune. He learned to curse violently and continually; he learned the devious tricks of the practiced poker player; and by the end of the war, after fourteen months on Bougainville and Green Island, he had acquired the character he would display to the end of his life. All his links with the Quaker faith were snapped. He became a dedicated gambler, his eyes on the main chance, with an ugly tongue and no moral purpose. What was interesting about him was precisely that he was a man without a faith and without a purpose.

Chance, which can be manipulated in stud poker and in life, brought Nixon's name to the attention of some Whittier bankers and real estate operators searching for a Republican candidate for Congress against the popular Democratic incumbent Jerry Voorhis. The bankers and real estate operators called themselves the Committee of 100. They wanted a Republican congressman they could dominate, and they chose Richard Nixon because he was an accomplished debater, because he was a veteran who talked easily about the opinions of the GI's he had met in the foxholes, and because they knew they could control him. Since he had done no fighting, the speeches built around his conversations in the foxholes were curiously inadequate. The speeches built around the theme of Jerry Voorhis as a Communist sympathizer were equally without foundation but were more effective. Nixon's hard-hitting style pleased the Republicans, and by repeating the charge that Voorhis was a Red often enough, Nixon won the election.

He repeated the same stratagem in 1950 when he ran for the Senate seat held by Helen Gahagan Douglas. The charge that she was a Red and deserved to be hounded out of office was not true and Nixon knew it was not true, but he was not concerned with truth. His stratagem worked again, and he won the Senate seat. In 1952 Thomas E. Dewey chose Senator Nixon to be the Republican vice-presidential candidate. He was climbing the Republican ladder at extraordinary speed. His addiction to gambling for high stakes enabled him to pass through the Area of Confusion with the greatest ease, and his journey into Toward Absolute Corruption was conducted without hesitation, almost without thought, as though it was a duty imposed upon him.

The sources of Nixon's political strength are difficult to discover, for he had no roots anywhere, not even in Yorba Linda where he was born, and therefore no natural constituency. He appealed to those who were alienated, who felt imperiled by Communism, who desperately wanted law and order even at the sacrifice of freedoms. The Middle West regarded him as the champion of conservatism. His defense of Whittaker Chambers, the confessed Communist agent, against Alger Hiss, who may or may not have been a Communist agent—the murky affair still remains unresolved—had catapulted him into a useful notoriety. His "Checkers Speech" was a masterpiece of vulgarity. As General Eisenhower's vice-president he fell once more into obscurity; and when he ran for the presidency against John Kennedy in 1960 and failed, it seemed that he had exhausted his last hopes for high political office. Lyndon Johnson's long presidency and the proliferation of the war in Vietnam beyond all reason still further reduced Nixon to the status of an outsider. His gambles had failed. People remembered the strange confrontation with journalists at the Beverly Hills Hotel when, having lost the election for governor of California, he turned on them and said with bared teeth, "You won't have Nixon to kick around anymore, because, gentlemen, this is my last press conference." He was a bad loser who had never learned the lesson that to lose badly is to lose twice over.

The Vietnam War, the longest, the most expensive, and the most unjustifiable of any war fought by the United States, was the single most important cause of Nixon's return to power. The mood of the country was bitterly hostile to Lyndon Johnson, who sent half a million troops into Vietnam. Weariness had set in. Someone new was wanted; new programs were needed; the misery of Vietnam must be redeemed. As the Republican candidate for president, Nixon presented himself as "the man with the most experience." He promised to end the Vietnam War. In fact he had very little experience, and his promise to end the war was merely a pretext to discredit the Democrats, for he had no idea how the war could be ended. In the eyes of Republicans of the extreme right he was an admirable candidate, for he could be relied upon to protect their interests. This was all they needed. And so once more, as in 1946, when the Committee of 100 chose him to be the Republican candidate in Whittier, so now in New York, Chicago, Houston, San Francisco, and Washington, wherever there were vast monied interests to be defended and protected, committees arose with the single purpose of ensuring his election. They were prepared to spend millions of dollars to put their candidate in the White House.

In *The Selling of the President 1968* Joe McGinniss describes in great detail the fraudulent techniques employed in order to portray on television an image of Nixon that had not the slightest relation to reality, a Madison Avenue composite calculated to appeal to the largest number of people. He was sold in the same way that deodorants are sold. The barkers and the hucksters were in control.

When Nixon assumed the presidency, they were still in control. The operating cabinet, the people to whom he delegated the largest powers, consisted of a small group of mercenary men, nearly all of them with German names, men without any experience of practical politics, without roots, without honor, determined to rule America with exactly the kind of heavy-handedness that might be expected when hucksters and advertising agents are in charge.

Ron Ziegler, the president's press representative, had formerly worked at the Los Angeles branch of the J. Walter Thompson advertising agency. He had also been a barker at Disneyland and had driven the Jungle Cruise boat through the pasteboard tropics, delivering the appropriate patter: "Welcome aboard, folks. My name's Ron. I'm your skipper and guide down the River of Adventure. . . . Note the alligators. Please keep your hands inside the boat. They're always looking for a handout."

H. R. Haldeman, who became Nixon's chief of staff, and John Ehrlichman, who was Nixon's chief adviser on domestic affairs and therefore possessed many of the powers of a home secretary, came from the same agency. Haldeman had a degree in business administration from the University of California at Los Angeles. At J. Walter Thompson he had worked on the accounts of Seven-Up, Sani-Flush, Black Flag insecticide, and Diaper Sweet. Ehrlichman, a close friend of Haldeman, had been a zoning lawyer in Seattle, a profession that had also been followed by Nixon's vice-president, Spiro Agnew, a man so incompetent, mercenary, and felonious that he continued to extort large sums of money from Maryland builders and contractors long after he had been granted the second highest position in the land. John Mitchell, who became attorney general in the new administration, was a member of Nixon's old law firm who had specialized in bond sales.

Henry Kissinger, who became Nixon's foreign affairs adviser, was a protégé of Nelson Rockefeller; upon entering his new post he was given $50,000 by his protector. He was the author of heavy Germanic books on Metternich and foreign policy. Born Heinz Kissinger in Germany, of Jewish parents, he had a difficult youth in New York, for a time sold brushes for a living, and then went into the army, where he served in military intelligence. One of his chief tasks in postwar Germany was to round up Gestapo agents, a task he carried out with considerable success by using their own techniques against them. An unhappy marriage led to a divorce; he enjoyed the company of belly dancers, starlets, and female journalists, a fact he publicized to a quite extraordinary degree. To a female

Italian journalist he compared himself to a cowboy leading a wagon train astride his horse, entering a city alone without even a pistol, a romantic out of the Wild West. He could be very cynical. "The illegal we do immediately," he said. "The unconstitutional takes a little longer." He lied repeatedly. While Nixon and Kissinger were busily aiding Pakistan against India, he declared with a straight face: "There have been some comments that the Nixon administration is anti-Indian. This is totally inaccurate." He lied about so many things that lying appeared to be his natural practice; to find the truth it was necessary only to reverse what he said.

This rat pack governed America. The White House was the headquarters of a mafia with vast powers and far-reaching interests. The rulers were without any carefully considered philosophy, without chivalry, without any feeling for the people. Each was dedicated to the enlargement of his personal empire. Collectively and individually they were more intelligent than the corrupt president. The scandal of Watergate, when it came, surprised no one. In the murderous corridors of power there are always booby traps.

What Nixon and his accomplices possessed to an extraordinary degree is best characterized by the Russian word *poshlost,* which implies a fearful, cruel, and interminable vulgarity. They had no grace of mind, no intellectual vigor, no concern for their country. Their concern was to save their skins. The tape recordings of their conversations show them busily preparing scenarios designed to disgrace and ruin their opponents and to prevent the truth from being known; but since it was beyond the wit of man to think of all the possible permutations and combinations of their opponents' position, they inevitably forgot many important aspects of the game plan, and often failed to take the most elementary precautions. The reading of the transcripts of their conversations is a frightening and salutary experience. They show a group of men, all corrupt in their different ways, each one determined to save his skin, each determined to outwit the others, each pretending to be serving the sacred cause of the presidency while serving his own interests. Corruption had taken up its abode in the Oval Office, and from this office the contagion spread throughout the entire executive branch of the government.

If the conversations recorded on the presidential tapes had concerned a large industrial enterprise or a banana republic, they would not have been of any great importance and no one would ever have heard about them. But they did not occur in an industrial organization where the cutting of throats and the fight for power produce a continual civil war, or in a banana republic, where the army rules, ballot boxes are stuffed, and foreign interference is expected and welcomed because it increases the wealth of the rulers. The transcripts record conversations that took place in the white and gold office, which had hitherto been regarded as the place where American power was generated.

In these conversations Richard Nixon speaks like a Mafia chieftain with two very formidable assistants, Haldeman and Ehrlichman, who reply to him as equals, never deferring to him, and always talking in tones of monotonous vulgarity and brutality. There is a glint in their eyes as they sharpen their axes and think fondly of the utter destruction of their enemies or—and this happens more often —of the people they imagine to be their enemies. Listen to Nixon, Haldeman, Ehrlichman, and John Dean, Nixon's legal adviser, at 5:30 on the afternoon of September 15, 1972, plotting the downfall of Washington lawyer Edward Bennett Williams:

> *Nixon:* I wouldn't want to be in Edward Bennett Williams's position after the election—none of these bastards!
> *Dean:* Williams has done some rather unethical things.
> *Haldeman:* Keep a log on all that.
> *Dean:* Oh, we are, indeed, yeah.
> *Haldeman:* Because afterwards, that's the guy—that's the guy we've got to ruin.
> *Nixon:* We're going after him.
> *Haldeman:* That's the guy we've got to ruin.
> *Nixon:* You want to remember, too, he's an attorney for the *Washington Post.*
> *Dean:* I'm well aware of that.
> *Nixon:* I think we are going to fix the son-of-a-bitch.

Nixon's crudity as he plotted the downfall of real or imagined enemies was not so surprising as his ferocious, anarchic rage, his determination *to annihilate.* He had the power to destroy; the gang of burglars known as "the plumbers" were his tools of destruction, and there was no saying where the destruction would end or when they would undertake sterner tasks than forcing entry into houses and bugging. The Mafia chieftain has always believed he possesses the right to destroy. Nixon's associates were well aware that he became enthusiastic whenever the question arose of punishing their enemies, and when there was a pause in the conversation it was the practice to remind him of the fate reserved for his enemies. On the same day that he plotted the downfall of Edward Bennett Williams, Dean dropped a hint about the enemies list:

> *Nixon:* We are all in it together. This is a war. We take a few shots and it will be over. We will give them a few shots and it will be over. Don't worry. I wouldn't want to be on the other side right now, would you?
>
> *Dean:* Along that line, one of the things I've tried to do, I have begun to keep notes on a lot of people who are emerging as less than our friends because this will be over some day and we shouldn't forget the way some of them have treated us.
>
> *Nixon:* I want the most comprehensive notes on all those who tried to do us in. They didn't have to do it. If we had had a very close election and they were playing the other side I would understand this. No—they were doing this quite deliberately and they are asking for it and they are going to get it. We have not used the power in this first four years as you know. We have never used it. We have not used the Bureau and we have not used the Justice Department but things are going to change now.

Things did change, but not necessarily in the way Nixon wanted. He became more and more involved in the intricacies of the conspiracy, and when he spoke of "power" he meant the power to ruin the individuals who had annoyed him or were thought to be annoying him, not the power of the presidency to direct affairs of state and to bring prosperity to a people harrassed by growing inflation. Nixon was perfectly serious when he said he intended to use the Federal Bureau of Investigation and the Justice Department for his own private ends. He compiled an enemies list; wiretaps were installed; tax returns were examined and reexamined; newspapers carried stories against the men he had "fingered." He thought he was working in secrecy, but inevitably the number of conspirators increased, and it became more and more difficult to control them and to ensure their silence. The conspiracy was falling apart. Everything in Nixon's manner and in his public speeches manifested guilt. He began to look less like a Mafia chieftain than like a small-town gambler drinking himself into incoherence as he contemplates the advantages of taking the 12:05 train out of town before the sheriff gets him.

He had always been a nervous, suspicious, and deeply frustrated man, and he became more nervous, more suspicious, and more deeply frustrated as the Watergate scandal continued. How reclusive he was we learn from John Dean's interrogation by the Senate Watergate Committee. Dean depicted him becoming more and more isolated from the world, at the mercy of sudden pathological rages, unsure of himself and as though about to break up mentally and physically. He became enraged at the sight of a single hostile demonstrator who held up a ten-foot sign in front of Lafayette Park, clearly visible from the White House. Haldeman was summoned by Nixon and ordered to see that the sign was removed. Haldeman passed the order on to Dwight Chapin, another former colleague from the J. Walter Thompson agency in Los Angeles, who offered to get some "thugs" to remove the offending sign by force. Dean said this would probably not be necessary; there were other ways of handling the problem. Chapin was concerned because it would take some time to round up the "thugs." Finally it was decided that the park police could deal with the situation by convincing the protester that he should go elsewhere. One does not argue with an armed policeman; the protester moved away; his constitutional rights had been violated; the president's rage subsided. He guarded his own constitutional rights closely but was not deeply concerned about the rights of others.

Nor were the constitutional rights of the people of Chile of the least interest to him. President Salvador Allende's government offended him; this, too, had to be removed, as the protester was removed. The simplest way was to pour unlimited funds into the hands of extreme rightist groups and to create economic turmoil in a country already afflicted with inflation. The State Department and the CIA objected, but were overruled by Nixon and Kissinger. At a meeting of the secret 40 Committee, which was answerable only to the president, it was decided to embark on a full-scale program to destroy the existing Chilean government and replace it by a military junta. "I don't see why we need to stand by and watch a country go Communist due to the irresponsibility of its own people," said Kissinger in the authentic tones of Hitler announcing the forthcoming destruction of one more state on his borders. Ray Cline, the CIA official entrusted with the task of destroying Allende's government, said later: "I'm not happy about the way things turned out in Chile, but I can defend them because I think our strategy was not unreasonable or immoral. It was our duty to preserve institutions which we call free." The military junta took over; Allende was shot to death in the presidential palace; "the institutions which we call free" vanished from Chile. A corrupt U.S. president had brought into being one more military tyranny in a world that already has more than enough military tyrannies. Kissinger repeatedly denied that American money and energy had been spent in toppling the Allende government. Thirty thousand people perished in the bloodbath ordered by the military dictators.

Nixon took comfort from his management of foreign affairs. In this field he could show himself as a man of decision and imagination, playing an important role on the world stage. There remained the possibility that people would lose interest in the Watergate scandal if he could accomplish resounding successes in foreign affairs. Kissinger's reputation as a man of inflexible principles and irreproachable morality sustained him, but Kissinger's flair for self-advertisement and his cautious efforts to dissociate himself from Watergate proved to be less sustaining. Nixon's foreign policy was Kissinger's foreign policy. They worked together as a pair like Tweedledum and Tweedledee, with Nixon pushing for dramatic confrontations that would bring his name to the front pages of the newspapers, while Kissinger, with his vastly greater knowledge of the workings of the ordinary human mind, reached the front pages of the newspapers with sensational interviews and disclosures about secret journeys. Kissinger found democracies boring and enthusiastically supported the military dictatorships of Vietnam, Korea, Chile, Greece, Spain, Portugal, and Pakistan. Nixon and Kissinger formed a duumvirate; sometimes they acted together while at other times they played puppet-and-master, and it was not always possible to discern which was puppet and which was master.

"I have sworn," wrote Thomas Jefferson in 1800, "upon the altar of God eternal hostility against every form of tyranny over the mind of man." Under the duumvirate of Nixon and Kissinger the care and cultivation of military tyrannies, even the most bloodthirsty tyrannies, were practiced with unswerving devotion, with particular reference to the military dictatorships of Vietnam and Korea. At no time did either Nixon or Kissinger raise his voice even to the level of a whisper to protest the ferocious inhumanity of these countries' secret police, the mass arrests, the tiger cages, the torture chambers. They reveled in their close connections with military dictatorships. In private both were foul-tempered, brusque, and dictatorial; in public they presented themselves as men who carried the world's weight on their shoulders and must not be questioned lest they stumble.

They were corrupt in different ways. Kissinger was corrupted by intellectual arrogance, by a talent for hair-splitting that could reduce all problems to theses, countertheses, subtheses, and every imaginable form of subsubthesis, following the Germanic pattern, and by his concept of the world as made up of huge power blocs destined to rule the rest. He saw himself as another Metternich, another Bismarck. Nixon lacked intellectual arrogance because he lacked intellect. He was financially corrupt; he was corrupt in his political dealings; he had an instinct for choosing corrupt men to serve him and knew how to manage them, using their corruption for his own purposes; and he degraded the presidency to the level of a Mafia chieftaincy. Both men were without honor, for they lied repeatedly.

Among Nixon and his advisers, lying became so habitual that it assumed something of the appearance of a familiar game with certain well-defined rules:

1. Lie wholeheartedly.
2. If it is absolutely necessary to tell the truth, surround the truth with so many lies that it will appear to be a lie and therefore of the same texture as all other lies.
3. Consult the appropriate scenario before telling a lie, so that all lies form a consistent pattern.
4. Leave margins for error. Never be precise. Give the lie room to swing.
5. All lies are interchangeable with other lies.

This systematic lying was carried on with deadly monotony throughout Nixon's presidential reign and culminated in the extraordinary speeches he delivered during his last six months in office, when he was confronted with mounting evidence of his guilt. He denied everything, pictured himself as a valiant man misunderstood by his critics, and implied that he was as pure as new-fallen snow.

"In wartime," Winston Churchill once said to Stalin, "truth is so precious that she should always be attended by a bodyguard of lies." The remark was unworthy of Churchill and wasted on Stalin. Nixon did not have the excuse that he was speaking in wartime; he was speaking to save his own neck, delivering speeches carefully constructed by armies of speechwriters. As he delivered them in prime time on television, his hands shook, a muscle in his upper lip twitched, and his eyes usually blinked whenever he was about to utter one of his more palpable lies, either because the sheer enormity of the lie frightened him or because in this way he hoped to summon the energy to speak the lie more convincingly. Nixon's speeches in his defense were well rehearsed; he rarely stumbled over words, but the blinking had a shattering effect on the onlooker, who found himself in the position of someone suddenly privileged to enter the mind of a crook of prodigious proportions—a crook who had somehow contrived to become president of the United States. The blinking resembled the sudden stirring of signals and piercing whistles as a train is about to enter a tunnel. Then it was all darkness, wind, gusts of smoke, and greasy air. Then came the platitudes. Then more lies. Then platitudes again. Then lies followed by more platitudes, so that it was difficult to know whether he was lying by habit or by design.

The speeches Nixon delivered during this period broke at the seams because so many writers had worked on them, but the president's own contributions could be readily recognized. When journalists pointed out that his statements of fact included many errors, Ronald Ziegler, the presidential press secretary, reluctantly agreed that there had been some minor inexactitudes because precise information was not readily available at the time. On one famous occasion he announced blandly: "This is the operative statement. The others are inoperative." A shutter suddenly opened up to reveal the dialectics of presidential gamesmanship. *Operative* and *inoperative* followed the laws of indeterminacy; no one could possibly guess what was true at any given time because the truth was the least important factor in the game plan, and at all costs it was necessary to conceal the truth that the president had had full knowledge of all the details of the scandal. The use of the word *inoperative,* which meant "untrue," showed what little respect the president's party had for the truth.

Nixon had reached that desperate stage when the corrupt man loses all sense of reality, that area I have called Toward Absolute Corruption, where there is no limit to human ambitions or to the risks a man will take in order to justify himself in his own eyes. Nixon told John Mitchell, the former attorney general: "I don't give a shit what happens. I want you all to stonewall it, let them plead the Fifth Amendment, cover up or anything else, if it'll save the plan." But the game plan was continually shifting now, the conspirators were beginning to talk to a grand jury, information was being leaked to the press from government departments, and Nixon's political life was in mortal peril. What he was hoping for was a great international coup that would elevate him above the petty quarrels of the Congress and the press. He hated the Congress and despised the press; this was dangerous; and soon, as he retreated deeper and deeper into a state of isolation, caring and not caring, at the mercy of the strange mental aberrations that develop in the higher reaches of corruption, he divorced himself completely from the real world. There was no presidency. In the Oval Office was a diseased man, putrefying with corruption, plagued with virtual immobility.

Nevertheless, this corpselike man was able to move spasmodically and from time to time to make abrupt and alarming gestures. On occasion he was heard to speak; his words were more lies, but they seemed superfluous. In any case he had never possessed an ability to organize his lies. From time to time photographs appeared in the newspapers showing him about to fly to his Florida estate in the company of his friend Bebe Rebozo or to the island off the Bahamas owned by another millionaire friend, Robert Abplanalp, a manufacturer of aerosol equipment, and these journeys into tropical landscapes left many people with the feeling that he might never return, that he might be washed away into the Atlantic or might simply vanish from sight. But he always returned, and his lawyers continued to issue statements in his name denying the criminal charges that were being examined by the House Judiciary Committee. The denials were so palpably untrue that even the lawyers seemed not to believe them. Finally, the committee voted to recommend Nixon's impeachment to the House of Representatives on charges of abuse of power and the cover-up of the Watergate conspiracy. Had he been impeached by the House, the way would have been open for a full-scale trial before the Senate, which would have inevitably led to his dismissal from office. On August 8, 1974, he resigned, admitting nothing except that his power base had shriveled—which was true— and acknowledging as his only fault his failure to act more forcefully in his management of the Watergate affair—which was not true, for he had acted so forcefully that he had almost torn the nation apart.

Although the House Judiciary Committee accused Nixon of many crimes, giving special emphasis to obstruction of justice, contempt of Congress, and abuse of presidential power, these are not the crimes for which he will be remembered in history. Far more atrocious crimes were committed by him; nor were they crimes that appear in any statute book. His worst crime was that he gave no hope to the young. A young man living in the Nixon era was confronted with a president totally concerned with his own financial and political profit, with neither the time nor the inclination to ponder the future of the country in terms of its just goals and moral responsibilities.

The young, who are the future, had no part in Nixon's scheme of things. He called them scum, because they were rebellious and because their idealism conflicted sharply with his own corrupted set of values. They were the enemy; he could not stamp them out, but he could refuse to see them and pretend that they did not exist. He failed them, as he failed the poor, the sick, the defenseless. He had nothing to say to them; it was as though they were strangers to him, speaking a language unknown to him, so far beyond the reach of his imaginative grasp that he was always tongue-tied in their presence on the rare occasions when, as though by chance, he encountered them. The young were not big business, were very rarely corporate lawyers, financiers, armaments manufacturers, generals. They brought him neither financial nor political profit: with little money, they could provide him with no tax advantages; with little political clout, they could provide him with no political advantages. Nevertheless, he did not entirely disregard their existence. He developed an unreasoning hatred and contempt for them. Since they refused to obey him or serve him, he decided that they must be punished, and he gave orders that their demonstrations must be broken up with whatever force was necessary, by which he meant the maximum force.

Among the many duties a president must assume none is more important than his duty to act as the moral leader of his nation. In the words of President Wilson, he must be "the spokesman for the real sentiment and purpose of the country." He is therefore the essential father figure, the protector and guide of the young, the leader of the multitudes who have grown to man's estate, the compassionate guardian of the aged. He must find the words and cultivate the acts that answer to their needs, and he has a very special duty toward the young not only because they are the future but also because it is the very nature of youth to be inexperienced and to need guidance. Not that a president should be like a schoolmaster giving moral lectures to children, but that in his life and actions he should be a moral example to all the nation. The president is the only father figure the American people have, and he has no higher duty than to play the role with all the dignity and chivalry he can muster.

But Nixon was quite incapable of playing the role. His instinct was always to strike out for his own advantage. He had no moral code and therefore could not present himself as a moral leader. He had no generosity of spirit or grace of mind. He was a divisive figure who rejoiced in his divisiveness, and he fell from power because he held fast to his own advantage and let the rest go hang.

Ultimately the most terrible thing about the Nixon administration is not that he wielded power incompetently and disastrously, or that he owed far too many debts to big business, which had given him his high office, or that he was incapable of telling the truth, or that he succeeded in gathering around him a multitude of sycophants, opportunists, and crooks, or that he bombed the civilians of Hanoi, or that he did not care about the people he ruled over with such a heavy hand. The most terrible thing is that a man who was corrupt on all levels, who corrupted and who was corrupted, was able to rise to a position of almost absolute power in the United States, and that the people permitted it to happen.

Nixon thought nothing of cheating the Internal Revenue Service of more than $400,000 and of spending a grand total of $17,000,000 of public funds on the improvement and embellishment of his private estates. But this was only the small change of his corruption. The real corruption lay in the stifling of every decent impulse for the improvement of the living standards of the nation, in the growing cynicism of the young who heard his lies and threw up their hands in despair, and in the growing horror of the old living on welfare who knew that Nixon would do nothing for them. Where there had been hope, there was now hopelessness. Where there had been courage, there was now cynicism. Where there had been life, there was a living death. During Nixon's reign, much of life in the United States was transformed into a nightmare.

History will judge Richard Nixon more sternly than we judge him now. There is evidence, and to spare, that he committed more crimes than the House Judiciary Committee was able to discover. Terrible things are still hidden in the black sack of mysteries that history will open in her own good time. The clock is ticking, the time is coming, when the black sack will be thrown wide open and we shall see things we never dreamed of.

The characteristics of the absolutely corrupt man are well known to historians. There comes a stage in the soaring progress of an absolutely corrupt man when he realizes that all things are permitted to him, and it is all one to him whether he commits a small crime or an absolutely intolerable crime. He can steal a dime from a blind newsstand operator as easily and readily as he steals from the nation's treasury; and he can kill a man as easily and readily as he orders bombers to attack a nation's capital. There are no fine distinctions among the absolutely corrupt. A man who can wage a secret war in Cambodia and lie repeatedly to his own people about it can wage a secret war against Americans and think nothing of it. Covering up becomes habitual; lies are his daily bread; he practices deceit because he is incapable of speaking honestly. If he wanted to speak honestly, he would find the effort too much for him.

To a remarkable degree Nixon succeeded in stamping his peculiar characteristics on officialdom all over the United States. Officials who saw how well he was faring in bending the laws to his own purposes began to imitate him; illegality became habitual; the Justice Department, which should have fought him, assisted him; congressmen announced without having heard the incriminating tapes that he was as clean as a hound's tooth when they knew very well that he was guilty—and if they did not know, they were either fools or hypocrites.

In those years one could feel the spirit of the country being sapped away. It was no accident that crime increased to fantastic proportions during Nixon's presidency, for a criminal was in the White House. He left America divided against itself, weak and irresolute, at a time of terrible dangers; and while there were few who still defended him—the evidence of high crimes and misdemeanors was irrefutable—the conditions that permitted him to arise were still present. Corruption did not cease when he fell from power. The black miasma was still spreading across the country, and the young felt as helpless and powerless as they did before.

Nixon's successor was Gerald Ford, the vice-president who had been hand-picked by Nixon and therefore possessed no mandate from the people. He is one of those who defended Nixon on all occasions. They were sympathetic to one another and understood one another. Even when Nixon's guilt was recognized by the vast majority of the American people, Ford persisted in declaring his innocence, and even when he was shown irrefutable proof of Nixon's criminality, he went on making speeches saying that there was no proof, that Nixon had been maligned, that the country should continue to have confidence in his leadership. Almost as soon as he was installed in the presidency, Ford exercised the presidential right of pardon, vested in him by the Constitution. Nixon was pardoned for all crimes, known and unknown, committed during his presidency. But in the Constitution it is clearly stated that the president's power to pardon is limited, for it says, "He shall have power to grant reprieves and pardons for offenses against the United States, except in cases of impeachment." And Nixon's case—in which a bill of particulars had been drawn up against him by the House Judiciary Committee and was about to be submitted to the House—was certain to become "a case of impeachment." Thus the Senate's judgment of the innumerable corrupt acts committed by Nixon was precluded, and justice was denied, by a final act of corruption by his successor; expediency once more defeated truth.

For the United States the future was dark; too many hostages had been given to adversity; the embittered youth of the nation had turned away from politics, despising politicians who had shown themselves to be too often corrupt or incompetent or both; the mood of the country favored a thorough cleansing, but there was no broom large enough to sweep the evils away. At the height of the American Civil War Abraham Lincoln said: "In giving freedom to the slave, we assure freedom to the free—honorable alike in what we give and what we preserve. We shall nobly save or meanly lose the last, best hope of earth." But now the last, best hope was ebbing away, and a country that was once the freest in the world, possessing a rugged democracy, became under Nixon a plutocracy, cruel, capable of atrocities that have darkened its image all over the world, wearing on its brow the sign of corruption. A giant in chains, wonderfully fashioned, went stumbling toward a troubled future.

A Vision of the
Uncorrupted Society

W̲e live on a tragic earth, where half the population walks barefoot, three-quarters of the countries of the world are ruled by dictatorships, and twenty million people rot in prison. We live in an
age of catastrophes, many of them engineered by men corrupted by
the desire for wealth and power. If we are sometimes permitted to
live peacefully, it is because we have achieved a balance of terror.
The game of power is played remorselessly by men who have not the
slightest knowledge of, or interest in, the way ordinary people live,
and the ordinary people are too terrified to protest. Even if we pro-
tested, it would do us no good. Change, if it comes at all, will have
to come from the top, with the knowledge that the game of power
is being played by people who use power to their own advantage.
We have suffered long enough at the hands of our rulers, and change
is long overdue.

The world is divided into two camps: the corrupt and the uncorrupted. The corrupt are not very numerous compared to the rest of
the world's population but they wield an influence out of all propor-

tion to their numbers. Like a poisonous gas, they seep into the places of power, and the harm they do is incalculable.

Corruption is an ever-present element in modern civilization, as prevalent in democracies as in military dictatorships. There are differences of degree, of kind, of nature. A military dictatorship is corrupted by the presence of huge concentration camps and torture chambers; it uses naked force and murder to impose its will. We measure the degree of corruption in a military dictatorship by counting the number of people living at starvation level, the number of people in prison for crimes against the state, the number of people executed, the wealth of the elite that rules the country. In democracies, too, we can make statistical summaries. Again, we can count the number of people living at starvation level, the wealth of the rulers, the bribes received by politicians, bureaucrats, judges, the police, and by all those in positions of authority who demand bribes as a matter of principle. Exact figures will not be available, but very close approximations can be made. There are even some corrupt practices prevalent in democracies that scarcely exist under military dictatorships. Building inspectors employed by the city of New York regularly demand handouts from builders; in a single year about forty million dollars goes into their pockets. It is unlikely that any military dictatorship would permit these things to happen.

Corruption, wherever it takes places, impoverishes the people. The spiritual and mental damage cannot be estimated, but the physical damage is obvious. The building inspector who takes bribes is adding to the cost of housing, making it vastly more difficult for people to find houses and apartments at rents they can afford; and for the poor the problem of housing becomes a perennial tragedy. What goes on in the mind of the policeman who seizes a thousand glassine envelopes of heroin from a drug trafficker and then recycles it by selling it to another drug trafficker? He knows—he cannot help knowing—the consequences of his act. He knows he has contributed to murders, to suicides, to maimed and broken bodies. After the abortive assassination attempt in 1944, Hitler ordered the execution of everyone who was even remotely involved. They were hanged with piano wire, and he watched the hangings on film projected in his own screening room, sitting comfortably in an armchair. There is not very much difference between Hitler watching these executions, so coldly indifferent to the fate of his victims, and the policeman who recycles heroin. The ultimate power is the power to reduce men to corpses.

It is not only national dictators who punish and maim and torture gratuitously. Petty dictators—bureaucrats, judges, politicians, inspectors, heads of regulatory agencies—find it difficult to resist the impulse to punish gratuitously. They are well equipped to punish, they can interpret the laws and the statutes as they please, and they are well protected. They are not military dictators but they share the same mentality. Power streams from their five-bladed hands, and power is profitable. The fact that they are paid from the public treasury is a matter of very little significance to them, and they fall easily into the sin of pride, by which the angels fell. From pride comes contempt for one's fellow men, and from contempt comes destructiveness. To compare the self-regarding politician in a democracy to Hitler may seem an exercise in flattery, but in his small way the politician also contributes to the death of a city or a state. He is indifferent to the tragedies he causes. He says: "Of course there are abuses of power, but my dear good people, I am one of those who have the people's interests at heart. Trust me!" That is the trouble. The people have no one else to trust and they follow him blindly until he is caught with his hand in the till. Then he may be brought up for trial, given a short sentence in prison, and soon enough he is back in politics.

While corruption is profitable to the few, it is a source of great suffering to the many. The evil lies in the degradation, the poverty, the accumulation of deceit; and if it is more terrible under a military dictatorship, it is intolerable in a democracy. All suffer when politicians are corrupt. Mostly they suffer in silence; they have no recourse, no court of appeal. Under a dictatorship, all men, even the dictator's closest followers, are reduced to a state of desperation. The dictator rejoices in the fact that the arrest of one man produces a shock wave felt by at least twenty persons. Punishment must be memorable and must deeply affect as many people as possible. It is a matter of indifference to him that a wife is forced into prostitution to support her children. This, too, is part of the punishment.

The game of power is played according to accepted laws sanctified by tradition. The game is played ruthlessly and cynically. The first rule of the game is "People do not matter." The second rule is "People must be bent to the dictator's will." The third rule is "If they do not obey, they must be punished." The fourth rule is "Loot them." Meanwhile the propaganda machine announces that everything is being done for the good of the people.

Surprisingly often the dictators portray themselves as men dedicated to the service of the people, suffering immeasurably on behalf of the popular cause. Yet they know very well that they are benefiting themselves, and they are prepared to practice any deceit in order to keep the people quiet and obedient. If the people are unruly and disobedient, the tyrant possesses well-tried instruments to silence them and make them obedient. Concentration camps with forced labor can break a man's spirit and transform him into a mindless robot. This is only one short step from being a corpse.

Military power in today's world has widened its scope to produce more suffering than anyone could have dreamed of in the last century. In the past, wars were fought between soldiers; today there is total war, and the soldiers turn on the civilians. The dictator at war has total power, and the totality of his power totally corrupts him. The soldiers too are corrupted; they massacre defenseless civilians and think nothing of it. This used to be called cowardice. Soon enough the soldiers lose those human qualities that alone give them human dignity; they become robots mechanically obeying orders. Massacre becomes part of the day's work, and it is all one to them whether they massacre their traditional enemies or their own people. Lenin once wrote, "The standing army everywhere and in all countries is intended for use not so much against the external as the internal enemy." It was not true when he wrote these words; no divisions of the imperial Russian army were thrown against the Mensheviks, the Bolsheviks, or the Socialist Revolutionaries. But in our own age the standing army has become a threat to civilian populations.

Wealth and power go hand in hand; the corrupt man, once he has achieved power, quickly amasses a fortune. He may announce that he is ascetic by nature and despises wealth because he is wholly at the service of the people and is dedicated to their interests and to their interests alone, but he always succumbs to the temptations of wealth. A Communist dictator lacks a Swiss bank account; little money passes through his hands; nevertheless, he possesses wealth in abundance. He has his fleet of airplanes, his choice of country houses and summer palaces, as many automobiles as he pleases, and servants beyond counting because he can enlist everyone in the nation in his service. It cost the Russian people the equivalent of a million dollars a year to maintain Stalin in comfort; even Lenin rejoiced in a sumptuous country villa and a Rolls Royce. Hitler, describing himself publicly as an ascetic who ate no meat, drank no alcohol, and eschewed women, succeeded in convincing a whole generation of Germans that the pleasures of life had no meaning for him and that he was dedicated only to their interests. In fact he reveled in sausages and beer, and there was always a woman available when he wanted one. He announced that he would accept no payment from the state and lived instead on the royalties of *Mein Kampf*. Since nearly everyone in Germany was forced to own a copy of the book, his royalties amounted to considerably more than the normal income of a head of state.

Wealth and power are the main sources of corruption. They are the cesspools pouring out an endless flow of corruption. The rich, simply by being rich, are infected with corruption. Their overwhelming desire is to grow richer, but they can do this only at the expense of those who are poorer than themselves. Their interests conflict with the interests of the greater number, and since they live in a world apart, remote from the constant anxieties of the poor and incapable of understanding them, they cultivate a cynicism that serves to protect them from the world around them. Inevitably they come to fear and distrust the poor, and just as inevitably their fear and distrust are translated into legislation that protects them against the poor. They have no difficulty in buying politicians or filling the regulatory agencies with their own agents. They buy votes, ambassadorships, governorships, even presidencies. Totally unscrupulous in the uses of wealth, and not bound by any moral code, they come to regard the existing government as something that can be bought piecemeal.

The mere presence of the rich is corrupting. Their habits, their moral codes, their delight in conspicuous consumption are permanent affronts to the rest of humanity. Vast inequalities of wealth are intolerable in any decent society. In the United States more than a third of the private wealth is possessed by less than 5 per cent of the population, while about a fifth of the population is living at the poverty level. The tendency is toward greater and greater concentrations of wealth in private hands. Unless this accumulation is checked by law or by violent social change, about two-thirds of the national wealth will be in the hands of 5 per cent of the population in the year 2000, while at the same time considerably more than half the population will be below or near the starvation level. These estimates portend disaster.

Nor is there any likelihood that the rich will plow back their money into services to ensure the general good. They have rarely demonstrated social responsibility, and they are much more likely to hold on to their wealth at all costs than to renounce any part of it. Like the tyrant who lives in a world wholly remote from the world of the people, shielded and protected from all outside influences, the rich are usually the last to observe the social pressures rising from below, and when these social pressures reach flashpoint, it is too late to call in the police or the army. The tyrant dies; the police and the army go over to the revolutionaries; and the new government dispossesses the rich by decree. A single authoritative sentence suffices to expunge all private wealth and restore it to the service of the nation.

A nation's wealth is too serious a matter to be left to the wealthy. The riches of a nation belong to all, to be shared among all for the general welfare. Unless there is at least an effort toward a general leveling of incomes, there can be no social peace. A country ruled by a small nucleus of rich men is obviously in a state of crisis; such a government cannot endure except by the use of armed force and draconian laws. Ultimately those instruments prove to be ineffective and useless.

For nearly everyone except the rich and the upper classes the world is an intolerable place. For the poor, the very poor, it is more than intolerable. Poverty is an enemy to be fought every day without hope and in the knowledge of certain defeat. To such people the mere existence of the rich is an affront, and when they ask why they are suffering when the rich live without any suffering at all, luxuriating in their wealth, they are well aware that it is not because the rich have some God-given right to their luxuries. Undernourished children, unemployed workmen, and old people living on cat food ask hard questions and receive no answers.

But the poor have a right to hope. They hope for an uncorrupted society where there are no rich and no poor, where the president works for all people and not only for the vested interests, where the representatives are truly representative, where the bureaucrats are trained to be the servants of the people, where the rich share their riches, and they know that all this is within their grasp if only they will reach out for it. Concerning the president, the Congress, the bureaucrats, and the rich they have much to say and much to dream about.

THE PRESIDENT

The president embodies the sovereignty and dignity of the American people. Once in office, he must not be partisan, for he is the leader of all Americans. If he chooses to act as a party leader, he destroys those bonds that should unite him with members of the opposition party, and to the extent that those bonds are destroyed, so is his effectiveness. In the desperate age we are living in, it is all the more necessary that the president should be the president of all the people.

Richard Nixon was a travesty of a president. The qualities he possessed are precisely those to be avoided in future presidents. The nation cannot afford to have self-seeking presidents who enrich themselves in office, lie habitually, and abuse their presidential powers. He should have been hounded from the presidency at the first lie, for the damage done by a lying president is beyond calculation, and every lie weakens the moral basis of the government's authority. The Turks very sensibly hanged the prime minister, Menderes, when he was shown to be corrupt. Richard Nixon was pardoned for his crimes, given large sums of money by the government, and permitted to retain his ill-gotten wealth.

If the president is the president of all the people, he should be a man of the people. Plato proposed that neither rulers nor soldiers should be permitted to hold private property of their own for the simple reason that since they possess an abundance of power they are peculiarly susceptible to corruption. The president, therefore, should be removed from the temptations of wealth while in office and should live, as Thomas Jefferson lived, in the utmost simplicity. At the end of his tenure of office he should be no richer and no poorer than when he entered it.

The time-consuming entertainments and costly trappings of office dangerously interfere with the conduct of the presidency. An army of assistants now works for the president in the White House, getting in one another's way, all fighting for the president's ear, and obscuring the issues before they reach the president's desk. A president does not need an army of assistants. Our Founding Fathers envisaged the president as one man exerting his human powers on behalf of his country, not as the chairman of a board. The president should not need speech writers and gag writers; he should be intelligent enough to write his own speeches, and if he cannot write them he should resign from the job. It is perfectly possible to imagine a president working with a staff of about twenty people. The growth of the presidential staff to its present fantastic proportions is a sign not of the president's strength but of his weakness.

Long ago Ibn Khaldun pointed out the importance of the gatekeepers who stand guard outside the sultan's palace. At his own pleasure and for his own profit the gatekeeper can act as the traffic manager; some will be barred from the sultan's presence, others will be permitted to have a glimpse of him, others will be permitted to kneel at his feet, and only a few will be permitted to ask for favors.

Ibn Khaldun went on to ponder the consequences of appointing a second and third gatekeeper. The bribes increase; the protocol becomes more complex; the gatekeepers themselves are soon in a position to make important political maneuvers; and the sultan becomes more and more remote from the people.

In the same way every addition to the presidential staff increases the distance separating the president from the people.

In theory the people are sovereign; in fact the powers of the president are now so vast that they exceed those of a medieval monarch. Richard Nixon rode roughshod over the Congress and the sovereign will of the people. He was ultimately forced from office, but he would have retained his power if he had not acted with reckless stupidity by taping his discussions with his advisers, thus in due course revealing all his shoddy maneuvers, his shoddy language, and his shoddy accomplices. The discovery of the existence of the tapes was the purest luck. The sovereign president fell from power not because he was a sovereign but because he made mistakes that would not have occurred to a six-year-old child.

What is needed of a president is a vast humility and an absolute dedication to his task. If it means working himself to death, then he should work himself to death. In any intelligently run state he can have no secrets, for it is only by the utmost openness that he can ensure the trust of the people. He must ask himself continually, "Will this benefit the children of my country?" and he must remember always that a country's children are its most precious possession. By his example and by his use of the power entrusted to him he must show an extreme intolerance to corruption wherever it appears, for corruption is death and he represents or should represent to an extraordinary degree the living forces of the sovereign people.

THE CONGRESS

The essential element in a democracy is that the people should be able to vote freely and without any kind of restraint for the representative of their choice. If he fails them, then they are free to vote against him and remove him from office. His task is to represent them, their interests, and the interests of the district. He has been entrusted with a sacred mission, for he is their advocate, their messenger, their protector against the massive and domineering weight of the government. The people, by electing him, affirm their belief in his integrity and devotion to the electorate. It is not his task to amass a fortune by selling his political influence to the highest bidder or by supporting powerful vested interests against the people. The moral imperative demands that he should be wholly unself-seeking and should do his utmost to protect and guide his constituents. If he accepts bribes of any kind or in any form, he should be punished far more rigorously than ordinary bribe-takers. His major task is to protect the poor, for the rich can take care of themselves. A corrupt senator or congressman divorces himself from his sacred mission. He has become the representative, not of the electorate, but of criminal forces.

A senator or congressman is a kind of priest, mediating between the ordinary man and the center of power. Like a priest he should live modestly, be in continual contact with the people, and work tirelessly for their benefit. At the end of his tenure of office he should be no richer and no poorer than when he entered it.

In nearly all the few remaining democracies in the world, the elected representatives are paid adequately and live modestly. In the United States alone, the representatives have granted themselves fabulous salaries and perquisites, which immediately remove them from the run of ordinary people. Members of the House of Representatives are allowed sixteen full-time employees on their personal staffs, paid for by the government, and a senator may have as many employees as he wishes—some have as many as seventy. A good deal of the time of a senator or congressman is spent in managing these unwieldy staffs, attempting to justify their existence, or using them to create his own empire. Each congressman has his public relations officer, his speech writer, his army of secretaries. He is in business—the business of making himself important. With each addition to his staff he becomes less approachable, more isolated, more ignorant, and more prone to corruption. Special committees and subcommittees proliferate on an alarming scale. At the time of this writing there were two hundred and eighty committees, but not one of them was devoted to cutting down the number of committees. The House and Senate have sixteen thousand employees who are paid a total of $328 million from government funds, an average of $20,500 for each employee. License to proliferate was not granted by popular mandate; the Congress simply appropriated the money according to its right under the Constitution to appropriate money for the public welfare. The public felt that the Congress was more interested in its own welfare than in the public welfare.

In this way, in the years following World War II, the Congress became a plutocracy.

A surprisingly large number of senators are lawyers—nearly 70 per cent. About half the members of the House of Representatives are lawyers.* With very few exceptions, all the people who contributed to the Watergate scandal were lawyers, from the president and his assistants down to the leader of "the plumbers," the burglars who were responsible for the illegal break-ins ordered by the president. A cold, calculated, well-planned conspiracy was managed by cohorts of lawyers dedicated to the principle that the president was above the law. When the cover-up began, more cohorts of lawyers were employed by the president at government expense to defend him, to tell lies, to cloud every issue, to make it virtually impossible to track down the guilty. The public reached the inevitable conclusion that an aristocracy of lawyers surrounded the president and those with the greatest ability to tell lies were in the most powerful and favored positions.

It is no more rational to have lawyers in positions of power than it would be to have garbage collectors in positions of power. And in human terms garbage collectors would be preferable. In a democracy the rulers must be representative of the people, they must come from the people and from all ranks of the people, they must be close to the people, and they must not work for their own advantage. Lawyers are especially prone to making inhuman and rationalistic arguments; they form a closed society and act in secrecy, and they are in general the least capable of assuming responsible positions in a democratic government. In no other country in the world is there such a vast preponderance of lawyers in the government.

The American Bar Association publicly excoriated the lawyers who took part in the Watergate conspiracy. They were the black sheep who had brought dishonor to an honorable profession. But the disease goes much deeper. The lawyers, by seizing so much power in government, had made Watergate inevitable, and there will be more Watergates as long as they continue to hold power. The legal profession has been granted no God-given right to rule. They are fully represented in the Supreme Court, and it is beyond any reason that they should appropriate to themselves the presidency, the Senate and the House of Representatives as well.

A healthy democracy does not need lawyers so much as it needs ordinary men and women. It needs doctors, shipbuilders, shopkeepers, salesgirls, street vendors, fishermen, engineers, garbage collectors, housewives, butchers, bakers, farmers, laborers. But alas, until there is a change in the election laws giving everyone an opportunity

---

* According to the *Congressional Quarterly Almanac,* vol. 29, 1973, there were 221 lawyers in the House of Representatives and 68 lawyers in the Senate.

to run for office, it is unlikely that our representatives will be really representative. The cost of running for office has risen appreciably, and few congressmen and senators in recent years have not had to spend vast sums of money in their electoral campaigns. To raise the money they must make promises to the rich; a modern election is an exercise in controlled corruption. President Nixon collected $30 million for his election campaign, most of it from vested interests to whom he promised favorable treatment, though the mere promise of favors was an act of corruption. He sold ambassadorships to the highest bidder and prostituted the presidency for money.

There is a moral imperative to reduce the cost of the Congress, to cut down the vast congressional staffs, to make the legislature truly representative of the people, and to remove it from the powerful grip of a confederacy of self-seeking lawyers.

THE BUREAUCRACY

When Winston Churchill was prime minister of Great Britain during World War II he was also Member of Parliament for the small town and district of Woodford. People from his constituency would sometimes write to him about matters concerning the town, and he would sometimes reply to them, signing himself, "I remain, dear Sir, Your obedient Servant, WINSTON S. CHURCHILL."

He was not, of course, anyone's obedient servant, for he was one of the six or seven men who held the fate of the world in their hands, and he was well aware that he possessed virtually dictatorial power. Nevertheless he enjoyed this pleasant and polite fiction and talked about it surprisingly often, saying that it amused him to add these words to his letters.

The fiction had a history. It was first observed during the period of the Restoration, when the government of Charles II consisted of polite rogues who delighted in flowery forms of address; these became codified during the later years of the seventeenth century. The form was splendid and the substance immaterial. In much the same way the pope, believing himself to be the anointed successor of Saint Peter and in full possession of the keys given to the saint by Christ, sometimes calls himself "the servant of the servants of God."

Churchill, roaring with laughter at the thought of calling himself "Your obedient servant," was being remarkably uncharitable. Every member of the House of Commons is elected to serve a constituency; without his promise to serve the electors to the best of his ability he will not be elected. Churchill consistently served his own interests. He was in his twenties when he announced his ambition to become prime minister. Ambition ruled him. The "obedient servant" saw himself as the commander-in-chief of vast and victorious armies, like his ancestor the duke of Marlborough, and as the destined master of Britain and perhaps Europe.

This is the trouble with politicians and bureaucrats. Although paid from the public treasury to serve the people, they quickly learn to become the people's masters. They have many weapons: they can keep people waiting indefinitely, withhold documents, write in a language impenetrable except to other bureaucrats, and serve their own interests while pretending to serve the interests of the community. They are confronted daily with the temptations of corruption. If they are weak-willed and studious, they can usually find in the laws an area so ill defined that it permits them to act arbitrarily; if they are merely weak-willed, uncomfortable in the exercise of authority, they become the victims of corrupt men; and if they lack willpower, they will seek to placate as many interests as possible, submitting to all, diffusing their authority, and arriving at no conclusions; from being amiable nonentities they become hopelessly corrupt.

Why a man becomes a bureaucrat is something of a mystery: a safe job, a secure pension, a modest standard of living, the possibility of rising step by step according to established rules of seniority, and the assurance of two or three weeks' vacation every year. His life is bounded by laws, statutes, and instructions; if he follows them, he is in no danger of making mistakes. He stands outside the stream of ordinary life. He says of himself: "I have a supervisory capacity. I am keeping the stream from overflowing its banks." In his office there is a safe where he keeps his most secret documents: they are his source of power. He smiles indulgently at the long line of people waiting to see him. He says: "They can wait a little while longer. Why not? They are only vermin." To keep them waiting still longer, he carefully trims his fingernails, telephones his broker, tells a long joke to his secretary, who has heard it a hundred times before, and finally says, "The first one can come in now."

For the long-suffering public these are not minor irritations. The character of bureaucrats is a massive irritation. Power corrupts them, destroys their humanity, blunts their imaginations. Dehumanization in various degrees attacks all but the strongest and most imaginative, so that even the post office clerk selling stamps smiles with pleasure when he sees a long line of people in front of his cage.

In *State and Revolution* Lenin decreed that the state would serve simply as an accounting facility, a kind of computer answering to people's essential needs. Instead of the accounting facility there arose armies upon armies of rigid bureaucrats who wore uniforms and derived their chief pleasure from punishing people for not carrying out their work norms, for not working in the manner stipulated in the laws, for not being robots. Poets, translators, painters, and sculptors were parasites; they had no place in the community. Writers were not permitted to publish their works, languished in prison or fled to foreign countries. The bureaucrats standing outside the stream of life have little understanding of the arts; for them a work of art is merely an object to be numbered and properly accounted for in the appropriate files.

The moral imperative demands that bureaucrats regard themselves as servants, not as masters. There are perfectly practical methods to make them aware of the human condition. The ombudsman who defends the people against bureaucratic tyranny fulfills an essential function. Judges can be made to serve a prison term, welfare officers can be made to stand in line for welfare checks, high officers of the agricultural department can be made to work a month every year in the fields. Paperwork dehumanizes; the living earth and human society humanize. There is a growing need to humanize bureaucracies and to put an end to the intolerable suffering they cause.

Everyone knows that the presidency, the Congress, the bureaucracy, and the rich contain within themselves the seeds of corruption and that corruption would be even more extensive than it is but for an aroused press. An open and free press remains our only guarantee against government corruption, and one would suppose that an intelligent government would do everything possible to assist the press in rooting out corruption, and not only because there exists a moral imperative to destroy corruption at its source. No government in a free society can afford to be corrupt: the price is too high. The real authority derives from the people's trust in government, and there can be no trust without openness. A government that stamps all its documents SECRET is not a government but a secret, conspiratorial society. A government that tells lies is already on its way to becoming a military dictatorship. Corruption is the lie in action.

One would have thought that the experience of Watergate would have profoundly affected the nature of American government by introducing substantial changes, a new openness, a new effort to change the electoral laws, a new determination to act with humanity and grace, a new program to remove the heavy burdens from the poor, the old, and the sick. One would have thought that there would be a new sense of a common human purpose. For two years the nation was stupefied by the Watergate conspiracy, but when it was over there was a collective sigh of relief that a scoundrel had been thrown out of office, and then everything went on as before.

THE RICH AND THE POOR

Western civilization, as we have known it, is on the eve of its death, for it is lacking in the one thing essential for survival—the *asabiyya* that Ibn Khaldun described at length. Western civilization is dying, not because it is confronted by the powerful emerging civilizations, but because it lacks the inner cohesion and moral vigor necessary for a civilization to survive. The governments no longer govern; the representatives are no longer representative; the people have no common cause and are helplessly divided.

Once Christianity provided the focus for men's dreams and actions; it was the standard to which men could repair. But Christianity no longer provides the essential cohesion that encourages every man to regard himself as the brother of every other man; nor does it permit us any longer in the hard, impersonal world of modern industrial society to regard every individual soul as possessing an infinite value. Men have become statistics served by a government that is increasingly remote from them. In the Middle Ages the king offered protection to his subjects in return for their loyalty, and the subjects were doubly protected, for the church also sheltered them. The need for shelter—for a father image that cares and hopefully will provide and give some meaning to human lives—remains as real as it was in the Middle Ages, but modern technocracy has no place for either the father or the church and provides no substitute.

There were many in the early years of the Industrial Revolution who wondered what would happen if Industry itself, that cavernous, clanking, steam-belching instrument, eventually ruled over the world. During the nineteenth century Western civilization grew rich because industry was harnessed to raw materials from the expanding colonies, and no one troubled to ask what would happen when the supply of raw materials diminished, or when the colonies became independent, or when the raw materials became too expensive to buy. Industry depended upon coal, copper, iron, cheap labor. The superb machinery perished unless it was fed with coal or oil. What happened when the price of coal or oil became prohibitive? And, more especially, what happened when the sources of cheap labor dried up? During the nineteenth century in the United States cheap labor was supplied in the South by slaves and in the North by vast numbers of immigrants from Russia, Central Europe, and Ireland. In Western Europe cheap labor was provided by immigrants from the colonies and by Europeans working in conditions not far removed from slave labor. Industry was ruling the world.

Much sooner than anyone expected, Industry was polarizing the world into the rich and the poor, the possessors and the possessed, the masters and the slaves. Industry provided cheap goods, but it could not provide for the human purposes of ordinary men and women caught up in the hard world of machinery, conveyor belts, automatism, computers. It was not a father, and it was not a religion. The machine did not care, and to the extent that it was not concerned with human lives, it was death-dealing and corrupt.

Most of the great fortunes in the world arose from industry; and while industry proliferated, so did the fortunes, and so did the naked power of those who owned the fortunes. Rich men were able to dominate politics in a manner that was totally undemocratic. Nelson Rockefeller spent $27 million in order to retain his position as governor of New York State; and there is a sense in which all this money went toward corrupting the citizens into accepting him as governor. It has been argued that the very rich are free of the taint of financial corruption; they are not likely to steal from the public till; their freedom from financial pressure grants them a kind of immunity from greed. But the rich by their very presence are corrupting. Their riches remove them from the human world, and like the machines they own, they do not care. "For me," said Nelson Rockefeller, "a hundred thousand dollars is like ten dollars for ordinary people." So it may be; but by that admission he removes himself far from the realm of ordinary people and the right to interfere in their affairs. We cannot demand of such men that they place their wealth in the service of constructive human purposes; their aim is only to increase their wealth and their power. The rich are a crushing weight on society.

The rich are an anomaly in a world where the only safety lies in achieving an egalitarian society. A class society is no longer viable in the closing years of the twentieth century, nor indeed has it ever been viable in human terms. "Your riches are corrupted," says the terrible text of the Epistle of Saint James; and in the long history of Christianity there has been general agreement that the rich are tainted with a disease and that the desire for luxury must be counted among the deadly sins. The rich, we are told, will enter heaven only as often as a camel will pass through the eye of a needle, which is to say that heaven is forever barred to them. They are barred from the human community as well. Wealth corrupts; great wealth corrupts greatly; and the greater the wealth, the more does society find itself in debt to it. One of the major tasks of Western civilization is to break the stranglehold of wealth and to equalize the incomes of the people, not because wealth is intrinsically bad but because it is brutally unfair and because it inevitably becomes a seedbed of corruption.

Thorstein Veblen spoke quite accurately when he said that the chief diversion of the rich is to advertise their wealth through conspicuous consumption. Like the Kwakiutl Indians of the Northwest, they have a fondness for staging banquets that are orgies of meaningless display and senseless giving of presents. They form a closed society with many tribes, each with its appropriate totem, its own language, and its own laws. The tribes are conspiratorial and make very little effort to conceal their conspiratorial nature. But their desire to perpetuate themselves is based on the theory that wealth in the modern world is in fact something that can be perpetuated; that there are no obstacles to the increase of private wealth; that the existing society will continue to tolerate their existence; and that they possess, as though by divine gift, the right to the free use of their wealth for their private purposes without any regard for their social responsibilities.

It is at this point that the theory fails, for increasingly it is coming to be realized that social responsibilities are paramount. The maharajas of India also believed that they possessed the right to accumulate wealth in their treasuries by taxing their oppressed subjects to the utmost conceivable limits. In 1946 the Chamber of Princes represented a formidable concentration of power and influence. By 1950 most of the maharajas had lost their states, and in the following years they lost their twenty-one gun salutes, their incomes, and their titles. The government of India wisely withdrew their privileges by the simple process of passing laws, and from being generators of power they became footnotes to history. They had been a corrupting influence and now they were no longer in a position to corrupt.

For a little while longer the game will be played according to the rules laid down by the millionaires. For a little while longer they will rule like kings, appoint their own governors and representatives, bribe, corrupt, impede justice, avoid paying their proper share of taxes, dominate the regulatory agencies, and proclaim self-righteously that the free-enterprise system permits them to do anything they please. But social justice has a higher claim on any government than the claims of the millionaires. Above all, social justice demands that corruption within the government and in the election of representatives must cease; for it is to the advantage of all that it should cease, and it is to the advantage of the few that it should continue.

There exist medicines for the cure of corruption. These medicines have a bitter taste and must be taken in large doses. Because corruption is so dangerous to the community it becomes necessary to give the corrupters lengthy terms of imprisonment so that they are effectively removed from their trade. The time has passed when corrupt men can be dealt with leniently. The Nixons and Agnews of this world deserve condign punishment, for as long as they are left unpunished they encourage other corrupt men to pursue the same courses. Nixon and Agnew were enemies of the society that gave them wealth, influence, and power. They deserve the punishment that is usually meted out to enemies of society.

In the United States corruption has gone beyond all tolerable limits. The nation simply cannot afford the drain of money and human energy and human hopes sacrificed to the corruptors. Corruption needs to be fought on all fronts with the same vigor and urgency that men bring to fighting a plague. It is not enough to deplore corruption; it must be rooted out. The subject should be taught in schools; there should be chairs for the study of corruption in universities; grand juries should be in permanent session to enquire into corruption wherever it occurs. Heavy punishments for the corrupt and an expanding program of education are needed, and at the very least it is necessary to set up a permanent commission within the government to draw up laws that will make it impossibly difficult for corrupt men to engage in corrupt practices in the affairs of government. For it is here, in the heart of the government and in the bureaucracy, that corruption does its greatest damage. When a president or a regulatory agency head receives a bribe in return for agreeing to an increase in the price of milk or bread or electricity or any of the many other things that directly affect the lives of people, he is committing an act of treason against those whom he has sworn to defend and assist to the utmost of his power. There can be no forgiveness for such a crime. A new ethic is needed asserting that the old ways must be abandoned and that everyone must realize the necessity of working for the benefit of society as a whole; otherwise the society will perish of its own heartlessness, its own inadequacies.

The truth is that we are making very little headway against corrupters. The Watergate scandal showed the extent of the crimes committed by the president against the people; the public was engrossed in the spectacle of the unfolding tragedy. But when some of the felons were given comparatively short terms of imprisonment, the public assumed—rightly—that very little had changed, that such things could happen again, and that in any case they could do little to prevent it. Cynicism was bred in them, and this is perhaps the most disheartening thing of all. As long as the public tolerates corruption, then corruption will persist. If the public rose up and said, as it has a perfect right to say: "This is shameful and must stop! It is destroying us, and there is no reason at all why we should tolerate it any longer!" then it would discover that it has the power to rid the country of the tyranny of corrupt men.

We have seen that it is not enough to punish the corrupters; the conditions that permit and favor corruption must be changed. Today corruption is still practiced successfully on a massive scale, to the danger and detriment of the entire nation. "Whatever power gives us life, and for whatever purpose," wrote Charles Dickens, "it was given to us on the understanding that we defend it to the last breath." We have a right to strike vigorously against the corruption that poisons the very roots of life.

Nor is it difficult to recognize when the time is ripe for attack. During the last months of his life the Danish philosopher Søren Kierkegaard wrote in his notebook:

> The sign by which it may be known whether a given condition is ripe for decline:
> If the conditions at a certain time are such that almost everyone knows *privately* that the whole thing is wrong, is untrue, while no one will say so *officially;* when the tactic used by the leaders is: Let us simply hold on, behave as though nothing had happened, answer every attack with silence, because we ourselves know only too well that everything is rotten, that we are playing false: then in that case the conditions are *eo ipso* condemned, and they will crash. Just as one says that death has marked a man, so we recognize the symptoms which unquestionably demand to be attacked. It is a battle against lies.

Kierkegaard was writing about the situation of the Protestant church in Denmark in the middle years of the nineteenth century, but he might have been writing about our modern corruptions. A church and a state are very similar organisms; they suffer from similar corruptions, and the same tests apply. The lie in action leaves its long trail of lies, which appear to be produced spontaneously by parthenogenesis. There is no end to them, and the more the officials lie the more they are caught in contradictions and confusions. Ultimately they must either admit defeat or they must elevate their lies into dogma.

It is perfectly possible to imagine a man going insane, quietly, determinedly, without equivocation, simply because he can no longer believe the lies told to him by governments, simply because he rejects the all-encompassing corruption of governments. Lies pour out of government propaganda machines like dung, bureaucrats build up their little empires, the television screen portrays a president whose shifty eyes betray his lies even before they are delivered. All this is familiar, and even commonplace. It is equally possible to imagine men rising out of their stupor and oppression to tear the liars and the corrupters out of government and all the places of power. Nor is it impossible to believe that these things will happen in our lifetime.

We have no reason to be especially proud of our sojourn on earth, for we have done little good to one another. We have permitted corruption. We have not fought it as desperately as it should be fought, and we have not always recognized the enemy when he was standing in front of us with a drawn gun, smiling triumphantly. But increasingly we are becoming aware that corruption is an enemy of all, even of the corrupters themselves, because it is deathly. Corruption kills, but not cleanly. It offers a slow and agonizing death to all classes and to all citizens, and dries up the nerves of human sympathy, which alone makes life tolerable. Because corruption is death, and always death, and because it is so widespread in our time, our generation is confronted with the task of rooting it out wherever it appears and at whatever risk. The military dictatorships, where corruption is most rampant, must be smashed; the arrogance of wealth must vanish; corruption, wherever it appears, must be burned out. If these things are not done, then the springs of life will never again flow unimpeded, and for all the foreseeable future humanity will be at the mercy of its corrupters.

Selected Bibliography

ACTON, LORD. *Essays on Freedom and Power.* Boston, Beacon Press, 1948.
ANDICS, HELLMUT. *Rule of Terror.* New York, Holt, Rinehart & Winston, 1969.
ANGLO, SYDNEY. *Machiavelli: A Dissection.* London, Paladin, 1971.
AUGUSTINE, SAINT. *The Confessions.* Translated by E. B. Pusey. New York, E. P. Dutton, 1910.
BAUDELAIRE, CHARLES. *Le Spleen de Paris.* Paris, Librairie Générale Française, 1964.
BRECHT, BERTOLT. *Mother Courage.* Translated by Eric Bentley. New York, Grove Press, 1966.
CHURCHILL, WINSTON. *Savrola: A Tale of the Revolution of Laurania.* New York, Random House, 1956.
COULTON, G. G. *The Inquisition.* London, Ernest Benn, 1929.
DIDEROT, DENIS. *Rameau's Nephew and Other Works.* Translated by Jacques Barzun and Ralph H. Bowen. New York, Doubleday, 1956.
DONNE, JOHN. *Poetry and Prose of John Donne.* Edited by A. Desmond Hawkins. London, Thomas Nelson, 1938.
ENAN, MOHAMMAD ABDULLAH. *Ibn Khaldun: His Life and Work.* Lahore, Sh. Muhammad Ashraf, 1969.
FISCHEL, WALTER J. *Ibn Khaldun in Egypt.* Berkeley, University of California Press, 1967.
GIDE, ANDRÉ. *Lafcadio's Adventures.* Translated by Dorothy Bussy. New York, Vintage Books, n.d.

GORKY, MAXIM. *Untimely Thoughts.* Translated by Herman Ermolaev. New York, P. S. Eriksson, 1968.

HALBERSTAM, DAVID. *The Best and the Brightest.* New York, Random House, 1972.

HIMMELFARB, GERTRUDE. *Lord Acton.* London, Routledge & Kegan Paul, 1952.

IBN KHALDUN. *The Muqaddimah.* Translated by Franz Rosenthal. New York, Pantheon, 1958.

ISSAWI, CHARLES. *An Arab Philosophy of History.* New York, Paragon Book Gallery, 1969.

KIERKEGAARD, SØREN. *The Journals.* Translated by Alexander Dru. London, Oxford University Press, 1938.

KNAPP, WHITMAN. *Commission to Investigate Allegations of Police Corruption.* New York, Mayor's Office, 1972.

LACOSTE, YVES. *Ibn Khaldun.* Paris, François Maspero, 1966.

MACHIAVELLI, NICCOLÒ. *The Prince and the Discourses.* New York, Modern Library, 1950.

MAHDI, MUHSIN. *Ibn Khaldun's Philosophy of History.* Chicago, University of Chicago Press, 1964.

MANN, THOMAS. *Death in Venice and Seven Other Stories.* Translated by H. T. Lowe-Porter. New York, Vintage Books, 1954.

————. *The Magic Mountain.* Translated by H. T. Lowe-Porter. New York, Alfred A. Knopf, 1953.

MEDVEDEV, ROY A. *Let History Judge.* New York, Alfred A. Knopf, 1972.

MONTESQUIEU, BARON DE. *Considérations sur les Causes de la Grandeur des Romains et de Leur Décadence.* Paris, Garnier, 1967.

————. *De l'Ésprit des Lois.* Paris, Garnier, 1973.

NIETZSCHE, FRIEDRICH. *On the Genealogy of Morals.* Translated by Walter Kaufman. New York, Vintage Books, 1969.

————. *The Will to Power.* Translated by Walter Kaufman and R. J. Hollingdale. New York, Vintage Books, 1968.

NORTON, LUCY (ed.). *Saint-Simon at Versailles.* New York, Harper & Brothers, 1958.

ORWELL, GEORGE. *1984.* New York, Harcourt Brace Jovanovich, 1949.

PAN KU. *History of the Former Han Dynasty.* Translated by Homer H. Dubs. Baltimore, Waverly Press, 1938–55.

PARETO, VILFREDO. *The Rise and Fall of the Élites.* Totowa, N.J., Bedminster Press, 1968.

PAYNE, ROBERT. *The Life and Death of Adolf Hitler.* New York, Praeger, 1973.

————. *The Life and Death of Lenin.* New York, Simon & Schuster, 1964.

————. *The Life and Death of Stalin.* New York, Simon & Schuster, 1965.

————. *The Roman Triumph.* London, Robert Hale, 1962.

————. *Zero: The Story of Terrorism.* New York, John Day, 1950.

PHILLIPS, PETER. *The Tragedy of Nazi Germany.* New York, Praeger, 1969.

RAUSCHNING, HERMANN. *Hitler Speaks.* London, Thornton Butterworth, 1939.

REITLINGER, GERALD. *The Final Solution.* New York, Thomas Yoseloff, 1961.

SCHAPIRO, LEONARD, and PETER REDDAWAY (eds.). *Lenin: The Man, the Theorist, the Leader.* New York, Praeger, 1967.

SCHWEITZER, ALBERT. *The Decay and Restoration of Civilization.* London, Adam & Charles Black, 1932.

SHUB, DAVID. *Lenin.* New York, Doubleday, 1943.

SOLZHENITSYN, ALEXANDER. *One Day in the Life of Ivan Denisovich.* New York, Praeger, 1963.

SPENGLER, OSWALD. *The Decline of the West.* New York, Alfred A. Knopf, 1957.

TURNBULL, COLIN. *The Mountain People.* New York, Simon & Schuster, 1972.

VALÉRY, PAUL. *Regards sur le Monde Actuel.* Paris, Gallimard, 1945.

VICO, GIOVANNI BATTISTA. *The New Science.* Translated by T. G. Bergin and M. H. Fisch. Garden City, N.Y., Doubleday, 1961.

VYVERBERG, HENRY. *Historical Pessimism in the French Enlightenment.* Cambridge, Mass., Harvard University Press, 1958.

WEIL, SIMONE. *Intimations of Christianity.* Translated by E. C. Geissbuhler. Boston, Beacon Press, 1958.

WILSON, EDMUND. *To the Finland Station.* New York, Doubleday, 1953.

WISE, DAVID. *The Politics of Lying.* New York, Random House, 1973.

ZIMMERN, ALFRED. *The Greek Commonwealth.* New York, Modern Library, 1956.

Index